The Muslim World
in Post-9/11 American Cinema

# The Muslim World in Post–9/11 American Cinema
## *A Critical Study, 2001–2011*

KEREM BAYRAKTAROĞLU

McFarland & Company, Inc., Publishers
*Jefferson, North Carolina*

ISBN (print) 978-1-4766-6667-9
ISBN (ebook) 978-1-4766-3363-3

LIBRARY OF CONGRESS CATALOGUING DATA ARE AVAILABLE

BRITISH LIBRARY CATALOGUING DATA ARE AVAILABLE

© 2018 Kerem Bayraktaroğlu. All rights reserved

*No part of this book may be reproduced or transmitted in any form or by any means, electronic or mechanical, including photocopying or recording, or by any information storage and retrieval system, without permission in writing from the publisher.*

Front cover image of *Babel*, 2006 (Paramount Pictures/Photofest)

Printed in the United States of America

*McFarland & Company, Inc., Publishers*
  *Box 611, Jefferson, North Carolina 28640*
    *www.mcfarlandpub.com*

To all those left behind

# Acknowledgments

This book could not have been accomplished without those who have generously spared their time to guide me towards my target. Therefore, I would like to express my gratitude from a chronological perspective.

Firstly, I would like to thank the team at a U.S. film company for leaving me behind during my internship in New York City, after we had witnessed the 9/11 attacks on TV from the safety of our hotel rooms at the 2001 Toronto Film Festival. Being neither a Middle Easterner nor a follower of any religion, I was made to feel "Othered" on grounds of no grounds, and returned to New York alone. This experience sparked the incentive to turn a personal experience into something positive, and gave me the determination to look beyond what is obvious as far as the East's projection on the big screen is concerned.

I am grateful to the organizers of the 2008 Middle East International Film Festival in Abu Dhabi for inviting me to sit on a panel to discuss "Challenging Muslim and Arab Stereotypes in Hollywood." The event, which took place before I embarked on my academic journey, gave me the opportunity to contemplate the importance of this area from a humanistic point of view.

Special gratitude and thanks are due to Professor Gerald MacLean and Dr. James Lyons, who provided me with the invaluable academic tools that acted as sidelights illuminating my route. I cannot thank Mac enough for his continuous support, generosity and input throughout the research period of this work.

Last but definitely not least, I am grateful for the encouragement I received from Dr. Jack G. Shaheen whose work on Arab and Muslim representations in film formed the backbone of my research and findings. Sadly, he left this world before I could give him a copy of this book as an appreciation of our discussions. May he rest in peace.

# Table of Contents

*Acknowledgments* — vi
*Preface* — 1
*Introduction* — 3

1. Building a "Muslim World" for the Large Screen — 11
2. Muslim Space Before and After 9/11 — 27
3. The Muslim Male Character Typology — 65
4. White Female and Muslim Male Characters — 97
5. From Stereotype to "New" Muslim Woman — 124
6. Muslim Children — 150
7. The Normalization of the Muslim World — 179
8. "Be sincere, be brief, be seated" — 188

*Filmography* — 199
*Chapter Notes* — 205
*Works Cited* — 209
*Index* — 219

# Preface

This study is an odyssey to trace the effects, as reflected in cinema, of the worst ever attack on America's national pride and physical being, and covers the ten-year period following the events of 11 September 2001. Its premise is that these events are bound to have profoundly affected how screen representations of believers in Islam needed to be altered to match the political climate, even though the culprits of this unprecedented disaster were only a handful of religious extremists.

Following C. Fred Alford (2016), it is plausible to assume that trauma often urges a willed ignorance of traumatic experience, and stimulates avoidance of the actuality that has generated it. It is, therefore, reasonable to expect that a social ordeal, like that caused by 9/11, eventually penetrates the social consciousness and leaks into all possible forms of social, political and artistic output, including feature films. This may follow a period of silence during which the shock and numbness work towards comprehending the magnitude of the impact. The healing powers of time may lessen the pain but what caused it in the first place is not totally forgotten. Although the magnitude of this event has come to be encapsulated in the cursory reference "9/11," its mention nonetheless creates a fission into countless memories and never becomes totally meaningless. In the course of this process, the psychological states of complete oblivion and forgiveness are out of the question. As Thomas Brudholm (2010), studying the life experience of the Holocaust victim Jean Amery, powerfully argues, the preservation of resentment is a natural human reaction to a traumatic past. This resentment, when coupled with the centuries-long tradition of Orientalist stereotyping, is bound to yield a fertile area where social, artistic and political backlash can be traced, not only during the lifetime of the current generation, but for many generations to come. Registering repercussions, therefore, is a long-term endeavor and the current study aims to uncover, in a modest way, the first phase of this post-traumatic expression.

# Introduction

Since the end of the decade under scrutiny in this book, that is, the year 2011, there have been many changes in world politics and the American presence in Muslim lands, mainly in the Middle East and the Gulf. Battles have been fought, migrations have been forced, national frontiers have been endangered, among other unfortunate phenomena. The effects of these events on American cinema could form the basis of a subsequent book, thus providing a framework for observing how stereotypes of the Muslim world have evolved (or as the case may be, regressed) over the course of subsequent decades. Our present concern, however, is to turn the spotlight on the way national cinema represented the Muslim world in the first decade after 9/11, when recollection of the event was probably strongest.

The book investigates what traditional conventions have been used and what innovative means have been created for the depiction of Muslims and Islam, which sometimes favors harsh, insensitive criticism and, at other times, sympathetic and accurate representations that are relatively free from previously held preconceived ideas. The use of comparative analysis helps to highlight innovations, changes, modifications and reformulations of stereotypes. The findings are intended to show how American cinema re-shapes its material to reflect the changes taking place in the way society looks at itself and the world.

The questions for which answers are sought are numerous: Have there been any alterations in the representation of Islam in American cinema since the crucial events of 11 September 2001? If changes have taken place, what current philosophical thinking, social tendencies and artistic trends are traceable in the framing of Muslim spaces and their inhabitants, apart from the political reactions that these events precipitated? Can the durability of long-sustained habits of looking at the East contemptuously be overridden—if not completely, at least in part—by effectively campaigned new doctrines such as feminism, post-colonialism and transnationalism? What is "Muslim space" and how indigenous is its representation in recent films? Do globalization and an increased awareness of the world necessitate an updated look at the interface of cultures? Is American cinema presently enlarging the picture of Islam to such an extent that previously underdeveloped features like women and children are now becoming unavoidable? How do these newly formulated images compare with those of the past?

In an effort to answer these and similar inquiries, sections focus on distinct areas, which are nonetheless connected and complementary. In order to map changes during the post–9/11 decade, each chapter examines the characteristics attached to Muslims and Islam through comparison and contrast with the depiction of location and characters on the screen before 9/11. The only missing element in the films made before the pivotal date is the Muslim male character developed to incite pity, rather than anger or fear, in the viewer, and used as an innocent coward to be victimized, crushed or ridiculed by a formidable American female character (Chapter 4).

The book is comprised of eight chapters. The first starts with a definition of the focal point of the study—what the filmic scenes of the "Muslim world" entail and what aspects are evaluated as having "Muslimness." Relevant concepts, "Othering" and "stereotypes" are explained in light of existing academic literature that delves into the factors that cause stereotypes to be created, developed, changed and/or discarded. In the same vein, attention is drawn to the parameters that influence the shaping of the filmic Muslim world and its people, namely Orientalism, feminism and the effects of globalization on movies (transnational cinema). While these currents of thought are not specific to the reflection of Islam on the screen, as a review of Hollywood's fixation with ethnic and cultural stereotypes shows, the observations of Jack Shaheen (2003a) confirm that Muslims are the only out-group whose cinematic vilification had been persistently damaging until the events of 9/11.

In Chapter 2, the analysis looks at the settings, locale, landscape and space displayed on the theatrical screen. Muslim space as represented in the past and present is examined through two distinct locations in the "Orient"—the desert and the city of Baghdad. These sites have been chosen because of their enduring representation in U.S. cinema. Since location—the spaces in which Muslims are represented on the screen—helps shape characterization, the chapter also examines how Muslim characters living in the United States are distinguished from other ethnic and racial minorities. The chapter is also significant for its discovery that Muslim spaces that simply provided a setting for the action in the past are now acknowledged in terms of their interaction with their inhabitants, regardless of their race and beliefs.

In much the same way that landscapes have been adapted from cinematic depictions of the pre–9/11 period, male and female characters are found, in Chapters 3, 4 and 5, to be constructed through a new perspective, allowing them to look more "human" compared to their monolithic antecedents. Following on from the analysis of changes in the depiction of Muslim male characters and documenting historical progress in a varied typology (Chapter 3), a remarkable innovation in films is noted: the portrayal of the Muslim man as a victim of the formidable American woman, which is analyzed in depth in Chapter 4. This overturns the earlier practice of the primitive male Muslim preying on an innocent white woman—for example, Rudolph Valentino in *The Sheik* (1921) who keeps a British aristocrat, Lady Diana Mayo, captive against her will (initially)—and replaces it with the imprisonment of a (presumably) innocent Arab man—such as Anwar El-Ibrahimi (Omar Metwally) in *Rendition* (2007) who is arrested on the orders of the ruthless head of Homeland Security, Corrine Whitman (Meryl Streep). Such a reversal is not pertinent to a single film but is recurrently practiced, and the trend is examined in four films of the decade.

In Chapter 5, the analysis centers on the characterizations of Muslim women, who have transformed from the former figures serving as decorative background fillers or colorful lusty dancers, invariably subservient to and at the mercy of merciless Muslim men, into new images of equal partners with ambitions of their own. The Muslim woman is now molded into a fully independent character who takes control of her emotional life and, in some instances, even dares to choose and guide her sexual partner.

Chapter 6 traces radical changes in the depiction of Muslim children after 9/11, moving from past depictions of amazingly eloquent or voiceless protagonist aides to youngsters whose search for identity and whose childhood loyalty, disloyalty and redemption are fully explored and sympathetically narrated. Themes of childhood loyalty, disloyalty and redemption are explored in the case of Muslim youngsters, while the Muslim American youth is presented as the "hybrid Other" desperately in search of his or her complex identity. Although there still exist examples of utilizing the overseas Muslim minor as a product of religious fanaticism, 9/11 initiated a new way of looking at the Muslim child. Artistic devices that have found their way into the commercial crop of U.S. movies include inner and external focalization, thus encouraging audiences' empathy for the child who had until recently been treated as an image on the screen rather than a character in the narrative.

All these findings indicate that, during the decade under consideration, American cinema has not drawn as sharp a cultural line between the "Orient" and the "Occident" as it used to. There are many reasons for this, and Chapter 7 explores and collates views and arguments raised by academics and analysts.

Finally, Chapter 8 provides an overview of the findings, with the hope that the evolution is not limited to a passing phase, and will not become obsolete in time. To ensure this, the United States needs to take large strides to close the gap between its people and the rest of the world, especially the Muslim world. In an era when challenges to America's world leadership are emerging, no margin of error will be tolerated. Comparative studies such as this, with a focus on past and present cinematic depictions of the followers of Islam, help show that there is eagerness in the United States to explore and reflect more on the characteristics of the Muslim "Other"—an eagerness which will prove, in the long run, to be in the interests of both the East and the West. Furthermore, such studies are a positive contribution to the humanities, the objective of which is to further knowledge and understanding of different cultures so that the world will be more favorable for all.

In terms of methodology, different disciplines are said to have been traditionally associated with particular methods of analysis. Sarah Pink (2008, 129), for instance, observes that "social anthropology was historically associated with the long-term fieldwork method developed since the mid–twentieth century (although it is less so now) and sociology with interviewing and survey methods." In terms of analytical methods and methodology, the humanities in general and film studies in particular have been eclectic, a fact confirmed by Jackie Stacey (1993, 260): "Film studies (unlike sociology) typically falls into the group which rarely debates questions of methodology." In the absence of pressure to choose this or that method, film analysts have utilized a variety, depending on whether they have taken a quantitative approach with statistical information, or a qualitative approach concentrating on the merits or shortcomings of the data.

Whatever method is adopted, an analysis of film has to take into account the complex nature of this art form, which is not simply "talking pictures" but a combination of both narrative and audio-visual elements. Scholars of cultural studies, who may come from a background in the humanities, generally use hermeneutic methods typically employed in literary analysis. As researchers, we all aim to prove a point in our studies. We have to have something to say and we use our analysis of media and culture to support our claims. We have to present our work in such a way that any reasonable person reading it will agree with our conclusions based on the evidence we have presented. A film as a "text" may be scrutinized in its entirety or in parts/frames but the resulting interpretation has to be acceptable and make sense to others, in whose interests the interpretation is made. Following McKee (2003), we can note that while individuals often casually interpret films in their daily life, textual analysis, which is conducted for academic purposes, requires a more learned and systematic approach both in terms of what is selected and how it is interpreted.

The analysis in this book adopts an inductive approach and considers the most likely interpretations of the texts. It observes interesting features regarding how Muslim space and its inhabitants (men, women, children, animals, location, fauna and flora, and so on) are projected and how congruent this depiction is with the tradition of reflecting such elements in earlier films. Points of interest consist of image formation through (a) narrative, setting, character and characterization, which are variable depending on geographical specifics (Islam in the United States, Islam in the Middle East, Islam elsewhere), and (b) cinematic effects (sound, light, use of the camera). Bearing in mind that the focus is on the changeability of image formation as well as on the symbolic meanings that are conveyed (such as people praying on a rug, the call to prayer or an image of a mosque in close proximity or in the distance, and so on), this approach can be defined as "interpretative" in nature, as opposed to "quantitative." Outstanding features of the film in terms of those listed above are described in detail but, as all description is largely subjective, the author has benefited from discussions and brainstorming with two regular co-viewers, one of whom describes herself as a "liberal Muslim," while the other self-identifies as a "Christian."

On the subject of the adopted analytic approach, it is worth adding that the concern here is with what appears on the screen, with regard to its ideological standing, story building, character development, and space/inhabitant interaction, rather than on audience response. The emphasis is therefore on "production," not "reception."

At this point, some explanation about the choice of films for analytical purposes would be beneficial. There are 167 films cited in this survey. In assembling a representative pre–9/11 selection, 10 films, from *The Sheik* (1921) to *Malcolm X* (1992), are revisited on account of their significant Muslim content and contexts that establish existing conventions and directions before the events of 9/11. These and 19 other films launched after 9/11 make a total of 29 productions which are presented in bold in the Filmography and analyzed in detail in the course of the study. The remaining 138 films are simply mentioned in passing to develop the argument.

There are advantages and disadvantages of including so much data in the analysis. Analysts have usually concentrated on two or three films at a time in their search for Muslim clichés. Semmerling (2006), for instance, looks at two pre–9/11 productions, *Three Kings* (1999) and *Rules of Engagement* (2000), to trace examples of Muslim savagery. Elouardaoui (2011) also focuses on three examples of positive characters: the Moroccan guide Anwar who goes out of his way to help Richard and his seriously wounded wife in *Babel* (2006); the personable and elegant Colonel Faris whose benevolent qualities are exposed in exchanges with the American soldiers in *The Kingdom* (2007); and Abasi Fawal, the cruel interrogator "with extremely humane personal characteristics" (Elouardaoui 2011, 8) in *Rendition* (2007). Sultana (2013) bases her argument on the same films and characters selected by Elouardaoui (2011), almost with the same results. The reason why the number of character types is so low in these studies may be explained by the limitations imposed by the use of a small number of movies. The inclusion of 29 case studies expands the scope significantly, which means that while some finer points in each film have to be ignored, repetitive elements can be more easily underlined in a convincingly varied selection.

In deciding which films to include/exclude, attention has been paid not only to the amount of screen time and dialogue the Muslim characters have, but also to whether they are drawn in substantial depth or superficially. From this perspective, the Muslims in *United 93* (2007) or *Team America: World Police* (2004) are not found to be fully realized characters, nor are the Bosnian Muslims in *The Hunting Party* (2007), hence their exclusion from the analysis.

The selected films range from independently financed movies distributed by smaller Hollywood studios to the grandiose productions we are accustomed to seeing at our local multiplex cinema. While the term "American cinema" can be considered too general to encapsulate the numerous case studies under scrutiny here, this expression is used because these films were financed and produced by American companies. The case studies have been selected on this basis despite their occasionally having a British director or cast. Furthermore, these quintessentially U.S. films indicate and reflect the cultural and ideological essence of what it means to be American, handling the narrative from a wider American public's point of view.

It is common knowledge that in terms of production American cinema has two distinct channels, namely the commercial and independent film sectors, which echo various political nuances present in the country's multiethnic and diverse society. A thumbnail explanation of the respective peculiarities of low-budget independent cinema and studio-produced multi-dollar mainstream films is that while the former aims to make its audiences think about national and international problems, the latter intends to provide spectators with escapism or entertainment through colorful, dazzling productions based on traditional narrative formulae. Borne out of this duality, independently financed cinema is associated with a more liberal mindset and political stance, but the commercial sector (as in the studio system) manufactures content geared towards a more generalized reading of the political sentiments within the country. As a result, while studio productions do not necessarily make claims to authenticity, indie movies' interest in real-life situations gives them a semi-documentary flavor. In the words of Katja Hettich (2013, 154–155), independent films "claim an 'authenticity' that implies a high degree of loyalty to the norms of cultural verisimilitude, hence the 'realistic' discourse, that makes audiences evaluate the fictional representation as satisfactorily valid and thus pleasurable."

Probably due to limited finance, independent films avoid filming overseas and tend to reflect Muslim integration or non-integration in the United

States instead. In comparison, commercial cinema is not financially restricted in the same way and can produce high-budget movies set overseas. Yet, the depiction of the Muslim world does not demonstrate clearly observable differences in the approach taken by these two strands of the film industry. The reason for such a negligible variation can probably be found in the fact that the mainstream film industry, having seen the success of indie productions with younger audiences, as well as their outstanding financial rewards, has decided to change its demographic appeal and generic formations, so much so that the categorical peculiarities of each sector have become less conspicuous over time. As Geoff King (2005, 261) writes, "[t]he lines between the independent sector and Hollywood are in many places blurred, the difference between one and the other being sometimes radical, sometimes far less clear-cut."

In the course of selecting films for the current study, it has been noticed that a large number contain narratives revolving around a re-analysis of domestic American cultural identity during wartime. From *Ali* (2001) to *Sorry, Haters* (2005), and from *Towelhead* (2007) to *You Don't Mess with the Zohan* (2008), Hollywood has been quick to portray a complex hybrid of standards that either conform or clash with U.S. cultural ideologies. For this reason, the portrayals of Muslim entities inside and outside the United States are observed separately.

Finally, an explanation is due regarding the choice of adjectives in the evaluation of film characters. Following scholars whose views have been essential for the current analysis (Said 2003 [first published 1978]; Hall 1997a and 1997b; Semmerling 2006; Morey 2010; Morey and Yaqin 2011; Shaheen 1993, 2000, 2003a, 2003b, 2008a and 2008b), characters are frequently described as "good" and "bad" as well as "positive" and "negative" in this study, not only in the main text, but also in quotations from other scholars. According to what criteria scholars distinguish the "good" from "bad" is not always clear, but the answer is most likely to lie in what Morey (2010) calls "ethnonormativity," that is, they acquire their meaning from the relative distance at which the film's Muslim characters are placed from "normalized" spectators:

> The ethnonormative space is the viewing space called into being by the narrative tension between the contending groups depicted (host community versus alien wedge). Its lineaments trace cultural fault lines that are visually translated in ethnic terms and its political animus is defined according to whether the viewer is empowered to recognize ambiguities and ambivalences, or whether s/he is merely expected to choose between predetermined ideological positions. This is the difference between the comparative banality of the "good guy/bad guy" paradigm and more sophisticated modes where some degree of self-reflection about the national normalization project is evident [ibid., 252–253].

# 1
# Building a "Muslim World" for the Large Screen

If a successful film is one which provides an alternative reality populated with convincing characters, and a platform satisfying the spectators' need for escapism from the daily order of life, as claimed by various authors (Holbrook and Hirschman 1982; Stacey 2002), then we have to be provided in the film with a "world" other than our own to escape into. This made-up world, with all its physical and normative characteristics, its animate and inanimate beings, its textures, sounds and colors, even with the clear or overcast sky it is enveloped in, can be an appealing place. Alternatively, it can be an environment where human misery is exhibited, a clash of ideologies or religions is staged, wars are fought or violence and cruelty are exercised. Nonetheless, stepping into it still promises satisfaction for the audience, for it is a place to be rescued by the protagonist, with whom the viewer has an affinity. The "Muslim world" is an example of this. It is a phrase used in this study to refer to the aspects immediately associated in the Western mind with Islam and Muslims, and not to a power bloc trying to outweigh the political and economic superiority of the West.

The interpretation of Muslimness in U.S. cinema tends to be based on an ideological construct through which the filmmaker or writer projects his or her understanding of Muslim characteristics in a narrative form. While their intentions may or may not be honorable, they cannot be impartial—their dominant ideological input shapes this creation. The result may be incompatible with what Jean-Louis Baudry (1986, 17) refers to as an "objective reality," and thus deviate from "real-life." In order to trace deviations from "objective reality" in numerous films that portray Muslims post 9/11, one must assess whether any similarities or assumptions exist in the imageology of the Muslim character. The immediate observation to be made regarding the spatial and character-related features of this Muslim world is the manner in which their "Oriental" identity is acknowledged. The genesis of this approach can be attributed to Edward Said's theory of Orientalism in which Islam/the East is seen as a weaker peripheral culture in relation to the central dominant Christian/Western culture.

We therefore need to pay attention to what lies outside "objective reality": the same features attributed to a particular world through centuries of repetition in verbal folklore, books, paintings and photographs, which have also been used in films for the last 100 years or so to build and rebuild Muslimness. The filmic representation of Muslimness has always carried signs of the social, economic and political influences of the time. Therefore, the images produced in the decade after 9/11 are affected by the ongoing ideologies of Orientalism, gender politics and feminism, as well as the effects of globalization on filmmaking.

In terms of *mise-en-scène*, the current analysis is sensitive to what Shohat and Stam (2014) call "spatial tropes," which produce symbolic hierarchies through the use of light and darkness in representation. They propose that spatial tropes are used to position European life as central and non–European life as peripheral, despite the fact that all life, wherever it is lived, is central. Through Western lenses, although light triumphs over dark in a number of other areas (e.g., light skin over dark skin, day over night, and so on), paradoxically what lies under a sunny Mediterranean sky is presented as inferior when compared to the cold and cloudy North, which, according to Shohat and Stam (*ibid.*, 141), is "the locus of rationality and morality, while the jungle and wilderness are projected as tangled sites of violent impulse and anarchic lust." Thus, as well as such spatial tropes, to make sense of the representation of Muslim space and characters, technical aspects are noted at appropriate points, bearing in mind that in today's filmography "[d]ark and light are still used through lighting and clothing, as well as music in order to further facilitate the audience's ability in deciphering who the villain is in comparison to the hero" (*ibid.*).

The analysis also pays attention to the film characters' physical attributes in line with the ideas of Haake and Gulz (2008), who propose that "the visual appearance can be used to suggest the internal traits … in order to function as shorthand for understanding and predicting the character" (5). Some of the static aspects they list include body and face properties, skin, hair and haircut, clothes and attributes. Appearance as well as behavior are, in fact, a concern not only for Haake and Gulz but for many other analysts. Mastro and Greenberg (2000, 693), for instance, see these as "primary components of image formation and stereotyping." Their categories can be useful, as they have been in the current study, for deciphering the "Muslimness" of film characters. These are: (1) physical/appearance attributes, including but not limited to weight, height, skin color, hair color and accent, as well as attire (traditional vs. Western) and grooming; and (2) behavioral attributes, including but not limited to intelligence, aggressiveness, subversiveness, laziness, truthfulness, altruism and likeability.

In short, similarly to other undesirable film settings (the old Soviet bloc, Nazi Germany, 1960s' Vietnam, and so on), the Muslim world, too, is found to be ripe with preconceived, essentialized notions. This is another way of saying that it is a world belonging to the "Other." To study the Muslim world and its fossilized representations, one needs to look more closely to what "Othering" and "stereotypes" are.

## *"Othering" and Stereotypes*

The terms "Other" and "Othering" have been utilized by different philosophers but not always with the same intent. Although there is no consensus as to who exactly used the terms for the first time, a number of sources point to the philosopher Hegel's *Philosophy of Mind* (1971, 3).[1] The idea was later developed by Jacques Lacan (1977, 6) who distinguishes between "other," that is, the alternative "self," and "Other" (with a capital O), standing for "*le grande Autre*," the "great Other." The latter is said to be formed through the gaze of the looker, whether it is the "self" or the "other" performing the act of looking. This notion of the "great Other," despite the criticism it has received from some scholars,[2] has generally been accepted and utilized in the literature, especially in psychoanalysis.

Theorists differ with regard to the reasons why individuals are urged to make a distinction between "self" and "Other." Homi Bhabha (1994) argues that the concept of "Othering" is important because an apparatus of power, which we call stereotyping, develops from it. The term "stereotype," however, existed before Bhabha mentioned it, despite the fact that it had a confusing start. Walter Lippmann (1967), its creator, explains it as both an overcondensed formulation, which does not represent reality, and an inevitable means for making sense of the world, which can otherwise be overwhelming. On the one hand, it is claimed to be used to ease the burden on the mind, and on the other, it is presented as unreliable because of its deceptive nature. These definitions have been developed over a couple of decades, especially in the area of social psychology.

Stereotypes are said to be acquired through living in the common environment, socialization and upbringing (Tajfel 1981a, 148). While cultural immersion explains how individuals are endowed with commonly accepted/utilized stereotypes, it does not account for the origins, changeability and demise of these fixed ideas within the culture. Although stereotypes can be complimentary among non-competing groups, hostile stereotypes emerge when there is a claim by different sides to the same resources or rewards.

This point is empirically verified by Sherif (1966) as a result of his experiments in a boy scout camp. In this experiment, 22 12-year-old boys, who were complete strangers to one another, were divided into two groups and asked to compete in sports and other mental tasks with a reward at the end. During the contest, the boys exhibited hostility to those in the other group, calling each other "stinkers," "braggers," "sissies" and many considerably worse names, but when they were asked to achieve tasks requiring the two groups to unite, the hostility disappeared and they worked together to bring the task to a successful end. This experiment verified that stereotypes can be created without much effort as long as the clash of group ideologies necessitates it; however, there are contradictory views about how easy it is to change, modify or eradicate deep-seated stereotypes. Allport (1954, 189), for instance, alleges that "it is possible for a stereotype to grow in defiance of all evidence." Tajfel (1981b), on the other hand, approaches the subject with more caution. According to him, when people have accepted stereotypes as the reality, their "rigidity and resistance to information which contradicts them is undoubtedly one of their most salient features," but a change is not completely out of the question (133). Despite reservations expressed by some scholars regarding the changeability of stereotypes, research now indicates that when low-prejudiced individuals possess the time and cognitive capacity necessary to engage in controlled processing, they are able to inhibit the automatically activated stereotype and respond according to their personal beliefs (Devine 1989).

Stereotypes find a habitat in all forms of communication, verbal or nonverbal, but the most effective medium for their representation seems to be the visual. Image making and breaking in the contemporary world goes through a route whereby cinematic artistry reflects stereotypes as shaped by selective images in TV news programs and on social media and the internet. Pickering's (2001) observations in this area are revelatory. He notes that in all forms of visual media with a latent political message, that is, news narratives, social documentaries, films and advertising, representation is achieved either by speaking for (sometimes in favor) or speaking of (sometimes in opposition) others, following specific conventions. If such symbolic representations with accounts or images of others are based on actual or assumed difference in social power, these may entail under-representation, over-representation or misrepresentation (xiii). American cinema involves a high degree of stereotypical representation as a tradition, with implications for the cinematic depiction of the Muslim world. This study additionally shows that the representation of this world in the post–9/11 era carries the imprint of the parameters not only of Orientalism, but also feminism and globalization.

## Orientalism

The systematically downgraded Muslim representations in various forms of art including filmmaking can best be explained by the theory of Orientalism (Said 2003, first published 1978). Said suggests that the word "Orient" refers to a virtual territory, created by the West to include India, the Silk Route, the Levant, the Arabian Peninsula and Arabic-speaking lands, North Africa and Egypt. In the tradition of Foucault (1977), Said (2003, 36) argues that "knowledge gives power, more power requires more knowledge ... in an increasingly profitable dialectic of information and control." However, the study of the East had been carried out in the past by the academic from his armchair, without firsthand knowledge, or with the firsthand knowledge of a short-term traveller who did not have a genuine opportunity to come to grips with the local cultures. The collection of tropes and false knowledge produced by the Orientalist academicians became, in time, a tradition or, as Michel Foucault (1977) calls it, "the discourse." The motive for this changed into colonialism in the nineteenth century, when the scholarly discourse became an imperialistic undertaking. As a result of the "maps of meaning" introduced by colonizers as a means to make sense of other lands, such as the Middle East, countries became subjective creations and their inhabitants despicable humans, compared to the Westerners. Said (2003, 40) writes: "The Oriental is irrational, depraved (fallen), childlike, 'different,'" thus "the European is rational, virtuous, mature, 'normal.'" This comparison, Said claims, is the outcome of the fear of Islam in modern times, precipitating the mental division of geographies into the West and the East. The driving forces behind the evolvement of Orientalism, therefore, have been the West's feelings of curiosity regarding the unknown, contempt for what is different, ambitions for power and fear for safety.

Said's sharp division between the actual West and the imaginary East has developed into a concern, as expressed by post-colonialists (cf. Bhabha 1994, Spivak 1985, Hall 1997a and 1997b), whose literature is rich with criticism of the practice of differentiating between cultures and cultural geographies. Bhabha (1994) in particular claims that the enunciation of cultural difference is problematic because it rests on making sense of the present by using elements of the past and thus presenting a disruption in place and time. Termed the "Third Space" of enunciation, this practice of cultural differentiation ensures "that the meaning and symbols of culture have no primordial unity or fixity, that even the same signs can be appropriated, translated, re-historicised and read anew" (55).

Any cinematic character creates an opportunity for identification by a spectator influenced by his or her own personal ego, yet in the case of the Muslim character this identification represents a more difficult challenge, for

Muslim characters are entities constructed to create "Other" spaces. In other words, the "Orient" is territorialized by showing how the inhabitants of that territory act for the purpose of implicating Islam. However, territorialization through the actions of inhabitants has different readings for different viewers, as exemplified by Said himself. In his book *Covering Islam: How the Media and the Experts Determine How We See the Rest of the World* (1997), he mentions the film *Death of a Princess* (1980). Apparently, at the time of its launch, this docudrama created many diplomatic problems between the United Kingdom and the United States on the one hand, and Saudi Arabia on the other, while causing different reactions in other Muslim countries such as Lebanon and Palestine. The behavior associated with the "Orient" at large, therefore, does not produce the same reactions in different societies, even if they are of the same or similar cultures.

Orientalism as structured by Said (2003) has been criticized by Bernard Lewis (1993) for the fact that, while accusing the West of the creation of an imaginary territory, he similarly redesigns geography to fit his scope of argument, almost totally ignoring the Ottoman Empire, for instance, the most important Muslim power for 400 years until the nineteenth century, and leaving out non–Arab Muslims of Asia, concentrating only on the Middle East and Egypt. While Lewis' criticism may be justified from a historical point of view, Said's restricted approach in correlating Islam only with Arabs is not completely out of place when film depictions of the Muslim world are considered. Said (2003, 286) himself alleges, albeit with no concrete examples, that in the representations drawn in films and on television the Muslim is portrayed in the form of an Arab who is "associated either with lechery or bloodthirsty dishonesty" among other degrading qualities. His comments are corroborated by Shaheen (2003a) who proves that in the majority of almost 1,000 films made in the period 1896–2001, Muslim characters are mainly of Arab origin and almost all of them are vilified. Shaheen's work will be looked at later in this chapter, in the section "The Depiction of Muslims."

## *"Waves" of Feminism*

Out of the consecutive "waves" of feminism that have contributed to critical thinking since the twentieth century, only the first seems to have fulfilled its motivations and completed its cycle. With the acceptance in 1920 of the 19th Amendment in the United States, and the 1928 Equal Franchise Act in the United Kingdom, women's suffrage was guaranteed and thus the primary demand of the first-wave feminists for gender equality was put to rest, at least in the Anglo-American Western world.

The start of the second wave (1960–1980) coincided with the period when black Americans were struggling for their civil rights. The fervor must have kindled feminist activists who wished to expand on the demands of the first-wavers. They turned their attention to anti-discrimination, men's and women's roles in society, equality in the workplace and in the family. They protested against women being treated as sexual objects and subjected to domestic violence and rape. It was during this period that new meanings were attached to the terms "sex" and "gender," with "sex" being considered a static biological fact and gender a changeable status dependent on the roles cut out for male and female participants in society and the family. On the whole, second-wave feminism was a pluralist movement, but it was limited by the self-centered concerns of Euro-American women in the West.

The third-wave feminism of the 1990s is a reaction to the second wave, not only in its attention to the status of women regardless of color and culture, but also in its insistence on intersectionality and individualist identity. The main issues raised are unequal privileges, essentialism and forced binary thinking. Heteronormativity is queried, thus raising questions about what is "normative" and what is "deviant," although both are looked at from the restricted perspectives of socially created binaries. Consequently, differences in ethnicity, sexual orientation and social class are celebrated. It is argued that women can have "feminine" qualities like being desirable, as well as "masculine" qualities such as being decision makers, resilient and intelligent. Based on this new understanding, femininity and masculinity have had to be redesigned. Chandra T. Mohanty (2003) claims that re-masculinization is orchestrated by exploring various forms of Western feminist attributes and placing them within the context of a Muslim narrative in film. The result not only polarizes patriarchal opposites of rival nation-states, but justifies a need to impose an incompatible Western feminist framework upon Muslim values. This outcome is translated into cinema as the female antagonization of the Muslim male character, whereby the latter is subjected to a process that feminizes his "inferior masculinity" and demoted to a despicable disposition in the hands, or through the eyes, of a Western female character (Sjoberg 2007, 95). The empowerment claimed by third-wave feminism, and its filmic realizations, are noticeable in the characters present in the case studies. Thus, the formidable white woman exercising her superiority over an inept Muslim male is a theme that has found popularity in recent narrative cinema.

Discussions about some of the issues underlined during these three phases of feminism are still very much alive; at the same time, feminists have plunged into an additional struggle on behalf of the voiceless Muslim woman. This is what Chandra T. Mohanty (2003) refers to as the discursive colonization of the experiences of the constructed "third world woman," a device used to perpetuate hierarchies not only between genders, but also between women (333). Armed with the idea of "global sisterhood" without frontiers, Western feminists turned their attention to the alleged sexual oppression of Muslim women by Muslim men, delineating their efforts as a "rescue mission" to emancipate their Muslim counterparts from the patriarchy of their backward societies. Their argument rests on the idea that women of the East have as much right to use their body and sexuality as Western women do. It is interesting that, possibly encouraged by the new feminists' enthusiasm to free the world of impositions on all women—who should have a say in the design of their public and private lives—the depiction of Muslim female characters in films has changed after 9/11, portraying them as individuals with the strength to decide how to feel, behave, dress and make use of their body. However, the concern for gender issues regardless of national and cultural boundaries has not been readily welcomed. The gains or losses created in the Muslim world as a result of militant feminism are still at the core of academic discussions, while further concerns regarding the universal applicability of feminist debates have also been voiced. Kimberle Crenshaw (1991), for instance, claims that mainstream feminism cannot progress universally because it cannot be applied to the multifaceted lifestyles of all women. In the same vein, Judith Butler (1999, 6) argues that a universal and cross-cultural female identity is questionable. She claims that gender differences are culturally contrasted identity markers that are not fixed or distinct. Similarly, Jane Gerhard (2005, 37) asserts that "gender" is resistant to different interpretations in different parts of the world. Therefore, while women across the world might be of the same biological sex, the demand that female sexuality should be lived in the same way falls into the domain of imperialism. The imperialist agenda could be assessed on the basis of its intention to utilize all forms of feminism as a means of "collectivism," but this overlooks the fact that women are of "many colors, ethnicities, nationalities, religions and cultural backgrounds" (Botz-Bornstein 2015, 24). What is applicable to one set of women may be inapplicable to others. This again brings us back to the fine line between sex and gender. It is true that female behavior can vary in different parts of the world as a result of cultural impositions and expectations, but the functionality and needs of the female body are the same world over. It is an interesting undertaking to study how sensitive or insensitive the American filmmaker has been since 9/11 to this fine line in the representation of the Muslim female character's overall behavior, including her sexual behavior and control over her own body.

## *Effects of Globalization: Transnational Cinema*

Mobility, forced economic migration and globalization have created a change in the idiosyncratic characteristics of nations and cultures. The study of immigrant Muslims coming in large numbers to live in America has called for a theoretical perspective on the duality of their status. Transnationalism, a term developed by Basch et al. (1994), responds to this need and refers to the processes by which immigrants "sustain multi-stranded social relations that link together their societies of origin and settlement," regardless of geographic, cultural and political borders (7).

Transnational cinema, which came into being in the early twenty-first century (Shohat and Stam 2014; Durovicová and Newman 2009; Shaw 2013), is not limited to the representation of immigrants but is concerned with many cultural and financial aspects of filmmaking. While what is covered by transnational cinema is still under discussion in academia, the cultural aspects, which are our concern, seem to be influenced by one of the five "scapes" introduced by Arjun Appadurai (1996). Calling this the "ethnoscape," Appudurai explains that, due to increased mobility in the world, landscapes are "no longer tightly territorialized, spatially bounded, historically unselfconscious, or culturally homogeneous" (48). We see in our case studies the effects of transnational cinema, in the hybrid approach necessitated by ethnoscapes, resulting in blurred landscapes and obscured inhabitants, lacking some of the clear-cut qualities that were previously considered indigenous. The fusion that is present in some cases, identified mainly in our discussion about the Muslim "space," makes it difficult nowadays to correlate a place with a set of people, or a specific attire with a certain culture, although in the past it was easy to recognize the links between them. The interrelationship in question is similar to that existing between a desert (place) and horse-riding Arabs (people), or a veil (attire) and an Eastern woman (Muslim culture). However, because the old rigidity in the use of stereotypes has now relaxed to an extent, the filmic depiction of the Muslim/Arab is not as clear-cut as it used to be. The desert can now provide a natural setting for the car-racing Euro-American bourgeoisie, as we see in *Sahara* (1983), or a Muslim woman can be indistinguishable from her Western counterparts in the haute couture clothing she dons, as in *House of Sand and Fog* (2003). Past Hollywood projections of Orientalist imagery have not been abandoned completely, but the more recent visual formulation of "Other" places and characters with some unorthodox qualities reflects the modern world better than filmmakers' unsubstantiable fantasies in the 1930s, 40s, and 50s, and mirrors more clearly the "objective reality" mentioned earlier.

## *Hollywood's Fixation with Ethnic and Cultural Stereotypes*

Hollywood has always showcased a wide range of ethnic stereotypes. While the nation prides itself on the cultural diversity and depth of its cosmopolitan citizenship, the film industry has progressively represented these ethnicities as sub-cultural, as Friedman (1991, 22) complains: "Hollywood films assign easily recognizable signs (e.g., speech, dress, food choices and mannerisms) which when taken together function as overt codes that apparently signify divergent ethnic cultures."

In terms of evolution, a racial/cultural stereotype is said to move along a predetermined path, starting with a phase of disapproval and progressing to one of approval. Clark (1969), for instance, compiles a list of stages through which the representation of minorities in the entertainment industry progresses. These linear stages are "non-recognition" (a given minority group is not acknowledged by the dominant media even to exist), "ridicule" (the group members are stupid, silly, lazy, irrational or simply laughable), and "regulation" (minority group members are shown to be engaged in regulatory positions, for example as police officers, military officers, teachers, and so on, upholding the white society's norms). The final stage is "respect," where the minority group in question is portrayed no differently than the dominant white in-group (18–22).

Fitzgerald (2010) applies Clark's model to his data on a television series depicting African Americans and concludes that the model adequately reflects the progress of the filmic stereotyping of this minority group. On closer inspection, however, one can see that Clark's study falls short of a wider analysis because it does not cater for various movements and socio-political trends in cinema. For example, the Blaxploitation movement and the elevation of the Jewish character, as personified in the all–American hero, have raised both minorities above the "dominant" group. These characterizations have surpassed how these minorities were initially perceived to such an extent that a shift in the hierarchal order has occurred. Furthermore, the progress from "non-recognition" to "respect" envisaged by Clark does not take into account the fact that sometimes stereotypes go from favorable to unfavorable, or fluctuate between the two, as in the case of the Muslim Arab. It is common knowledge that in the 1940s, when American viewers were fascinated by *Arabian Nights*–inspired films, there was a variation in how the East was depicted, deplorable images appearing alongside respectable ones. In the 1960s, respectability disappeared almost completely, being replaced by the "Othering" of everything that was associated with the East. As for the second half of the decade following 9/11, it can be argued that the rigid confrontation with Muslim culture is, to an extent, easing yet again. This is not how other racial/cultural representations have developed.

In cinema, the Native American's identity and image have often been juxtaposed with the white Western heroic male whose role has been to reinforce the notion of American self-definition. In this manner, the Native American has been reduced to the savage "Other," while the protagonist affirms his place in the dominant value structure. In her book *Celluloid Indians: Native Americans and Film*, Jacquelyn Kilpatrick (1999, xvii) identifies three common stereotypes that the Native American has been locked into: "mental, sexual and spiritual." Furthermore, although they may be seen as spiritual, Native Americans' practices and nature-based nobility are commonly projected in many run-of-the-mill westerns as primitive and heathen. However, Kilpatrick (*ibid.*) states that later the image has generally been transformed to shed its derogatory implications and the spiritual character has evolved into a natural ecologist warrior (e.g., *Dances with Wolves* [1990], *Little Big Man* [1972], *Last of the Mohicans* [1992] and *Hidalgo* [2004]). She connects this to the white man's gradual acknowledgment and acceptance of the natives' territorial claims and hereditary rights.

Despite this change in Native Americans' image on the screen, there are analysts who claim that stereotypical representations have not disappeared entirely.[3] For instance, Rinne (2001, 3) observes that "[n]ot until the revisionist westerns of the 1970s did Hollywood begin to offer slightly more complex and accurate American Indian characters, but Hollywood representations of American Indians still remain problematic at best."

In contrast to all the outsiders coming to settle in the United States, some of whom are regarded as interesting because of their "immigrant experience," the African American's image has developed far more tenaciously, which may in part be attributable to economic trends and themes as well as the political discourse of the time. While in the early days the "Negro" stereotype played to comic effect or was presented as a servant in upper-class settings, this demeaning portrayal was later revised to include other characteristics. With regard to the evolution of the African American's film image, Stuart Hall's (1997a) views deserve a mention. Referring to the stereotypical molds for black people, namely those inhabited by "Uncle Toms" (the harassed but selfless good negro), "coons" (the unreliable and crooked liars), "the tragic mulattoes" (the mixed-race and sexy heroines), "Mammies" (the fat and loyal female servants) and "bad bucks" (physically big and over-sexed savages), Hall (*ibid.*, 252) asserts that "there have been many twists and turns in the ways in which the black experience was represented in mainstream American cinema. But the repertoire of stereotypical figures drawn from 'slavery days' has never entirely disappeared." In his view the casting out of demeaning stereotypes started cautiously in the 1950s and 60s with the appearance of a few respectable character types such as those played by Sidney Poitier (*ibid.*, 270). Later, the traditional representation of black people changed rapidly with the arrival in the industry of new black directors such as Spike Lee, who, with their "revenge films" (*ibid.*, 271), as referred to by Hall, reversed the white-hero, black-antagonist formula, showing good blacks triumphing over white antagonists. This paved the way for portraying characters in various ways regardless of their skin color, but as Hall (*ibid.*, 272) attests, "[e]scaping the grip of one stereotypical extreme (blacks are poor, childish, subservient...) may simply mean being trapped in its stereotypical alternative (blacks are motivated by money, love bossing white people around, perpetrate violence and crime...)." Further on, Hall (*ibid.*, 274) expresses his reservations about the face-boosting characterization of African Americans entering the filmmaker's stockpile:

> The problem with this strategy is that adding positive images to the largely negative repertoire of the dominant regime of representation increases the diversity of the ways in which "being black" is represented, but does not necessarily displace the negative. Since the binaries remain in place, meaning continues to be "framed" by them. The strategy challenges the binaries but it does not undermine them. The peace-loving child-caring Rastafarian [Afro-Caribbean] can still appear in the following day's newspaper as an exotic and violent black stereotype.

When it comes to Asian film characters the situation is not any better. Nittle (2014) observes that a similar binary structure applies to them. She notes that American cinema in its early days tended to shape the Asian in the guise of "dragon ladies," "Kung Fu fighters," "geeks," "prostitutes" and "foreigners" (presumably as the tourist abroad). However, she says little regarding the historical factors that led to the formation of these images. Over time, the Asian stereotype has evolved into two contrasting categories, which can be labeled as either the "yellow peril" or "model minority," and in terms of cinema these differing portraits have led to the embodiment of an Oriental figure who has struggled to maintain their social hierarchy within the framework of a cosmopolitan American landscape. While the "yellow peril" is perceived in those Asian characters who have lived outside America and principally pose a threat to U.S. sovereignty, the "model minority" is quite the opposite, being identified as immigrants whose lifestyles are deemed to be most exemplary by the dominant white governing race. This contradictory representation, however, has been short-lived, with new interpretations of the Asian character emerging. In his book *Orientals: Asian Americans in Popular Culture*, Robert G. Lee (1999, 8–9) identifies four more faces of the Oriental that have been imposed on the American nation's psyche: "The pollutant," "the coolie," "the deviant" and "the gook." Lee claims that the "pollutant" and "coolie" stereotypes are primarily Asian identities that originated in mid-nineteenth-century California and are synonymous with films that deal with the historic progress of the post–Civil War era and Western expansion. The "deviant" character has been portrayed either as the Asian prostitute or gangster. Perhaps the most common stereotype that the Asian has fallen victim to is that of "the gook," especially in films that have dealt with the conflicts in Japan, Korea and Vietnam. Furthermore, Asians have also been portrayed as comedic fools or wise and mystic teachers, but always asexual in order not to pose a threat. Characters such as the Chinese detective Charlie Chan, or

Mr. Yunioshi in *Breakfast at Tiffany's* (1961) affirm the demeaning means of representation that were being orchestrated at the expense of the Asian American, which also shows that Hollywood now uses a combination of contrasting character types when depicting Native Americans, African Americans and Asians. Representations of the "Jew," however, do not fit this progression.

Hollywood portrayed the arrival of European immigrants in a favorable light, romanticizing their "immigrant experience" (Kracauer 1959, 259), but Jewish immigrants, though also from Europe, are a special case. Friedman (1982) manages to categorize this historical screen evolution by dividing the image of the Jew into alliterative periods: "The silent stereotype," "the timid thirties," "the fashionable forties," "the frightened fifties," "the self-conscious sixties," "the self-centered seventies" and "the emerging eighties." Each chapter summarizes various artistic devices and means by which Jewish characters' sensibilities are evoked. While focusing on the representation of the Jew from the silent period of filmmaking, Friedman (*ibid.*, 10) claims that this character was mostly shown in the worst possible light to "occupy lower-class positions, with several occupations recurring in the early films such as pawn shop owners, clothing merchants, money brokers, sweat shop workers, peddlers, tailors, and grocery store/delicatessen owners."

The outbreak and consequences of World War II brought about a relatively sympathetic portrait. Holocaust films and films that centered on the Israeli conflict introduced a character whose humanity required the empathetic involvement of the cinema audience. From the 1950s, things began to go the other way, as the studios which had been mainly founded by European Jewish émigrés were gradually bought up by corporations that tended to avoid depicting Jewish ethnicity if at all possible. Things changed again in the 1960s and 70s when the self-conscious/centered portraits of Jewish stereotypes started appearing with the likes of Woody Allen (Friedman 1982). Filmmakers such as Steven Spielberg helped the Jewish character take on a dominant role in which even the white post-colonialist would be subjected to criticism. Recent attempts to play upon past misrepresentations in a post-modernist fashion have resulted in the establishment of the Jewish superheroic character, as conceived in *You Don't Mess with the Zohan* (2008). Zohan retains his capacity for self-depreciation and buffoonery but remains unique in his ability to parody his own past cinematic tropes. This is a distinct quality and achievement that clearly distinguishes him from other forms of cultural representation.

Do filmic stereotypes in time become extinct? The answer to this question should be in the affirmative in view of the existing examples. It seems that when differences between the in-group and out-group disappear, stereotypes become non-functional. One case to consider in this respect is that of the Irish immigrant, as we are reminded by Ramirez-Berg (2002). Apparently, during and just after the silent film era the monolithic representation of the

Irish immigrant was as a dumb police officer or an alcoholic, unemployed father, but when the later generation of Irish émigré families entered the social arena as "mainstream" American citizens (i.e., good looking, well educated, white, Christian, heterosexual), the need to treat them as the "Other" disappeared. This is exemplified by the main character in *Jerry Maguire* (1996), for instance, who is presented in the film as a respectable citizen wholly integrated into the social order in appearance, behavior, beliefs and aspirations.

As this overview shows, different racial/cultural communities have been represented through different stereotyping processes in American film, depending on their specific standing in terms of national interests, current ideologies and upheld values. The depiction of Native American, African American, Asian and Jewish characters in films has progressed along two paths: either favorable characters have been introduced to the repertoire to exist alongside unfavorable ones, or demeaning representations have stopped being practiced altogether. A common denominator for all these cases is that once the appealing character type has become the only fashionable form, as in the case of the Irish and the Jew, there has not been a return to showing this ethnic or cultural group in degrading terms. However, as is apparent in the following chapters, the depiction of the Muslim world has not followed this unidirectional route.

## *The Depiction of Muslims*

The theory of Orientalism (Said 2003), despite its abovementioned shortcomings,[4] offers a convincing motive for the systematically downgraded representations of Muslims in various forms of art including filmmaking. Shaheen (2003a) bases his encyclopedic work, *Reel Bad Arabs: How Hollywood Vilifies a People*, on Said's views about Muslim stereotypes being figments of the colonial mind, which is guilty of creating "imagined communities."[5] Associating the beginnings of the stereotype in American cinema with eighteenth- and nineteenth-century European paintings and literature, Shaheen echoes the argument developed by Said and replaces the colonialists' virtual "Orient" with the American filmmakers' "Arab-land." This is a recurrently and ruthlessly used mythical, illusory setting, functioning "as a make-believe theme park complete with shadowy, topsy-turvy sites ... populated with cafes and clubs like the 'Shish-Ka-Bob Café' and 'The Pink Camel Club.'" The locale is furnished with "instant Ali Baba kits consisting of curved daggers, scimitars, magic lamps, giant feather fans and nargelihs" (*ibid.*, 8). If the frame captures a desert scene, easily recognized features like the "oasis, oil wells, palm trees, tents, fantastically ornate palaces, sleek limousines, and, of course, camels" (*ibid.*) provide the décor.

The analytical section in Shaheen's exhaustive book of 574 pages takes up only 57 pages. The rest consists of brief explanatory notes about more than 900 American-made films (though a small number are of European origin), which were released between 1896 and 2001. They all contain Arab characters and the majority use the "Arab-land" as a setting. Although the Introduction to Shaheen's extensive study is brief, his indictment is clear and to the point, demonstrating in a somewhat journalistic style how Islam and its believers have been vilified by mainly American filmmakers in the history of this art form. "Islam," Shaheen (*ibid.*, 9) says, "comes in for unjust treatment. Today's imagemakers regularly link the Islamic faith with male supremacy, holy war, and acts of terror, depicting Arab Muslims as hostile alien intruders, and as lecherous, oily sheikhs intent on using nuclear weapons." The faithful are stereotyped as "brutal, heartless, uncivilized religious fanatics and money-mad cultural 'others,' bent on terrorizing civilized Westerners, especially Christians and Jews" (*ibid.*, 4). These characters appear in recognizable groups, as villains, sheikhs, maidens (of the harem), Egyptians and Palestinians. Their physical appearance is designed to induce disgust and fear in the case of the male Muslim, and pity and compassion in the case of the female. Arab men are played by robed actors "with dark glasses, fake black beards, exaggerated noses, worry beads and checkered burnooses" while women are provided with "chadors, hijabs, bellydancers' see-through pantaloons, veils and jewels for their navels" (*ibid.*, 8).

Vilification in films, Shaheen argues, is not only administered through visual elements, but also through speech. In hundreds of films, Arabs are referred to by white characters in derogatory terms. Those frequently used are "'assholes,' 'bastards,' 'pigs,' 'devil worshippers,' 'jackals,' 'rats,' 'rag heads,' 'towel-heads,' 'scum buckets,' 'sons of dogs,' etc." (*ibid.*, 11).

This degrading image has lingered stubbornly, even though "in the last third of the twentieth century Hollywood was steadily and increasingly eliminating stereotypical portraits of other groups" (*ibid.*, 6). While images of a variety of racial and cultural identities have been normalized over the years, the representation of Muslims has been uninfluenced by major international or domestic events, such as women's suffrage, the Great Depression, the civil rights movements, two world wars and the collapse of the Soviet Union. Thus, Muslims have remained lifeless, disposable caricatures in a world of rapid geopolitical change. In light of this persistence, Shaheen (*ibid.*, 4) asks: "Where are the movie Arabs and Muslims who are just ordinary people?" At another point, he continues: "Missing from the vast majority of scenarios are images of ordinary Arab men, women and children, living ordinary lives. Movies fail to project exchanges between friends, social and family events" (*ibid.*, 15).

The reason Shaheen gives for the enduring vilification of Arabs on the screen, while the rest of the minorities have been set free from the clutches of stereotype perpetuators, is "you can hit an Arab for free, they're free enemies, free villains—whereas you couldn't do it to a Jew or you can't do it to a black anymore" (*ibid.*, 6). Although this sounds like an emotional rather than an academic evaluation, the underlying message here points to the absence of protests from Islamic and Arab circles (at the time Shaheen was writing this) against filmmakers who continue to vilify Muslims. Indeed, as Shaheen points out, "ethnic stereotypes do not die off on their own, but are hunted down and terminated by those whom the stereotypes victimize" (*ibid.*, 51).

However, not all images of Arabs are equally offensive. Shaheen (*ibid.*, 18) admits that "some Arab portraits are dangerous and detestable and should be taken seriously, others are less offensive." Of the more than 900 films he scrutinizes, only six (made in the 1980s and 90s) feature heroic Arabs. Of these, the most notable is said to be *Three Kings* (1999), the credits of which list Jack Shaheen himself as Script Consultant.[6] Otherwise, the majority of images imply that "the only good Arab is the dead Arab" (*ibid.*, 18). On the other hand, in a later book Shaheen (2008a, xv) admits that out of all post-9/11 films portraying Arabs, about a third project them as worthy characters and decent Arab Americans. Bearing in mind that there have been about 100 such movies in total, Shaheen's findings confirm the analytical results of the present study. However, while the following chapters provide an extensive analysis of various aspects of the Muslim world represented in pre- and post-9/11 films, Shaheen (2003a) concentrates only on the depiction of character, neither dealing categorically with the representation of male, female and child characters, nor with the space these characters exist in.

Researching the world of a different religion and culture as projected onto a screen with settings and characters, be they male or female, adult or child, black or brown, sounds like an over-ambitious undertaking, bearing in mind the endless aspects that one can focus on in a world of this kind. On the other hand, considering that this special world is created by the filmmaker by building on a limited number of stereotypes, which have continued to be recirculated over the years with minor changes, the work becomes manageable and not so daunting. Existing theories and academic observations also help the analyst to make sense of the ways in which this world is constructed, its inhabitants created and its culture projected.

Now that we have established which theories and concepts are relevant to a study of this kind, and have looked at the functions and durability of stereotypes in general, and more specifically at stereotypes in American cinema with reference to Said's *Orientalism* (2003) and Shaheen's *Reel Bad Arabs* (2003a), our attention can now turn to how American cinema has represented Muslim space before and after 9/11.

# 2
# Muslim Space Before and After 9/11

When we refer to a special "world" with characteristics that distinguish it from other spheres, we are not equating it with "space," at least not in this study. Space exists in a "world" but is only one feature of it. Consequently, it is important to distinguish between the concept of the "Muslim world," which was introduced in the previous chapter, from that of "Muslim space." The "Muslim world" is the larger picture, as seen by non–Muslims, involving all the peculiarities associated with believers in Islam, whereas "Muslim space" is what the believer asserts a right to. This space may be in a Muslim country or elsewhere in the world, as Metcalf (1996, 4–5) explains:

> For a Muslim to feel at home or for a non–Muslim to recognize a Muslim space, the presence of certain spoken or written Arabic words is most telling. Even when they arrive in unknown places, familiar Arabic dicta greet Muslims from Arabia to China, from Detroit to Mali: "Bi'smi'llah (In the name of Allah), Al-hamdu'llah (Praise to Allah), Insha'llah (If Allah wills).... Photographs of calligraphy in a Muslim home in Canada and an African-American Muslim home in Philadelphia ... depict a use of sacred words widespread among Muslims everywhere."

This chapter focuses on the way Hollywood films have been representing Muslim space in the aftermath of 9/11. Inevitably, there are questions to be answered. Has the presentation in contemporary films of the desert, which has been portrayed as a typical Muslim location in the "Orient," been modified? Can we find any alterations in the cinematic presentation of Baghdad, thus manifesting a new perspective regarding Iraq, especially after its invasion by U.S. forces? Is the scene of the disaster, the city of New York, projected as a hostile place in films when looked at from the perspective of Muslim immigrants after 9/11? What aspects have been chosen to fill the background of the frame so that important implications about the local culture and people are deducible? What recent changes have integrated into the cinematic product that stand out in terms of transnational cinema? Does old-fashioned

Orientalism still exist in its full capacity or has it been mingled with a blurred correlation between man and nature? To respond to these queries, our case studies are *Hidalgo* (2004), set in the desert, and *Green Zone* (2010), set in Baghdad. However, before examining these films, it is useful to explore examples of narrative cinema with similar settings produced before 9/11, in order to provide a comparative framework through which recent changes become more observable. It is additionally illuminating to analyze the projection of New York in *Man Push Cart* (2005), to see how the relationship between the non-Muslim urban space and its Muslim citizens is reproduced.

## Initial Observations

In cinema, characters do not develop in a vacuum, but in settings determined by the narrative or considered by the filmmaker to be appropriate. Although locations can be selected from an infinite number of possibilities, there have been attempts to classify them. For example, McArthur's (1997, 20) list consists of "wilderness, pastoral landscapes, agrarian landscapes, villages, rural towns, suburbs, inner cities, and metropolises." At the extreme ends of this spectrum lie the wilderness and the city and the opposition between them, McArthur observes, is deeply rooted in American culture and surfaces in national cinema as two distinct genres specifically associated with traditional Hollywood films: gangster movies, which are predominantly set in a city, and cowboy films, set in the Wild West with its natural wilderness and shaky, dust-ridden small towns. The "urban space," defined by Mark Shiel (2001, 12) as a man-made environment mirroring social life and relationships, lifestyles and human conditions, has fascinated filmmakers and spectators, from the Lumière brothers' *Paris* (1895) to John Woo's Hong Kong depicted in *The Killer* (1989). The wilderness, on the other hand, with its contrasting qualities to the city, and its pristine (or desolate) lands where the laws of nature are in force, provides rich artistic material. As an entity, it is referred to by Laderman (2002, 8) as both "a savage space separate from and inferior to the realm of civilization," and a "romanticized space of tranquility." The image of nature therefore "bears within it a contradiction, that is, the need to conquer the wilderness as well as to celebrate it."

There is a consensus that in the selection of an environment as a backdrop for film characters and their actions, ideological and political considerations play an important part. For example, Natali (2006, 100) points out that Hollywood's dramatic figures featuring in the landscape are "iconological and political compositions that display uncanny likenesses, survivals, and returns from the past U.S. history and ideology. Film landscapes are neither purely narrative backgrounds nor simply distracting spectacular settings. They bear the traces of political projects and ideological messages."

That political concerns inform the projection of environment both in terms of the metropolis and wilderness is also echoed by McArthur (1997, 20), who proposes that "cities (and indeed all urban spaces and even natural landscapes) are always already social and ideological, immersed in narrative, constantly moving chess pieces, in the game of defining and redefining utopias and dystopias." Furthermore, for Ingram (2004, 31–32), landscape images "perpetuate bourgeois relationships to land, endorsing in particular the commodification and domination of nature." When applied to cinema this is in turn divided into two aspects: firstly, "[t]he notion that ideologies of dominance and mastery over nature are inevitably constructed by the camera itself"; and secondly, "[t]he theory that the perpetuation of those ideologies should be located within specific representational practices" (*ibid.*, 32).

The city being a playground for ideological messages finds evidence in Kääpä and Laine's (2013) work on a series of films set in Helsinki. Analyzing the dynamic and complex depiction of the cityscape in the Inspector Palma series, the authors observe, "At times very cosmopolitan, at others a brutally traditionalist and regressive space, the city in the films is a dynamic organic entity. It is also a space of the cultural battles of the era of generational and ideological clashes between different identity groups, ranging from youth culture to authoritarian figures, from modernist art to traditionalist family dynasties" (34). A longitudinal study of the Muslim-related wilderness, the desert, also demonstrates a different approach taken by filmmakers, in line with the existence or non-existence of ideological pressures. An example is cited by Shaheen (1993) who observes that while *The Desert Song* made in 1929 displays devout and daring Arabs who defeat evil French colonialists, the Arabs in two remakes of *The Desert Song*, in 1943 and 1953, respectively, are an "unruly, unkempt, feuding lot—one of them is even pro–Nazi" (8).

Khatib (2006, 31), in her analysis of the production of space in American films, observes: "While the exterior space of America is masculine, refusing to kneel down and non-penetrable, the exterior space of the 'Other' is feminized through mapping (*The Siege* [1998]), invasion (*In the Army Now* [1994]), and exploration (*Three Kings* [1999]). In other words, it is a 'passive space,' yielding to 'power, ideology, surveillance, and control.'" Despite the changes taking place in the Islamic world, especially in the oil-rich Arab lands, the message of American cinema has insistently relied on centuries-old stereotypes, sometimes in the hope that the projected images of the environment will convey to the spectator an inferior, bloodthirsty culture. As Semmerling (2006, 110) claims, "Arabs were likened to the American Indians in that the ideology of savagism and the basic orientation toward Indians were applied to the Arabs."

When it comes to the projection of Muslim lands in American cinema, Shaheen (1993, 80–85) points out that in ever-changing urban life, where skylines in most parts of the world have altered significantly, the Arab lands are shown to be as they were 90 years ago, if not worse. These images exhibiting properties of terror—guns, bombs, tanks and airbases—are not genuine representations of Arab settings and unless moviemakers educate themselves concerning the true appearance of such lands, they cannot escape accusations of prejudicial tendencies, to say the least. Shaheen's discontent resonates with McArthur (1997, 33–34), who argues, "Hollywood has created a series of 'Others' which in no sense relates to the self-definition of these diverse other places and peoples: rather they project the needs, fears, fantasies, and representations of particular American ideologies." What we can deduce from all this is that the Middle East, being at such political odds with the U.S. administration for so long, is one of these unhappy geographies that has, until recently, been denied a realistic representation.

## "Location" in Academic Studies

Establishing a connection between the movie actor and the movie setting is not a new venture. For instance, Chris Robe (2010, 199) reports that Jean Renoir talked about this connection while explaining the success of his masterpiece, *La Grand Illusion* (1937): "It has become clear to me that man is rooted in the soil that nourishes him. He is bound to the conditions that form his body and soul and chained to the landscape that dazzles his eyes." However, despite the popularity of connecting a location to its inhabitants, it is not always clear what the term "location" or its equivalents stand for. To be able to find one's way through a plethora of jargon, it is necessary to provide an overview of comments made by some researchers working in this area.

For Yi-Tu Fan (2011, 3), space and place are different entities, their difference being based on their contrasting offerings: "place (or location) represents a sense of attachment and security whereas space represents freedom." While we are attached to one we seem to yearn for the other and, in order to enhance and expand either of them, force, tools and machines are implemented by man. Firstly, according to Fan, space is a cloudy area of insufficient knowledge that surrounds the factually known; secondly, it is an area influenced by the conception of localized principles. He takes this rationale further by applying the paradigm to the general characteristics associated with an Oriental mythical space. He argues that we organize the forces of nature and society and associate the outcome with locations within the spatial system. This is an attempt "to make sense of the universe by classifying its components and suggesting that mutual influences exist among them. It imputes personality to space, thus transforming space in effect into place" (*ibid.*, 91).

For his part, Henri Lefebvre (1991, 33) defines space as a wide confine distinguished from "nothingness and uncertainty." Lefebvre, in this instance, is more concerned with the encapsulating quality of space, although he accepts that there are also other qualities within its confines. One of the entities falling into his definition of space is the landscape, which is quite a distinct concept. He accepts that the existence of landscape dates back to times when scenery came to be represented in its own right in a form of art, especially visual art. In the days when nature was depicted in paintings, and later in still photography, the term landscape referred to the depiction of natural space, with no inclusion of people or events. Even when these were included, they did not contribute much to the aesthetic message inherent in the image of the landscape. As moving pictures became a dominant art form, projecting a narrative with its own actors and locations, the term required a new definition vis-à-vis setting. Another scholar, Martin Lefebvre (2006), distinguishes between setting and landscape in terms of pictorial economy and proposes that "as long as natural space in a work is subservient to characters, events and action, as long as its function is to provide space for them, the work is not properly speaking a landscape" (64). Moreover, taking Freeburg's (1918) *The Art of Photoplay Making* as a starting point, Martin Lefebvre observes that the filmmaker uses the natural space as subservient to the projection of dramatic action, but this subservience varies in degrees between being "neutral, sympathetic, participating and informative." At one end of the spectrum lies the neutral setting, relating indifferently to the action or the characters (in this sense it is very close to the earlier definition of landscape), and at the other end is the informative setting that helps to express the character's state of mind (Lefebvre 2006, 64).

Other scholars are also attracted to the natural environment of the "wilderness," where there is no human involvement. One such scholar, Light (1999, 138), defines the wilderness along two lines: first, the classical version deriving its meaning from its etymological origin—"a wild area"—the conquest of which will be "a victory over the dark forces"; second, the romantic wilderness, which is "a form of nature that has remained close to its 'pristine' state and has not been corrupted by human intervention." Starting from the point that wilderness denotes savagery, Light (*ibid.*) applies the classical use of the term to the city and coins the hybrid phrase "urban wilderness" (a useful notion to denote the decadent aspects of a city with disturbing scenes and characters such as prostitutes, drunks, brutal husbands, young and old murderers, and so on). This is especially serviceable in the case of the *film noir* trend of the post–World War II period.

In an attempt to develop the concept of landscape, Melbye (2006) asserts that the mere presence of humankind in the spectacle makes an otherwise mute landscape "speak." Additionally, he remarks that the "language" of the landscape is idiosyncratic to the people who confront it and is understood through their common experience and imagination. Having built a metaphoric bridge between the landscape and the people who can make sense of its messages, he concludes: "This collective interpretation of the environment is referred to as *culture*—and the exploitation of a particular landscape's potential to convey meaning may vary drastically from one culture to the next" (3).

It is useful to clarify at this point that the term space is used in this chapter in the way defined by Henri Lefebvre (1991)—an entity encapsulating qualities of a particular kind (in this case the Muslim space)—while landscape is an "informative" space with cultural implications, to combine Henry Lefebvre's and Melbye's suggestions. In the case of sub-Saharan Africa, for instance, the environment is a natural wilderness but influences its dwellers or passers-through, who also leave their marks on it. The occasional use of the term wilderness in this study points to the image of the virgin desert as employed in some of the films cited.

It is also useful to add that when environment is represented on the screen, it reproduces an imaginary space that allows the story's organic narrative to function from within. The reframing of the world through the camera's penetration of a subjective reality may result in transforming cinemagoers' perceptions. The natural landscape may create a sense of pure nostalgia that conflicts with a spectator's sense of modernity and purports a more traditionalist viewpoint. If we are to presume that modernity and the urbanized city have become representations of human endeavors related to culture, then it can be concluded that nature has been surpassed. Although the ongoing debate over nature versus culture is an area that this study acknowledges, it would be unwise to extend its practical application any further. Suffice to say that nature that accommodates humans (in all its academic interpretations) cannot exist without culture and vice versa. What distinguishes one from the other is the manner in which each evokes a human interrelationship that has become dependent on its existence. For example, if we are to establish that modernity has been concerned with the eradication of all traces of ambivalence characterized by earlier modes of existence, then the natural landscape may arouse a sense of identity that harbors nationalism, as discussed below.

## *The Muslim Natural (Desert) Landscape Before 9/11*

In U.S. cinema the natural landscape and wilderness has classically been depicted in the western genre by the likes of John Ford as a means of evoking a nostalgic yearning riddled with national pride, and attributing the development and evolution of the country to man's taming of the Wild West. Films such as *The Searchers* (1956) have not only toyed with this understanding but have been responsible for shaping a misrepresentation of the native indigenous populations while paying homage and respect to the brutal colonization of these people and their land. As the American wilderness was represented as the basis from which U.S. history, culture and heritage derived, the western genre was used to illustrate the past and propagate this narrative. The grandiose landscape of the American West was accompanied by a similarly exaggerated soundtrack that heralded the majestic and self-proclaimed imperial disposition, probably as a device to cover up the sad historical facts of colonialism. With the decline of western films, American cinema needed a new wilderness to conquer. Zaccak (2003) points out that movies such as the British-made *Lawrence of Arabia* (1962) and *Three Kings* (1999), utilizing an "eastern gaze," are Orientalist adaptations of cowboy movies in which Arabs adopt the significant roles once played by Indians. Old habits of associating the Native American with nature to an almost mythical degree were carried over to this new landscape inhabited by desert Muslims.[1] The desert over time became such a space that not only through the *presence* of recognizable Islamic or Arabic tropes, but even in their *absence,* the view connoted Muslims. An empty desert with a camel on the horizon created the expectation in the viewer that Arabs would soon make their appearance in the frame. Thus, the *presence* of the stereotype was indicated by its *absence*. There is, however, some evidence in the films under observation here, that this strong correlation is weakening.

The use of the desert in films primarily serves the formation of a dichotomy between good and evil along the axis of East and West. Shohat (2006, 31) writes: "While the Arabs in such films as *Lawrence of Arabia, Exodus* (1960) and *The Raiders of the Lost Ark* (1981) are associated with images of underdevelopment, the Westerner, as the antithesis of the oriental desert, is associated with productive, creative pioneering, with the masculine redemption of the wilderness." Desert people, in comparison to heroic, self-righteous Westerners, are perceived as murderers and rapists. Said (2003, 287) observes that in films and on television, the Arab appears as an oversexed degenerate and reminds us of the words uttered by Valentino's suggestively leering Sheik to the English female character: "My men are going to kill you, but—they like to amuse themselves before."

Sexuality as the common denominator in most desert films has been viewed in various ways. Shohat (2006) analyzes desert films in terms of transsexuality and the gender differences projected through them. Using David Lean's Lawrence as an example, she purports that "despite his classical association with norms of heroic manliness" he is "portrayed in a homoerotic light" (53). This is obvious, Shohat says, especially when Lawrence is dressed all in white and delicately rides on a horse, looking like a bride. With repeat workings of the same kind of homoeroticism, the desert is made to look like "a sexually and morally imaginary territory" (54). It is also used by American film directors as a space for heterosexual and interracial infatuations, epitomized by *The Sheik* (1921), which, according to Hsu-Ming Teo (2012, 140), replaces the Latin lover with the Arab/Muslim. While it may extend an erotic invitation with a show of its smooth, whitish, feminine curves, the desert simultaneously sends out a silent warning charged with puritanical values: rebellious white women who venture into an unknown terrain in the name of self-determination run the risk of being raped by the savage men of the desert. Despite the underlying pedagogic discourse, however, romanticizing the Arabs/Muslims in the desert maintained its hold on the American audience, with sequels to *The Sheik* continuing to be produced until the middle of the twentieth century. After a short lull, American filmmakers returned in the 1980s to themes involving the Middle East, in the wake of the Iran hostage crisis, the Arab-Israeli conflict and the oil problems caused by OPEC. Teo (2012) proposes that revisiting the "Orient" with expensive productions was also influenced by the spectacular British Raj films portraying colonial India, such as David Attenborough's *Gandhi* (1982), James Ivory's *Heat and Dust* (1983), and David Lean's *A Passage to India* (1984). Americans sought to express their own colonial sentiments by recasting onto the screen the arid lands of the Middle East (Teo 2012, 140).

The cinematic desert wilderness is a landscape of extremities. At times, it is presented as an alternative world that appears to be menacing, a coarse arid expanse, a rocky and dusty terrain that implicates the brutality of nature and its inhabitants. The sun's anvil is ever present and is regularly portrayed in a blazing whiteness that rests on the surface of the cracked salt pan. The Muslim native inhabitants tend to be faceless effigies on horseback, their identity concealed behind head scarves, and their cloaks floating in the wind. Historically, the romantic cinematic depiction has tended to emphasize the triangular curvatures of the desert landscape, peaceful and gratifying, with the power to liberate city dwellers from the constrictive and institutionalized cultural structures of the metropolis. Yet, despite its often serene appearance on screen, the desert is not a static entity but a multifaceted phenomenon, constantly changing and interacting with those engulfed in it (Marks 2006). The best depiction of the desert's changeability and its effect on mankind is in *Lawrence of Arabia*, where the change in the land's temperament goes hand-in-hand with the protagonist's psychological mood. Kennedy (1994, 16) explains this interaction as a "profound change that takes place in Lawrence's relationship with himself and his relationship with the desert. It is a change from love to fear. Lawrence embraces the desert and through the intensity of his experiences is transformed, a transformation that results in a destruction of a part of himself." In the first half of the film, Kennedy (1994) notes, Lawrence is at ease with himself, confident that he can achieve his goal of bringing independence to Arabia, and he is filmed against a clean, heroic landscape full of beauty: "In medium-range shots, Lean makes extensive use of triangular composition—reflecting the forms in the landscape and indicating stability" (166). The desert is initially projected as a calm, reliable and assuring companion whose presence augments Lawrence's self-confidence. In the second half of the film, however, its "vertical and diagonal lines meet at odd angles, giving a sense of instability and chaos.... The landscapes are harsher, rocky, flat, full of dust, war, slaughter, suffering, death and flies" (*ibid.*). This is the period when Lawrence's relationships with those around him are disintegrating, a fact that eventually pushes him to the point of psychological breakdown. Lean's directorial achievement in *Lawrence of Arabia* is lauded by Aitken and Zonn (1994, 16) for presenting a convincing interplay between a schizophrenic character and a schizophrenic setting. His artistic skills in uniting the narrative, the character arcs and the scenery, as well as elevating the landscape to such a level that it looks as if the desert has a life of its own, are unique. Unfortunately, such mastery is not evident in the majority of American desert films, possibly because the United States is physically a much larger land mass than Britain, and Americans might be less vulnerable to the impositions of land and landscape. However, artistic sensibilities seem to be changing, as we shall see in *Hidalgo* (2004), where there is a superior handling of the desert's interaction with men. In the earlier films, the variations in the land were used either to signal the emergence of a romance, to serve a certain action, or to incite fear or excitement in the audience. In such films, the desert was a battleground for the "only good" and the "only bad" Arabs, although other races—black Africans, gypsies, Iranians and much later the Kurds, for instance—also occasionally entered the scene.[2] Westerners, especially Americans, becoming a warring side happens at a later stage in the aftermath of the Gulf Wars.

This is also the case when it comes to couples in love. Earlier films under the *Arabian Nights*' influence narrated love stories mainly between Arabs. In the desert romance films, on the other hand, the couples were either both European—for instance, in *The Garden of Allah* (1936) the male character is French and the female character German—or European and Arab, as in *The Son of Sinbad* (1955) where the male character is Arab and the female is Greek.

In the paragon of this genre of the silent-movie era, *The Sheik* (1921), the desert is presented as a large prison where Sheik Ahmed Bin Hassan (Rudolf Valentino) keeps an English woman, Lady Diana Mayo (Agnes Ayres), as "a helpless captive in the desert wastes," as described by one of the title cards. Another card tells us, "The desert is a great hiding place," and in another, the

Sheik tells his captive who is contemplating escape, "In that sand fury you will not live an hour." *The Sheik*'s desert is therefore a restrictive environment, barring free movement, a quality also referred to in other films.

In the action film *The Jewel of the Nile* (1985), the desert serves to enhance suspense. For example, a whole army of tribal fighters hides under heaps of sand and becomes indistinguishable from the khaki soil, only to pop up unexpectedly when the time is right. Also, the sandstorm provides invisibility to the protagonists escaping in a taxying jet plane that fails to take off, a horde of evil Arabs in their pursuit. A rocky mountain offers them a getaway route from the tanks chasing them. Walking across the arid land under a scorching sun is used merely as an excuse for the main character, Jack Colton (Michael Douglas), to scold his girlfriend Joan Wilder (Kathleen Turner) for causing their ordeal. The desert here is again projected as a location where different tribes fight over primitive causes, while its impassibility and threatening masculine nature are emphasized by the brutal ruler of a mud-built city: "Only a fool can go out to the desert alone."

On the other hand, the desert is also associated with submissiveness and femininity. In light of Khatib's (2006) comments concerning the feminization and passive characterization of the desert, we can say that the desert in *Three Kings* (1999), a satirical war comedy released only two years before 9/11, is made to look not only submissive but raped. The narrative is about four greedy American soldiers secretly departing their military camp under the leadership of Major Archie Gates (George Clooney) and going to a small village in the desert near Karbala to steal the gold that Saddam Hussein's army stole from Kuwait. As their search for the gold takes them to nearby villages, their mission unravels the extent of damage their war has caused in the desert. It is not a pristine landscape anymore—there are burning oil wells in the distance emitting black smoke into the air; petrol-filled ponds where dead or dying birds float; rotten human skeletons on the sand lying alongside a blood-stained ox head; an oil tanker with a hole in its side from which gallons of milk gush out and make anyone in its path fall; army vehicles turned upside down; abandoned artillery and damaged bunkers, and so on. The views of the desert in this film reveal the degree of damage and dilapidation that the American army has caused. There is no backlash from the land, no quicksand, no sandstorms, no desert creatures, just the static, flat and barren desert lying silently under the aircraft, tanks, jeeps, helicopters and army carriers. *Three Kings* bears the signs of American remorse for the destruction they have caused in the Muslim lands, although a different sentiment is expressed by Semmerling (2006, 133–134) who, in his analysis of the film, sees the blame for the destruction lying with the invaded, not the invading, party: "Cruz [the female journalist] ... and a male military escort find dying oil-soaked pelicans in an oil-contaminated marsh, and she breaks down in tears. This environmental disaster, along with the burning of oil wells in the prior scene, is meant to show an example of Arab savagery in the wilderness."

Semmerling argues that foregrounding Cruz's feminine weakness at this point, in such a sympathy-begging way, is intentional to clearly bring out the masculinity of the American soldiers and the revival of the victory-culture syndrome, but his analysis disregards the fact that the film also contains many other disturbing images of rotten human corpses and animal bodies, damaged artillery and similar war remnants polluting the desert, the blame for which lies with both the American and Iraqi armies.

*Sahara* (1983), a cross between a road movie and an action film, bound together by the adhesive force of a romantic love story, contains a number of familiar stereotypes, some taken straight from *The Sheik*.[3] It is the story of Dale (Brooke Shields), who is obliged to take her father's place in an international car race through the Sahara. Once she gets on her way in the race, discarding the men's clothes that she had to wear initially to claim eligibility in a strictly male-only activity, she is abducted by Rasoul (John Rhys-Davies) who takes her to his tribal camp, but his advances are prevented by his handsome nephew Jaffar (Lambert Wilson). A desert romance then develops between Dale and Jaffar. After being involved in a fight with another tribe and its ruthless chief, she returns to the car race to win it, but in the middle of the celebrations she decides to go back to Jaffar and the film ends with them riding on one horse against the red sunset, to the accompaniment of triumphant music. This spectacle replaces the lone ranger of the western films with male and female representatives of the East and West, heralding a happy future together.[4]

There are in the film some stereotypical scenes, such as when Dale is shown staggering along aimlessly in the vast, scorched desert under a sun at its zenith. The camera at this point is in flicker mode, underlining the instability of the air in the heat. Naturally, she loses her battle against nature and collapses, thus becoming easy prey to the evil tribal chief. The sandstorm is also a widely used desert feature, as we have seen many times before, and in this instance it rains on a racing car and engulfs it, knocking one of Dale's competitors out of the race. The action film presents an additional set of dilemmas: an army of scorpions approaching Dale's unconscious body; two leopards that are made to chase the harmless gypsies in the desert by the rival tribesmen; and large pieces of rock pushed from the top of a mountain cave by the same evil tribesmen to crush Jaffar's men below are some of the devices used to increase suspense and excitement. On the romantic side, a large oasis with a thicket of palm trees and a waterfall is offered as a location for the couple's first kiss. This hard-to-believe setting leads even Dale to remark, "A waterfall in the middle of the desert! It's breathtaking!"

Just as it is suggested that the wilderness is a space to be both conquered and worshipped, the desert in *Sahara* (1983) is used as a backdrop for the good and ugly actions of its inhabitants. The scene where the tribeswomen tear up Dale's clothes like wild animals is congruous with their cave habitat. Captives being thrown down a well where hungry leopards are waiting is another motif underlining the savagery associated with the place. On the other hand, the film also celebrates beauty and tranquility of the feminized desert with long aerial shots of the virgin sand dunes, one after the other, with their white, smooth and curvy surfaces.

More than any other film of the pre-9/11 period, *Sahara* is the most appropriate example to compare with *Hidalgo* to see what has changed in the post-9/11 era, because of the similarities in their narrative structure. Both films are about a race and the participants have to survive their journey through the desert to reach their destination. While in *Sahara* expensive cars are used for this purpose, in *Hidalgo* the racers compete on horseback. Despite this resemblance, however, the environment is depicted differently. As discussed above, the way the desert is projected in *Sahara* serves the stages of the love story and the battles fought for the sake of this love, and in this respect the location does not stand out on its own but provides a vehicle for the progress of the narrative. In comparison, in *Hidalgo* we see a mighty desert, like a living being, fiercely competing with the protagonist and pushing him almost to the point of extinction. In this sense, the Muslim space in *Hidalgo*, although marked by some of the clichés we have become accustomed to in the pre-9/11 period, is a richer and more novel depiction of the man-and-nature interaction.

## *The Desert After 9/11:* Hidalgo *(2004)*

*Hidalgo* tells a story involving a half–Native American man, Frank Hopkins (Viggo Mortensen), and his mustang, Hidalgo, being challenged to take part in a 3,000-mile survival race in the Najd region of Arabia. Despite the dangers created for him by his Bedouin competitors on Arabian horses, he wins the race and also the heart of the Sheikh's (Omar Sharif) daughter, Jazira (Zuleikha Robinson).

The film manages to identify typical key features that derive from the cinematic Native American character and attributes these to the Arab. Reminiscent of Mark Twain's comments, quoted by Hutchinson (1994, 17), regarding the similarities between Arabs and Native Americans—both being "infested with vermin"—the likeness between these two races is magnified in the film. Instead of being offered a peace pipe in a tepee, Frank is given a water pipe to smoke in a Bedouin tent, and the Arab Muslim, like the Native American, is portrayed in a patriarchal manner and considered to have similar traditional and spiritual affinities with horses, nature and God. The comparison is even made in an exchange between Jazira and Frank:

> JAZIRA: In this wild west there are nomads also. The red people like the Bedouin. They are a horse culture. Have you seen their vanishing kind?
> FRANK: I am their kind.

The spirit of the western genre, the plight of the black slave/Native American and the celebration of cultural diversity are all areas that nationalistically evoke sentiments of an American heritage. *Hidalgo* manages to capture each of these and build an overview that incorporates them within the scope of the desert. Its ideological premise is to adopt recognizable themes and establish them in an environment that would benefit from Western intervention. This moral justification and reasoning culminates in the heroism of Frank winning the race and achieving superiority in the Muslim space. However, it should be noted that this does not represent the superiority of Christianity over Islam. As Frank is someone brought up in the American wilderness, whose physical and psychological world consists of Native American norms, his triumph in the desert is attributed to his nationality rather than his religious inclinations. To the Arab characters in the film, he is a cowboy equivalent of Buffalo Bill. His presence is menacing—even when they hear the tune he plays in darkness on the harmonica, they are frightened to the extent that they respond by devising devilish traps.

Viewing *Hidalgo* in light of Ingram's (2004) abovementioned comments about bourgeois considerations, which are described in terms of men's ambition to conquer and dominate nature as seen through the lens of the camera, it is noticeable that these are addressed from the onset. The opening images of a snowy American forest gradually melting due to a seasonal change point to the significant role the natural wilderness will play throughout the course of the narrative. The constant orchestral and exaggerated soundtrack, as well as the sudden close-up of Hidalgo surrounded by a lush and picturesque pasture, at the beginning of the film evokes a stylized self-proclaimed belief that U.S. ideals are born from the expansive beauty of its wilderness. The spectral visions of the diverse landscapes in the States contrast with the later empty-looking desert environments, and it is this sense of ideological domination and the portrayal of the natural landscape that makes *Hidalgo* a modern-day exploration of forgotten U.S. ideals. While the climax of the film's race at the end focuses on the expansive nature of the blue Arabian Sea, in the waves of which Frank and Hidalgo celebrate their victory, it also manages to capture the rolling landscape of the desert to demonstrate the limitless and vast effect nature has on the human psyche. This is what Martin Lefebvre (2006) calls an "informative" setting, as discussed earlier, which helps to express the character's state of mind.

The film identifies common ailments in cultural ideologies and acknowledges Hollywood's historic Orientalist association with the Middle East. It assumes that the audience is able to recognize Orientalist character traits and locations from past Hollywood incarnations, alongside a current sociopolitical understanding of events post 9/11. To this effect, the usual tropes are present, such as the desert raiders, gypsy caravans, slave markets, desert falcons, scorpions and tattered grey tents. With mirages and thermal heat waves, the desert is projected as capable of distorting and confusing its entities, a force that cannot be tamed but can tame humans. In one take of a long shot exhibiting its expanse, the desert space gets smaller as a sandstorm approaches and swallows everything under it like a tsunami, ready to crush the tiny riders galloping for their lives. This demonstrates in the most dramatic way the extent of man's weakness when pitted against the rage of nature. The desert in *Hidalgo* also acts as an equalizer or cleanser for those characters who champion their own self-worth and ideology. The terrain is a means to motivate its protagonist and give him the required impetus not only to win the race, but also to morally justify his desire for recognition by his Arab contemporaries.

As Frank finds refuge from the climatic disruptions that occur, he contemplates his past. His vision/mirage towards the end gives him the required insight to understand himself and rediscover his identity, as a result of which he returns to live with his Native American soulmates. In contrast, to those who are unable to find refuge, the desert promises a more theatrical end like their space being enveloped by their environment and drowned in quicksand. The underlying message is that, in the Middle East, space works against those who inhabit it, while in America the focus is on a more harmonious relationship, although with similarly destructive results, reminding us that the Native Americans were subjected to spatial territorialization at the hands of the U.S. cavalry.

The film gives us examples to build a better understanding of different cultural landscapes and, in this respect, reflects the characteristics of transnational cinema. While Frank questions the role of the black slave (Jazira's manservant) in Arabia, he also acknowledges the restrictions placed upon their space in the United States. As his quest is to discover who he truly is, the Muslim space reminds, reinforces and reaffirms his desire to associate himself with the natural native inhabitants of his home.

Apart from the two contrasting yet in some ways similar spaces, i.e., the Middle East and the "Wild" West in the States, there is one more spatial point of comparison in the film, that is, the space of the colonialists. In the English characters, Lady Davenport and Major Timothy Dalton, we see colonialism personified; they are intentional reference points that remind the audience of the origins of the American military's massacre of Native Americans at the beginning of the film. Lady Davenport, with her ambition to get her horse to win at all costs, even having Frank murdered, is an example of a cold-blooded colonialist taking advantage of her power in a primitive location. Similarly, some iconic characters such as Buffalo Bill are considered just as critically in their association with and participation in the aforementioned massacre.

While *Hidalgo* captures and contrasts the wilderness landscape spaces in the United States and the Middle East, it also acknowledges the existence of a nearby Muslim city, adorned with all the familiar elements. The souk provides a stage for depicting stereotypically mischievous Muslim characters, intent on achieving personal gain whatever the consequence. Whether the emphasis is on a chaotic process of buying, selling and bargaining for goods, or on the protagonist rescuing the heroine, Orientalist images seem to be used in order to fill in the cinematographic tapestry of frame. They are not required to distract our attention from the spectacle, but to emphasize the filmic canvas and play to our familiarity with and expectations of the scene. In the film, various towns, souks and water wells are dominated by unsavory characters, be they Arab Muslim aides or corrupt British soldiers, motivated by payment from an equally corrupt Arab prince.

Each setting portrays an ancient lifestyle that contrasts with that of the U.S. landscape: the guarded and limited water hole in Arabia contrasts with the abundant and free-flowing rivers at the start of the film; the old and decrepit city that Frank rescues Princess Jazira from is the opposite of the modern clamor of New York City; and the derelict area where Frank seeks refuge from the hostile sandstorm contrasts with America's open plains and green pastures. Even the allusion to the enclosure and confines of a Bedouin tent is contrasted with the large and colorful circus marquee that Frank finds himself in while dreaming about his collaboration with Buffalo Bill.

These contrasting scenes continue throughout the film. One example is when the viewer is invited to compare the scenes in which the ship carrying Frank and Hidalgo leaves New York and arrives at an Arabian port. The departing steam liner is marred and stained with a grey and ominous looking undertone, which foreshadows the impending storm that lies ahead for the protagonists. The expansive ocean is rough and choppy. The Statue of Liberty, the familiar cinematic trope that has been used in many past U.S. films to romanticize an immigrants' arrival into the new world, now recedes in the background, a reminder of the county's nationalist legacy. The shot of the steam liner's arrival at the Arabian port reverses the cultural significance of traditionalism and modern industrial capitalism. The call to prayer now dominates the cinematic frame and a minaret assumes the same position and importance formerly held by the Statue of Liberty. However, in this instance the sea is calm, sedate and blue and the sky is lit with sunshine. Through these comparative shots, a thematic balance is established between the advantages and disadvantages of both locations. To achieve this, the filmmaker artificially creates the image of the ship arriving at the port using computer-generated imagery (in fact, this is the color version of the same still drawing that *The Sheik* opens with).

However, it must be said that the contrast between the Muslim desert and the U.S. territories in the film is not drawn crudely. In the same Eastern lands, the characters are shown as experiencing both the blazing desert during the race and the coolness of the Arabian sea during the end-of-race jubilations. The frames therefore capture not nationalistic divisions, but the interface between human sensations and the offerings of the environment, regardless of who is experiencing this interaction and where it is experienced.

In terms of gender, the veil brings a constrictive significance to the female spaces inhabited by either Lady Davenport or Jazira. Both require stimulation or an awakening by an American male, but while Jazira eventually dismisses the veil's social necessity and shows her face in full, Lady Davenport is seen adorning a Western-fashioned, transparent version following her failed attempt to seduce Frank. The contrast drawn here is that the desert, where the traditional restrictions of a city are absent, allows an Eastern woman to open up and a Western woman to close herself off, to the same end. The effect is of blurred identities, the West imitating the East and the East emulating the West.

*Hidalgo* also offers contrasting portraits of local people. There are two Bedouin tribes operating autonomously according to two separate ideologies, representing the new and the old. Their nomadic existence is examined within the scope of their desert landscape and hinges on the constant influence of

*Hidalgo* (Joe Johnston, 2004): Frank Hopkins (Viggo Mortensen) and his mustang are worn out in their struggle to survive the dangers thrown at them by a "capricious" desert of changing moods.

foreign sources—Sheikh Riyadh's partial devotion to Islam but also his childlike excitement at getting hold of Frank's Remington pistol is a case in point. Their habitat is devoid of life and their choice of structural dwelling—the tent—is indicative of their primordial lifestyle. In the same way that the tent represents an enclosed space that is easily transferable and practical, and thus able to adapt to the rapidly and unexpectedly changing moods of the desert and travel, the Arab characters are able to adapt to the numerous influences that coexist within the same location. The constant change in locale and region does eventually upset the hierarchical positioning of the Arab characters in the film, but this is primarily to do with the pressure Western characters exert on their status quo.

*Hidalgo* differs from earlier desert movies in the way it depicts the environment and personifies it with human qualities and temperaments. This is a wilderness that can be calm and inviting like Jazira, or harsh and atrocious like some of Frank's Arab competitors. To survive its ruthless changes in mood one needs accessories (binoculars, a compass, a cowboy's hat, a lasso, even the ruins of a deserted city); quick thinking (Frank feeds himself and his horse with the remnants of a desert locust swarm); spiritual opulence (he performs a "death dance" of the Native Americans at a point when all hope for survival is lost); and unconditional love (Frank lets the Arab who injured Hidalgo die in a booby trap, saying, "No one hurts my horse").

Frank is shown wrestling with the natural wilderness not for material gain, which is what motivates his co-racers, but for spiritual satisfaction. In this respect, the exchange he has with Sheikh Riyadh at the end of the race while giving him his pistol as a present is significant:

SHEIKH RIYADH: But I lost the race.
FRANK: Yes, but you gained a friend.

Frank's perseverance in surviving in the desert becomes more meaningful when, at the end of the film, he uses the prize money to buy all the wild mustangs that are about to be exterminated by the American cavalry and releases them back into the pastures, together with his much-loved Hidalgo. This, then, brings a new meaning to Hidalgo's appearance in the green opulence of the American West at the beginning of the film, and connects this richness more to the state of being peaceful and free than to being in his home country.

*Hidalgo* has attracted the attention of a number of analysts. On the linguistic credibility of the film, Tayyara (2014) suggests that both literary and colloquial Arabic are used to show the high and low functions of the language, and quotes from the conversation between Sheikh Riyadh and his daughter, noting that, in contrast to earlier films, the exchange reflects correct language use, with due observation of gender, age and social status:

> JAZĪRA: kunn hadhir idhan yā 'Johabī. La'anī akūn 'alā qimat sa'ādatī 'alā hīsān, arkab al-khayl haythu al-nisā' muharramāt (So be careful my father, what you wish for, because I am the happiest when I am on horseback when other women are forbidden to do so).
>
> SHEIKH RIYĀD: fī khaymatī 'āsifa jā'at bi-shakl ibnatī al-'azīza. Hall turīdīn an takūnī sabab fī tafjīr marāratī al-fāshila (In my tent there is a tempest in the shape of my beloved daughter. Do you want to be the cause of bursting my malfunctioning gall-bladder)? [7].

A point not underlined by Tayyara (2014), however, is that we are presented in this instance with a pair who break free from Muslim family stereotypes: a non-typical Muslim father who tries hard to convince his daughter to marry the man of his choice, not through force but by asking her to take pity on his health, and a daughter who is more akin to a Westerner than women in her environment.

An area that has received sparse attention in academic work, however, is the Muslim space captured by the film. Rather than the interaction between man and nature, some writers prefer attending to the synergy between man and animal. Helff (2016), for example, studies *Hidalgo* not from the viewpoint of man–environment interaction, but as an example of the man–animal relationship within the framework of transnational cinema. She claims that the film mixes genres in order to reach out emotionally to the cinemagoer. This newly created genre of the sport film-cum-adventure western may sound attractive and challenging but "emotional contact has always been, and still is, central in the visual narration of the horse–human relationship" (105). The changing moods of the desert are what affect the actions of the hero and move the narrative forward, but Helff's article is mainly interested in the solidarity between the rider protagonist and his horse, with no mention of the terrain they figuratively conquer.

The most extensive study of *Hidalgo* has been carried out by Susan Kollin (2015), who calls it an "Indian sympathy film." She says loyalties are divided in the film between whites and Native Americans, "acknowledging the complexities of racial identity in contemporary multicultural U.S. society" (102). Her focus remains on the narrative development more than on the accord between man and his space. She mentions that the hero, Frank Hopkins, faces challenges from treacherous opponents, thwarts the sexual demands of a female British horse owner and woos the daughter of an over-controlling father. Despite her divergent style, which wanders into the areas of Omar Sharif's career (he plays Sheikh Riyadh in the film), and the background story to the making of the Statue of Liberty, she also makes some useful observations. The gender politics displayed in the film, which are in accordance with "the complicated and contradictory post-feminism of the Bush administration" (*ibid.*, 109), and the struggle of the hero in his feat to tame the unruly racial "Others," are mentioned in passing. Additionally, there are references to the British colonial order—as represented by Lady Davenport—needing to be (symbolically) contained "in order for the American to assert his own national interests" (*ibid.*, 108). Hopkins' love interest, a "woman of cover" (Jazira), is mentioned as needing to be modernized, in line with Shohat's (1997) "colonial rescue fantasy," because she is a dark-skinned woman "trapped in [a] brutal retrograde society" (Kollin 2015, 11). However, while the narrative, characters and social/political/racial implications of the film are explained in 25 pages, Kollin has almost nothing to say about the desert in which the story unfolds. Only in one instance does she propose that in *Hidalgo* we are "constantly presented with symbols of decay, of relics and archaeological remains of long-gone civilizations, swallowed up by time and the desert" (*ibid.*, 111). Equating the role of the desert solely with the need for modernization of the Middle East, even though such modernization is overdue and seriously required, does injustice to the functional use of space in the film. It is in fact its play on the interface between man and his environment that makes *Hidalgo* a memorable product of filmic art. It is also right to say that, with its superb—sometimes real and sometimes digitally produced—views of the desert from artistic angles, the film makes the audience see that one can come out of the desert intact despite all the hindrances it may throw up. Survival for both locals and outsiders is through common sense and inner strength. The desert in the film, as an example of transnational cinema, is no longer an exclusive space for the uncivilized Muslim—it is now a space for every believer or non-believer, rewarding the respectful and punishing the disrespectful.

To conclude, it is right to say that, in the classical style filmmaking, the desert has been projected as a partly wild and partly romantic place wherein the qualities generally associated with Muslim Arabs can be magnified. Its wild characteristics have been highlighted to confirm Western preconceptions that desert inhabitants are in every way inferior. Their primitive world is comprised of primitive artifacts and governed by animal instincts for survival. On the other hand, the whipped-egg-white appearance of sand-dune tranquility, and oases blessed with water and palm trees have been used as a backdrop to monoracial or interracial romantic allegiances. In the period from the 1970s to the turn of the century, when the world came to be plagued with global oil shortages and the Arab-Israeli tug-of-war over Jerusalem, unsavory characters of international terrorism dominated the on-screen desert (e.g., *Raid on Entebbe* [1977]). However, later films, while reproducing earlier depictions, have been additionally marked by references to American victories in the Gulf Wars, which devastated not only the cities in Iraq, but also turned the desert into a wasteland.

*Hidalgo*, which was produced after 9/11, is the first American-made desert film where a psychological element is wrought into the spectacle, similarly to David Lean's *Lawrence of Arabia*. The desert has a designated role, as if it were a living being, kind to its worshippers and cruel to its enemies, be they Christian or Muslim. Projecting Frank and Hidalgo in extended takes in their lone journey across the Sahara, alternating between low- and high-angle shots, the filmmaker uses the desert as an animated force in close interaction with man and his horse. In fact, it is through the interaction of an extraordinary man with an extraordinary environment that the narrative develops, the man and the environment being at times in close harmony, and at others terrifyingly at odds.

## *The Muslim City (Baghdad) Before and After 9/11*

Unlike the previous section, where the correlations between the environmental landscape and its inhabitants are highlighted, this section assesses various features that are attributed in films over the course of time to a particular city, Baghdad, in the so-called "Orient." The city of Cairo has also appealed to many productions over the years but Baghdad is chosen as a case study in this instance because of its affiliation with the *Arabian Nights* stories, and also because it is recognizably an Arabian city, as Scurry (2010) rightly describes, while Cairo is quite often associated with ancient Egypt. In his analysis, Scurry also looks at films set in Jerusalem and Egypt alongside Baghdad but he says of the latter, "The Baghdad portrayed in American cinema is always depicted from an external perspective.[5] It is represented by outsiders, for outsiders, and no thought is given to how residents of Baghdad perceive their city" (18). To observe an up-to-date portrayal of Baghdad, he selects *Body of Lies* (2008); however, his interest is drawn not to the way the city is depicted as the story unfolds, but to the underlying message it carries in its criticism of American policies. He makes a reference to what can be termed "classical cinematic orientalism" and points out that "[t]he film includes many of the stock features of cinematic orientalism, such as torture and sinister Arab terrorists, but there is also an effort to move beyond stereotypes and blatant xenophobia" (Scurry 2010, 33).

While the city is not a relatively monotonous landscape like the desert, the aspects selected for the camera lens are still a crucial decision for the film director. In real life, there is a 360-degree interaction and two-way engagement between people and their surroundings, but a cinema audience is offered the 180-degree realization of the scene that the camera is turned towards. The features of the location transported to the screen can accentuate the underlying message that the filmmaker wishes to impart. The architectural location created in this way plays upon the multisensory and multidimensional experience of the film. Unlike the natural wilderness habitat, the city's presence and its landscapes, whether filmed in studio or on location, are responsible for stimulating the audience's memory of preconceptions, which in turn is directly attributable to the notion of how they perceive the city's organic foundation. However, in contrast to the natural wilderness, cities change in time as architectural and social needs dictate. This is a process that most well-known cities have undergone. Lisiak (2010, 185), for instance, observes that after the end of the Cold War, film portrayals of central European cities, such as Berlin, Prague, Budapest and Warsaw, have provided the audience with new images to make them aware of the transformations. Films have also taken into account changes in Western European capitals, such as London, Paris, Rome and Berlin, but the tendencies in presenting a Middle Eastern city such as Baghdad on screen, as noted by Shaheen (1993), cited above, have not changed, at least until recently.

A study of place depictions in films is not only beneficial for updating the public memory in terms of the urban characteristics of the same place, but can also reveal the evolution of filmmakers' approach over a period of time marked with fluctuations in ideologies. For this reason, the choice of films set in Baghdad—*Bagdad* (1949), *The Human Shield* (1991) and *Green Zone* (2010)—is important as they hold a mirror not only to changing habits in the use of artistic license but also to how the city is regarded in terms of its geopolitics.

### Adventurous Baghdad—Bagdad (1949)

The city of Baghdad in this film is depicted as a site of conspiracy and infidelity on the one hand, and mysticism and love on the other. It is described by one character, a suave representative of the Ottoman palace, pasha Ali Nadim (Vincent Price), as "Bagdad. The Arab's abode of peace. But for several centuries there has been no peace." This contradictory utterance foretells the opposition inherent in the movie. The setting, while used as a backdrop for a love story, also includes elements that nurture savagery.

The film was first screened in New York City on 13 December 1949; the next day *The New York Times* commented: "Old Bagdad, city of mystery and enchantment, is the locale of the new romantic adventure, called, appropriately enough, 'Bagdad,' which Universal-International presented yesterday at the Criterion. Done up in Technicolor and glittering like Broadway after dark, 'Bagdad' spins a familiar story of intrigue, revenge and, naturally, romance without making any attempt to apologize for its clichés. That's one point in its favor, at least."[6]

This cliché-ridden story, as it is rightly described above, involves a Hollywood-ized Muslim princess, Marjan (Maureen O'Hara), the daughter of a Bedouin leader, returning from her studies in England only to find out that her father was murdered in her absence. Determined to bring the murderer to justice, she gets involved in a confrontation between the Arabs and the Bedouin renegades, while at the same time being courted by the suave but corrupt pasha Ali Nadim. Upon her return to Baghdad she meets and falls for a prince of another Bedouin tribe, Hassan (Paul Christian), who is accused by his cousin, Raizul (John Sutton), of the murder of the princess' father, while in actual fact it was Raizul and his men of the Black Robes who had him killed. To find out who the culprit is, the main characters, as well as their henchmen, soldiers and guards, convene at an oasis in the desert. A fight breaks out between Raizul and Hassan, who is rescued by his father at the last minute, leading to a happy ending for him and Marjan.

Islamic "Otherness" is underlined as soon as the film's first light hits the screen. The opening credits (and also those at the end) pass over a picture of three mosques. Background commentary describes the location—"Bagdad, ageless city of intrigue and treachery.... Crossroads between the West and savage East"—followed by a shot of a minaret where an imam is chanting the call to prayer to the accompaniment of Middle Eastern music. Next, the camera captures a group of Arabs performing *namaz* in a desert, prostrate on the ground, their foreheads resting on the sand. They are the camel drivers of the caravan, carrying the belongings of Princess Marjan, who is on her way to Baghdad under the protection of the pasha's soldiers. Once they reach the entrance gates, the camera turns to a picture showing Baghdad as a small city inside a citadel, inhabited by Arabs, although the extras dressed in European clothing indicate that the city is not completely cut off from the rest of the world.

A Western audience can easily associate with the décor in closed environments such as the Ottoman pasha's palace and the hotel where Princess Marjan stays. Large entrance halls with chandeliers, marble floors and columns, spacious bedrooms with brocade curtains and king-size beds are familiar features. However, the mixture of East and West is taken to an absurd level in one of these settings, Café Ifrangi, a European restaurant which, it seems, the filmmaker is using in order to satisfy the audience's hunger for the Hollywood extravaganzas of the 1940s, but which in fact produces a most bizarre and unrealistic environment. This is intended to dazzle the audience, with line dances of semi-clad girls in colorful Eastern costumes and jewelry, and musicians seated cross-legged on the floor, accompanying Princess Marjan, who resembles a New York nightclub singer with her uncovered ginger hair, singing romantic ballads in the European fashion. The non–Arab customers are shown to be sitting at tables of normal height while most of the Arab guests are at dwarf tables and chairs, yet they too applaud most emphatically Princess Marjan's songs, which are delivered with no regard for her religion and culture. While the locals are shown drinking tea, champagne is served at the foreigners' tables, including that occupied by the pasha, the princess and Prince Hassan. The latter's white evening suit and Marjan's ball gown are completely inappropriate for Bedouin royalty—both of them, as well as the Ottoman pasha in his military regalia, are an irrational juxtaposition of elements in this bizarre setting.

Public places are also imaginary creations, putting on display all kinds of tropes associated with the "uncivilized" Orient: men relaxing over water pipes; beggars in rags and tatters calling for "alms for the love of Allah"; sand diviners with scruffy white hair and long white beards reading fortunes on the sand; an ox-drawn water mill in the middle of the square; baskets of cherries, oranges and pomegranates on sale; acrobats juggling fire rings; a barber shaving his customer in the open air; women wearing *burkas* and *niqabs*; men in clothes reflecting a wide geography from India to north Africa; donkeys, horses, goats, and dirty looking children all parade in front of the audience.

Outside the city gates, which are closed at night to keep away thieves and murderers because, as the Ottoman pasha puts it, "those savages stop at nothing," lies the arid, vast, sandy desert as an alien space. It harbors the same menace found in other desert films. A horde of bandits on horseback suddenly appears at the top of a sand dune when signaled by the gang leader, and charges at the protagonist(s). Desert people called the Black Robes invade the city, causing pandemonium with their archaic weaponry of knives and swords in an otherwise peacefully settled area, just like a group of bandits of Mexican or American origin in a western film, galloping into a dusty, shaky town to cause mayhem.

*Bagdad* (1949) is an example of the artistic visualization of a location put together with the help of imagination, old clichés and stereotypes as well as ploys for which financial return has proved to be high in the past. Common sense in creating utopias and dystopias cannot be questioned when there are no political pressures on the filmmakers or the audiences, who are there to entertain and be entertained; however, once political conjunctures require a more target-driven approach, the outcome may be a location which is depicted with a frenzy of propaganda and national fervor, as is the case in *The Human Shield* (1991).

### Depressive Baghdad—The Human Shield (1991)

This story begins with an incident in 1985. One of the Americans helping Iraqi forces with battle techniques, Colonel Doug Matthews (Michael Dudikoff), travels in an open jeep through the arid territory of Northern Iraq. By chance, he comes across a troop of Iraqi soldiers killing all the Kurds in a small village. He is told that these villagers have been collaborating with the fighters from neighboring Iran during the ongoing Iran-Iraq war. In his effort to stop the massacre, he engages in a fight with the leader of the troop, Ali Dallal (Steve Inwood), and slashes him across the face with a knife.

Five years later, while foreign nationals are leaving Iraq in fear of the looming First Gulf War, Doug's diabetic brother, Ben Matthews (Tommy Hinkley), is taken hostage by Iraqi soldiers at Baghdad airport on the orders of Ali, who has by now become the Chief of Staff. Ali hopes that by holding Ben in custody he will lure Doug back to Iraq for revenge. As expected, Doug returns to Baghdad and with the help of his former friend of Kurdish origin, Tanzi (Uri Gabriel), and the girlfriend he left behind, Lila Haddilh (Hanna Azoulay Hasfari), he rescues his brother from captivity, demolishes a huge chemical compound where Ben was kept and kills Ali.

The city of Baghdad in the film is projected more as a provincial town than the capital city of an oil-rich country. There are many scenes shot at night, showing different buildings of a contrasting nature: some are mansion-like lodgings or government offices, blazing with light and well guarded by the armed forces, such as the property owned by Ali; others are dilapidated, uninhabited, whitewashed constructions, giving the impression that they have been left unrepaired since the Iran-Iraq war. There are no views of the impressive looking palaces and monuments built during the Saddam era. The roads shown on the screen are narrow, lit only on one side by street lights and deserted, except for a few pedestrians, which adds to the gloomy atmosphere of the environment. Even on the main street where Ali's luxurious property is located, no other eye-catching buildings can be seen. In the side streets, there are worn-out, two-story dwellings where the city's poor probably live. Their shutters are kept closed even during the day, revealing no sign of life behind them. The city's icons, such as the Golden Gate Palace, Hands of Victory arches and other historical structures, do not feature in the film, not even in the distance. In *The Human Shield*, the message to the audience is that Baghdad has long lost its past glorious attraction and its citizens are sentenced to live a drab life with no place for leisure or entertainment.

The views of the metropolis during the daytime are similarly gloomy. There are no children or stray animals in sight, nor are there any street vendors, who are common in Baghdad, bringing energy and vitality to the capital. Soldiers in their brown uniforms are noticeable everywhere and it looks like there are more security forces in the city than citizens, despite the fact that at the time of shooting the population of Baghdad was around 7 million. At one point, the camera captures a plain-looking mosque, a favorite trope in films depicting the Middle East, but the river Tigris, which passes through Baghdad and brings dynamism to the city, is nowhere to be seen. Old-model automobiles as well as some occasional state cars are driven through the streets.

It is noticeable that a contrast is created in terms of locations, that is, between Baghdad and the Kurdish village where Tanzi takes Doug to hide. They arrive at the village when the birth of a baby is being celebrated in the communal tent with music and singing. It is a rocky area with goats and donkeys, the meager sources of income for the villagers, resting outside the tent's entrance. The Kurds welcome the newcomers and make them join the feast laid out on floor rugs. Tanzi and Doug sit side by side with men and women. This merry environment in the mountainous terrain is the opposite of the gloom surrounding the city.

There is also a noticeable contrast between costumes. The city dwellers wear plain-colored clothes, some in European style, some in Arabic fashion, long *thobes* as a cloak, and a *gutra* on their head secured with a black cord. Not counting the dull-looking military uniforms, Baghdad in this film gives the impression that it is a racially mixed city, comprising of Arabs, Kurds and the Turkmen. In comparison, the Kurdish village in the mountain has a more decisive character. Despite holding the celebrations inside the confines of the tent, the villagers all wear headgear, possibly to mark that it is a special occasion. This consists of a variety of turbans of different sizes for men, and colorful scarves for women, covering their hair as well as their forehead, adorned with gold coins or beads. The place buzzes with merriment, with no anticipation that the village will be ambushed the next morning by Ali's troops and all, except for Doug, will be killed.

The line between cruelty and benevolence in the film is drawn in an essentialist way, based not on religion but race. The harsh dictum prevailing in Baghdad at the time is spelt out by Ali when he says to Doug, "Insults here can only be washed away with blood." The protagonist is the target of an army of Iraqi Arabs who hunt him with the intent to kill, while the Kurdish villagers provide him with hospitality and refuge at the expense of losing their own lives. Yet, all those on either side of the line are believers in Islam, albeit from different sects. The film seems to have predicted in 1991 the developments that would take place in the second decade of the new century, when the United States helped the Kurds to become autonomous in Northern Iraq where important oil reservoirs are situated. Long shots are used when Doug is travelling through the vast plain in his jeep, capturing a large area within the frame and emphasizing its magnanimity as well as its tranquility. The only background noise is that of the jeep's engine. However, the city is filmed using medium or close-up shots, emphasizing its claustrophobic nature. The minaret is framed in a close upward shot which lasts only a couple of seconds, once more verifying that in this context it is not religion that is at the center of adversity.

Baghdad as portrayed in *The Human Shield* is not the Baghdad depicted in earlier periods (1910–1950). Gone are the days of *The Thief of*

*Baghdad* (1924) and *Kismet* (1944), when the city was reflected as a dazzling center of wealth, both in the physical and psychological sense, communicated through the use of color, dance, music, romanticism and mysticism. Instead, the Baghdad of the 1990s is made to disclose calm indifference and pessimism. While this is a noteworthy change, it should be borne in mind that Baghdad was not represented accurately in either of these periods (the 1920s–1940s and 1950s–1990s). It is noticeable that although in the films of these eras focusing on the desert—e.g., *The Garden of Allah* (1936) and *Lawrence of Arabia* (1962)—panoramic scenery is captured using long or aerial shots, only close-up shots are used in *Bagdad* and *The Human Shield*, suggesting that the city as shown in these two movies is what lies in the mind of the filmmaker and not how Baghdad actually was at the time. After 9/11 however, there is an obvious change in the filming of the city. The Iraqi capital is often shown from a bird's-eye view, depicting its many features in the same frame, with all its similar or opposing characteristics, as is the case in *Green Zone* (2010).

## "Shock and awe"—Green Zone (2010)

The subject of this film is "chaos" in everything that is connected with the invasion of Iraq in 2003. The Iraqis are in turmoil and rebellious because they have been bombarded day in, day out, and cut off from their lifelines; the Americans are divided among themselves—the Pentagon, the CIA and the military, each with different agendas for the future of Iraq. The city of Baghdad is projected as going through the most chaotic period in its history. It is as if there is an interface between the city and those who happen to be there, whether they are locals or Americans, each affecting the other in an antagonistic way. Greedy men destroy the environment, and the destroyed environment spurs animal-like behavior in men.

The film starts in the three-week period when Baghdad was undergoing an air attack by the U.S. Air Force. An Army chief warrant officer, Roy Miller (Matt Damon), who is on duty during this period to find weapons of mass destruction (WMDs), realizes that, on several occasions, he was given a false report about the site he was asked to investigate. While he and his platoon are in a city square digging holes in the ground to find biological weapons, he is informed by an Arab who introduces himself as Freddy (Khalid Abdalla) that Saddam Hussein's right-hand man, General Mohammed Al-Rawi (Yigal Naor), is holding a secret meeting with some Ba'ath Party leaders in a house somewhere in the city. Miller and his men ambush the house but Al-Rawi escapes. From a man taken hostage during this ambush, Miller learns that Al-Rawi disclosed to Pentagon officials several months ago in Jordan that all WMDs in Iraq had been destroyed and that there was nothing left in the country to cause concern for the United States or its allies. Realizing that the intelligence given to him for the search of WMDs does not have any substance, Miller wants to get hold of Al-Rawi so that the general can make public the details of his meeting with Pentagon representatives in Jordan. At the point when Miller finds Al-Rawi and is about to convince him to give himself up, Freddy, who appears to be a follower of the Shia sect of Islam and not a Sunni Muslim like Al-Rawi, shoots and kills him. The film ends with a long aerial shot capturing the American tanks moving into Baghdad, the Tigris and the suburbs of Baghdad on one side of the road and a huge oil refinery compound on the other, suggesting that in fact this, and not the WMDs, are the real reason for the invasion.

The opening scenes in the film show a city in complete disarray, caused by American soldiers rushing through the streets trying to find the snipers lurking in multistory, derelict constructions, while hundreds of looters run in all directions with goods they have recovered from the debris of the bomb-destroyed buildings. People pull and push one another, trying to make way for themselves while carrying their loads of pillows and bedding, large containers, paintings, furniture, urns, planks of wood and metal rods, among other things. It is even possible to see on screen the effects of a missile, creating a hole in a wall from which hundreds of concrete pieces spurt out in slow motion into the dusty air. The whole environment, with its roads and buildings, looks yellowish white, which is probably a ploy used to convey to the audience that in this environment nothing is free from a thick layer of dust. The sounds of guns firing, people shouting, engines running, and a CNN anchorwoman reporting the news, are all presented simultaneously as the background noise adds to the mayhem that unfolds in front of the audience's eyes. It is as if the day of apocalypse has come to Baghdad.

In one of the night scenes, the camera frames the Tigris river reflecting a city pounded by Tomahawk cruise missiles, with red flames and clouds of white smoke continuously popping up. The sky lights up with each explosion as the missiles hit the ground, as if hundreds of volcanoes are erupting one after the other. This mayhem, coupled with the sirens in the background, must be very close to the real-life experiences of the city at the time. The slipshod rockets hit the ground incessantly and the intensified bombing of civilian targets creates a humanitarian disaster.

The inclusion of modern technology, which governs the landscape in *Green Zone* points to the superiority of those who can manipulate its application. Through cyberspace, Miller is able to investigate and apprehend those who are eventually deemed guilty; through its domination of air space (which is never challenged in the sky, although later in the film a helicopter is attacked from a ground offensive), the U.S. military is able to maintain a stranglehold on the city. The air-force presence at Baghdad Airport, the helicopters taxying military personnel, the control centers, the tanks rolling on strategic roads, and the communication systems, all add up to resemble a "shock and awe" campaign. In the scene of the city square, where digging is carried out in search of biological weapons, a military helicopter suddenly rises up with a thundering noise, as if from the ground but from what turns out to be the cliff below, making three Muslim women in black *burka*s run for their lives.

A scene in which a U.S.-elected Iraqi leader is flown back to Baghdad airport projects the total territorialization of the city. The camera manages to capture the limitless sky intruded upon by military helicopters, and we are later reminded of this intrusion when the "deck of cards" (high-value targets) eliminator, Briggs' (Jason Isaacs) helicopter, lands in the middle of four high-rise residential blocks. In between these two contrasting scenes, the space, as the camera records it, is reduced. The technique of using low-level camera angles and wide-angle lenses in the airport scene, manages to capture the aerial activity and landscape of the location in full. Briggs' entrance is filmed from an aerial position in order to impede the abundant sky. This device is further elaborated in the execution of various ground-chase sequences filmed on the streets of Baghdad. The streets are made to resemble a maze where the characters are trapped as if within a labyrinth. The restriction of the city's environment and its effect on their personal space is evident in their inability to see the sky. The use of tight close-ups and the *cinéma vérité* style of capturing the scene not only accentuates the effect, but creates a sense of claustrophobia.

The projection of space is pivotal in the film. In the opening phase, a Muslim escaping from attack cries out to his compatriot, "Leave.... That space is limited!" This comment heralds the overall premise that each character has to fight for his or her space within a suppressive enclosure. In the course of the narrative, we are introduced to various forms of restrictive spaces, which the characters react to differently. The opening scene of a daytime traffic jam is used to illustrate the chaotic landscape that prohibits any form of mobility among its native inhabitants. Amidst this impasse, we are shown a montage of various Muslims reacting to encumbrance.

The experience of being bombarded every night and having their city turn to rubble might have been expected to create fear and subdued behavior among the people of Baghdad, but the filmmaker decides that a different type of reaction, that of anger and revolt, is more suitable. This is especially noticeable in the scene where the trucks carrying Miller's soldiers get stuck in the middle of a Gordian knot of traffic. It is a jam where every vehicle faces a different direction and every driver wants the right to pass. A large number of pedestrians caught inside the jam shout and gesticulate menacingly. Empty plastic water containers fly in the air, thrown by people protesting against the cut in the water supplies.

*Green Zone* (Paul Greengrass, 2010): The film, like the newsreels in 2003, realistically depicts Baghdad as a city where local Muslims and the invading forces experience chaos, frustration and fragmentation.

There are also aerial shots of a calm day with sunshine over the Republican Palace. The camera travels into Great Celebrations Square from the parade ground, lined on each side with tall palm trees, and then through the Victory Arch erected by Saddam Hussein to commemorate the Iran-Iraq war. It finally pans on the fairly damaged palace itself. On its way to the palace, the camera focuses on a dilapidated bridge that is the result of the air raid, its two feet still on either side of the street but the middle joining these supports now gone. Once the camera turns to show the interiors of the palace and its garden, we are presented with a totally different picture. Members of the international media and some American officers in leisurely clothes are around or in a large swimming pool, some sunbathing, some swimming, and others chatting over drinks. The serenity of the environment and the laid-back attitude of those present draw a striking contrast with earlier pictures of chaos in the city and create a surreal effect. The sense of relief released by the copious use of blue, as defined in the imagery of water, reinforces the idea of contrasting cultures in Baghdad and compensates for the dehydration invoked by the saturated yellow earlier on. While we are subjected to a decomposing city inhabited by Muslims, we are also given a perverse insight into locations soaked in recognizable Western trinkets representing America's global, economic and ideological dominance over the world.

The palace bedrooms are also shown in a way as to surprise viewers. A bed with a gold headboard in a stately room fit for a president is now used by Miller, while an oil painting in a golden frame rests against the wall on the floor. The great presidential hall with crystal chandeliers serves as a self-service canteen for the foreigners. The whole atmosphere surrounding the palace, inside and out, projects a world disclaimed by both cultures, with mismatched, contrasting arrangements. The same can also be observed outside, as in the square where the military excavators dig the ground on one side and Muslim children play football on the other, displaying a merger of two different worlds in the same frame.

The race between Miller's troops and the platoon activated by the Pentagon officer to capture Al-Rawi takes place in a suburban area of Baghdad. The demolition of the city center is something new and intentional, for which American foreign policy can be blamed, but the poverty and wretchedness, obvious in the peripheral areas, owe their existence to the neglect of the ousted regime. Here, the director chooses to film the area after dark, which adds to the ominous look of the place. Its narrow streets, black houses, the derelict, graffiti-covered bus-station wall, discarded pieces of cars, a pack of stray dogs that appear suddenly when Miller turns a corner, when all put together, increase the suspense that the environment creates. These scenes bring to mind Andrew Light's (1999) "urban wilderness," referred to earlier in this chapter.

*Green Zone* uses the souk to reinterpret a customary preconceived notion in a manner that almost deliberately provokes the audience to revaluate and reassess their indoctrinated understanding of the space. The film manages not only to stage its climactic sequence in the given space, but also deconstructs all previous realizations. This is orchestrated by the means in which the area is projected as desolate and devoid of human entities during the bombardment of the city at night. The commercial activity and frenzy of people is replaced with a chase sequence and aerial attack. Where there was once an abundance of color and commotion, only three solitary figures are seen. The cinematic frame is devoid of light and the color green is used to ominous and desolate effect.

*Green Zone* is a memorable film because of its stylistic photography, although some scenes must have been created as computer simulations. It has not been nominated for any major film awards, but in terms of visually and realistically replicating war-torn Iraq it is a commendable achievement. Almost all the scenes in the film focus on capturing the claustrophobia of and disarray in Baghdad from a street-level perspective. Some pictures showing the city from the air, for instance, the central areas under the air raid and the final scene with American tanks rolling into the city while an oil compound lies in the distance, are loaded with visual messages that are difficult to forget.

There are still the usual tropes associated with earlier Orientalist street views, such as women in black *burkas* and men in white *thobes*, but these are not used excessively. In any case, this is Baghdad and some citizens still wear traditional Islamic clothes. Yet, the film does not utilize the old-style religious elements that were popular to the point of predictability with filmmakers of the past. There are no mosques shown specifically, no calls to prayer, no old men squatting on pavements and counting their prayer beads and, quite surprisingly, no Middle Eastern music in the background.

While the fight for space takes place on the streets of Baghdad, the narrative and cinematographic focus tends to concentrate on idiosyncratic cultural contradictions within the given locations. The spoils and trappings of Western comforts are presented in an opaque city whose citizens are in turmoil. What prevails throughout all the chaotic clashes is the defiance that nature demonstrates. Among these different cultural and ideological conflicts, its presence and resistance to the ongoing destruction and deterioration is illustrated by the symmetrically aligned palm trees that line the dilapidated buildings and streets. Even oil (which in essence is a by-product of nature) can be associated with this notion. Its existence and influence are implicitly referenced in many of the films that deal with the Iraqi conflict, but in *Green Zone* this is even more pronounced in the opening and final manifestations of Baghdad. The city's architecture and infrastructure are also interpreted in terms of economic inequality. The ominous abstractions of the oil refineries, which are peripheral within the same landscape spectacle, create an all too familiar and foreboding impression of nature's hold over culture, despite its confinement to man-made refineries.

The transaction between behavior and environment is most skillfully demonstrated in *Green Zone*. Although the individuals in the film are shown to become uncontrollable when their location is devastated, we also see that the violence (or greed) present in the nature of man can destroy the environment. Baghdad in the film is such a confusing place that, outside the designated areas for Westerners, the behavior of both the extraordinary characters (the local Arabs) and the ordinary characters (the Americans themselves) becomes extraordinary, unrecognizable and chaotic. There is a "no-win" situation in the film and the audience is made to leave the theatre without feeling affinity with either side, having witnessed a prolonged and unfinished struggle.

Although there are some sporadic comments about *Green Zone* in the literature, not a great deal of academic material exists on the film. There are various sweeping remarks, such as those addressing the film's overall message, for example, "Released in 2010 *Green Zone* epitomizes the evolution of post–9/11 Hollywood films. The Iraqi voice ... is consistently portrayed as truthful and valid.... The Iraqi people are also humanized: A scene of aggression is explained as resulting from the lack of water" (Mingant 2014, 187–188), or those regarding the director's exceptional skills, as in McCarthy's (2010) online article: "Employing his customary whiplash style of shooting and editing, he [Greengrass] wants to plunk the viewer right down in the hellish anarchy that Baghdad soon became in 2003 after the Americans rolled in and were faced with far greater challenges on the ground than they anticipated."

However, any commentary about the man–environment interaction is nonexistent.

## The Muslim City in Conclusion

These three films, focusing on one Arabian city, Baghdad, expose the changes in how the Muslim world has been visualized and presented in American cinema over time. In the days when the name Baghdad brought to mind the *Arabian Nights* fables, it was possible to offer cinephiles, who had never visited Baghdad or seen it in the media, a city of extremes, where the rich and beautiful coexisted with the poor and ugly (e.g., *The Thief of Baghdad*, 1940), where romance could blossom easily (e.g., *Sinbad the Sailor*, 1947), and love could be declared under a French balcony (e.g., *Bagdad*, 1949), a fantasy land of white peacocks and pink parrots (*Kismet*), and also lavish palaces only a few yards away from camels and horses (e.g., *The Golden Blade*, 1955). The visual content was exaggerated with the inclusion of everything associated with the "Orient" from the Asian subcontinent to North Africa, so much so that it gave films a carnivalesque or circus-like quality. The only menace for the citizens of this picturesque and carefree Baghdad came from outside, either from the desert or further away (e.g., in *The Golden Blade* [1955] the antagonists are from Basra, fighting against the caliph of Baghdad).

As political conjunctures changed in the second half of the twentieth century, however, Baghdad came to be projected as a despondent city inhabited by perpetrators and victims of cruelty and violence, even when the narrative was about the Iran-Iraq war in which the United States was not explicitly involved. A tendency to focus on the clash between opposing states and values rather than between the religions of Islam and Christianity started developing at this stage, demonstrating conflicts stemming from race (Arabs vs. Kurds or Arabs vs. Iranians), location (the city of Baghdad vs. the countryside, i.e., the mountains or the desert) and social standing (civilians vs. national security forces). The city views were limited to the prerequisites of the narrative development, and the avoidance of wide-angle shots created a claustrophobic effect. The poor and the rich of the fairytale Baghdad were replaced with characters in more realistic garments such as Islamic attire, military uniforms and Western clothes. Human relations were shown to be under strain and even love had to be experienced in a clandestine fashion (e.g., Lila and Doug's romance in *The Human Shield*). It is, therefore, right to claim that Baghdad as depicted in the ten-year period after 2001 is the complete opposite of the extravagant city of the classical period. In *Green Zone*, the city appears to be in total disarray and chaos as a result of being turned to rubble by heavy air strikes. Its panic-stricken inhabitants run aimlessly, not knowing where they are heading. Even the American characters are shown to be at a loss, with no clear understanding of the purpose of the "shock and awe" campaign and its expected results. The film demonstrates that once you destroy the social order of a city, it turns into a wilderness where only savagery rules, regardless of who the savage side is. A transnational cinema approach in this case demonstrates how dynamic the individual–environment relationship is, both being responsible for the changes for the worse in each other. Finally, on a more socio-psychological note, it can be argued that the depiction of Baghdad in the films of the 2000s carries the signs of an American people's repentance over the metamorphosis they have caused in the dreamland of their childhood.

## *The Immigrants' City: New York Before and After 9/11*

The city of New York became closely associated with narrative cinema as early as the 1920s, when its rapidly changing skyline and verticality were accentuated in many films including Paul Strand and Charles Sheeler's *Manhattan* (1921). Christoph Lindner (2015) claims that this is the first avant-garde film recording images of the city from the perspective of high-rise buildings, underlining the disconnection between people and the new urban surroundings. A decade later, Elmer Rice's screenplay *Street Scene* was adapted for the screen (1931), portraying the drama of New York's tenement life and slums occupied by immigrants. Carr (2007) considers this film to be the first of its kind, carrying a message that the New York ghetto of poor immigrants was a breeding ground for anti-social behavior. In the decades to follow, many films mirroring the social, economic and assimilation difficulties of different immigrant groups were produced, including *America America* (1963), *The Molly Maguires* (1970), *Mean Streets* (1973), *The Godfather Part II* (1974) and *Hester Street* (1975) among others. While these films featured Greek, Jewish, Italian, Irish and Polish émigrés, for some reason a blind eye was turned by the film industry to the existence of Muslim people, who arrived in New York in large numbers between the turn of the last century and the 1920s. Shaheen, in his article "Arab Americans" (2003b, 218), informs us that "[l]ike all immigrants passing through Ellis Island, most Arab immigrants were desperately poor and discriminated against early on for the mere fact that they were foreigners." Apparently, the first film ever made about an Arab immigrant character in New York was *Anna Ascends* (1922), the rags-to-riches story of a Syrian girl who falls in love with and marries a rich American man. This was followed, after an incredibly long gap of 54 years, by *The Next Man* (1976) and *Wrong Is Right* (1982), briefly showing militant college kids of Middle

Eastern origin in political rallies. Then came a controversial film set in New York, *The Siege* (1998), in which a dubious Arab character appears in the form of a university professor who contrives with terrorists and gets killed in a clash with FBI agents. Just before the events of 9/11, *A Perfect Murder* (1998) was released, representing "Americans of Arab descent as everyday, neighborly Americans" (Shaheen 2003b, 223).

From this meager list, perhaps the most suitable film for comparison with *Man Push Cart* (2005), discussed in the next section, is *Quick Change* (1990). During the course of this narrative, the bank robbers get into a taxi but the driver turns out to be a dim-witted immigrant who "listens to Arab music and mumbles only in Arabic" (Shaheen 2003b, 221), thus frustrating his customers. However, the driver in *Quick Change* has a minor appearance in a comedy film, injected as a laughable element and, as such, is not comparable with the Muslim protagonist of *Man Push Cart*, which deserves to be discussed.

## Man Push Cart (2005)

*Man Push Cart*'s Ahmad (Ahmad Razvi) is a poor immigrant Muslim character from Pakistan, where he used to be a famous pop singer. In New York, he earns his living by selling coffee and bagels on a street corner. In order to get the rented cart from the depot to the location he conducts his business from, he leaves his tiny, candlelit room in the early hours of the morning and pushes the heavy cart through the streets, making his way by dangerously dodging the motorists in the heavy traffic. The mad race of the early morning drivers in an army of cars and buses with dazzling lights, disturbing engine sounds and roaring horns have a blinding and deafening effect on the senses.

Ahmad is all alone in New York City; the only companion he keeps is a kitten in a cardboard box, which shares his room. The film shows the difficulties that newly arrived immigrants face and how the city of New York is seen from their perspective. Interestingly, religion is not used in the portrayal of either Ahmad or the other Asian characters in the film, as the filmmaker's main purpose seems to be to show how hard the environment's conditions are for poor immigrants in the United States, where they have arrived with great expectations.

*Man Push Cart* relies heavily on the perpendicularity of the city of New York. Its portrayal illustrates a ground-view perspective, limited except for the availability of an open sky within the confines of its concrete structure. As in the film *Sorry, Haters* (2005), in which New York is revealed as a place of socio-economic hierarchy with its working-class underbelly, it is here reflected in its current multicultural diversity. Ahmad's recollections of his former colorful life are only briefly commented upon in a passing reference, but his understanding of his role and social standing in New York is echoed through his constant efforts to survive. Yet this energetic urban metropolis has not taken to him as much as he has to it. Colors are worn and pale, cinematography and framing exist primarily to describe it as an enclosed municipality. His world is restricted within the space of his cart's movements.

Resembling the theme explored in the Italian neo-realist film *Bicycle Thieves* (1948), *Man Push Cart* dwells on the cultural, social and economic burdens that a city places on individuals who rely on mobility to exist. Cinematic techniques employed in the film include the over-compensation of street noise that drowns out the monotone sparse dialogue during exterior scenes. This is especially noticeable when Ahmad becomes numb and introverted against the multi-sensory overload that New York City exudes. The only open space that he is filmed in is the car park where he meets his ex in-laws. Even this extended area has a concrete floor and is surrounded by iron bars, leaving no chance for the character to be released from frustration.

The spectacle of walls in films is considered to be significant. Schwarzer (2000, 208), for instance, claims that walls have been cinematographically useful in capturing a specific mood: "The blank walls of modernist architecture were polemical statements, the realization of a functionalist aesthetic that sought to reveal the materiality of pure surface and banish the pretense of historical ornament." In *Man Push Cart*, the walls of New York protrude and cast a menacing shadow over the characters. Establishing shots are limited and medium close-ups are favored in order to add to the city's claustrophobia-inducing atmosphere. The abundance of blank walls against which Ahmad positions himself (whether at work, on the corner of streets or within an interior location) is used to mute his feelings and distance him from others. Ahmad's Pakistani heritage has been replaced by a blank canvas of concrete that defines a new beginning in his life. It looks as though the film director aimed to address a background landscape populated by recently arrived immigrants and make them part of the foreground narrative, each equipped with conniving skills to cope with the city. The camera's depth of field and reflective light cast on flat concrete walls and indistinguishable people's faces are devices repeatedly employed by the filmmaker. We can see in this film similarities with the *Trümmerfilm* ("rubble film"), which was popular after World War II as a device for suggesting a new cultural and reconstructive beginning for the war-torn city's inhabitants. In *Man Push Cart*, cinematic techniques use the city's space and architecture to emphasize and enhance the perceptive gaze, which gives the impression that the characters are manipulated and exploited. It is no surprise in this environment that Ahmad is cheated by his compatriots and robbed of his coffee-cart business by fellow immigrants.

The plight of immigrants in the United States finds resonance in Scott's (2009) article "Neo Neo-Realism," which focuses on *Man Push Cart* (2005). Scott defines Ahmad as "a dreamer, a lover, a hustler, a former pop singer and, not incidentally, a Muslim man making his way through a city still gripped by post–9/11 anxiety." While he accepts that Ahmad's representation does not give any indication of his Islamic inclinations, he fails to mention that his pitiful existence is the outcome of New York City's darker side, which has no sympathy for hard-working poor immigrants. Indeed, New York is projected in the film as a city of not only dazzling wealth and attractions, but also of destructive malice. The problem is that while the former are only for the white professionals of the city, the latter are what the Muslim immigrants endure. All the characters in the film are placed in districts occupied by immigrants only and Ahmad's social environment is portrayed more like the "Orient" than the "Occident." Here, "liberty," which is the signature in stone of New York, is a relative notion as it does not apply to all its dwellers, especially if they are worshippers of Islam and have arrived in the land of opportunity with no material wealth of their own. In *Man Push Cart*, the Muslim man is not liberated but taken hostage by the epitomic city of capitalism. Looking at the film from this angle, its sympathetic way of interpreting the mark New York City leaves on its Muslim immigrants is a significant achievement, especially when the memory of the 9/11 disaster was so fresh in people's minds.

## *Conclusion*

Muslim spaces have generally been conceived as being as hostile as their inhabitants. Not counting the portrayal in classical Hollywood films of the desert wilderness, images since the 1960s have resembled those relayed via news networks reporting Middle Eastern wars. Common themes of Orientalism, i.e., despotism and savagery, have been impersonalized in characters such as corrupt and ruthless despots or terrorists. The arid and rocky terrain of the war-genre films has accentuated the abundance of "desolate spaces." Unlike the desert space, the protruding texture and shapes of which define the interaction between the individual and nature, the desolate space rids the background of the individual's meaningful bond with their environment. The city has similarly been subjected to ideological austerity, being turned into a claustrophobic confine just spacious enough to enable a chase between the protagonists and antagonists. The Muslim characters that exist in the films pre–9/11 range from faceless distortions of an assumed enemy to exaggerated Muslim caricatures that have been preconceived through the bias of a Westernized gaze. Similarly, the Middle Eastern space is acknowledged through a white American character's perception, both in the case of the natural landscape and the man-made city. Occasionally, as has been the case in the western genre, films have used the natural American wilderness to evoke a sense of traditional values to contrast with the bone-dry texture of the Arabian landscape.

Supporting the understanding that landscape is an important feature in shaping human character, *Hidalgo*, as a recent film featuring the Arabian desert, proves to be a significant source, for it not only pays homage to past Hollywood films that have romanticized the "Oriental" spectacle, but chooses to focus on the adversity between modernity and traditional existence, and how these are influenced by the milieu. Good and the evil exist simultaneously in the film, but these are treated as general human weaknesses or strengths rather than attributed to differences in race and/or culture. From this perspective, they are not old clichés but representations more akin to transnational cinema. Not all protagonists are white Christians, nor are all antagonists black Muslims. In this respect alone, *Hidalgo* (2004) stands out from the desert films of past eras, even if one ignores the captivating photographic instances of the desert in its changeable moods of docility and ferocity. Thus, the new desert belongs neither to the locals nor the rescuers, competing with or befriending both sides as it pleases.

As a film illustrating the individual-environment interaction in a city, *Green Zone* depicts a Baghdad pounded by missiles, causing both physical and psychological devastation. The only protection there seems to be granted to the foreign press in the "Green Zone" of the city, while everybody including the American soldiers outside this territory fights for survival. A surreal atmosphere is created in the film by showing the effects of the catastrophe but not its reasons—even the attackers do not know why they are there to cause this turmoil. The frames created through aerial shots, zoom-outs and a variety of camera movements highlight the process of destruction that is taking place. It is obvious that the filmmaker is casting a critical eye on the damage caused in Baghdad and on its civilians with no acceptable justification.

While the spatial landscape defines the native inhabitants of the desert and the city of Baghdad, the U.S. Muslim immigrant's landscape has been altered to accommodate the idea that the distribution of the American doctrine of opportunity, liberty and freedom is very selective. In this respect, *Man Push Cart* carries a touch of compassion. Here, the Muslim is conceived from a Westernized perspective but his space is interpreted with empathy for what it must be like for him to survive in this new environment. In *Man Push Cart*, the economic hardship of New York City is the motivational effect that underlines Ahmad's need to survive. The film offers variable takes on the immigrant perspective and presents to the audience an alternate existence.

In view of the findings reported in this chapter, it can be concluded that American films of the earlier age that depicted Muslim space were influenced by Orientalism to a large extent, but this was greatly softened by positively charged imaginative work as a result of the *Arabian Nights* stories, which became fashionable in Hollywood from the 1920s to the 1940s. With political interests developing in the Middle East in the second half of the twentieth century, American cinema became infested with state ideologies, and generated hard-core Orientalist films in which both the Muslim characters and their space were ruthlessly "Othered." The situation changed once again after the trauma of 9/11 and films started showing the people from the East and their space not as crudely factitious, as they did in the past, but through a transnational lens. Further research will reveal whether or not this novel approach to the Middle East and other Muslim lands will continue beyond the first ten years after the 9/11 trauma.

# 3
# The Muslim Male Character Typology[1]

More than any other aspect of the Muslim world, academic studies have shown interest in the representations of the "man from the East," particularly his physical appearance and one-dimensional behavioral pattern. The literature is rich with references to filmic representations of his primitive, evil nature, his dirty, repulsive appearance and his skin color and physical attributes, but perhaps the best summary is provided by Cones (2012, 26) who observes that Hollywood has always portrayed Arabs as "evil, barbaric, oversexed, depraved, villainous, shifty, possessed, hostile, fanatical, criminal, mystical, wicked, and crazed," as "kidnappers, enemies, mysterious, murderers, assassins, terrorists, blood-thirsty, saboteurs, extremists, cult-ridden, curse-stricken, oily, shifty-eyed, violent and as idiots."

Other analysts have concentrated mainly on the violent nature of cinematic Muslim Arabs. Alalawi (2015), for instance, argues that some of the old clichés of pre–9/11 representations, such as "savage-like," are still very much alive and gives the example of the scene in *The Kingdom* (2007) where a man is killed by terrorists in front of his young son. Semmerling (2006) similarly deciphers the Muslims in a number of films as savages, claiming that they portray "Palestinian Arabs as ruthless, vengeful, and indiscriminate killers" (96). On the other hand, while analyzing *Three Kings* (1999), he admits that "Arabs are still totalized into an exploitable Otherness. They are appropriated as pawns in the narrative to jeopardize the American myth so that the Americans can defend and reassert the myth for themselves" (*ibid.*, 161). Yet, despite the saturation of work on the Arab's timeless physical and behavioral disposition, there does not seem to be a single work examining in detail current character types in American cinema, as well as earlier representations; a work which would allow one to understand what has been carried over from earlier periods and what has been newly remodeled. Morey and Yaqin's (2011) "Use Value Muslim" and "Islamic Rage Boy" are groundbreaking terms in categorizing these two character types but the majority of analyses are restricted to the classification of male characters along a binary of "good" and "bad" descriptors. Shaheen's (2003a) catalogue of 900 films does not apply a systematic classification to Muslim characters other than a rough grouping consisting of sheikhs, maidens, Egyptians and Palestinians. It is obvious that a typology that reflects the current situation more widely is needed. Also required is an approach sensitive to differences in the Muslim world. The abovementioned studies, although providing a general evaluation of the celluloid character types, lack explanation of the finer nuances. A demographic classification of Muslim characters in films is non-existent although the representation of Muslims living outside the United States is not the same as that of Muslims in the United States. Furthermore, looking at the Muslims based in America, there is a difference in how African American Muslims and immigrant American Muslims are depicted. An awareness of these distinctions will produce a better and clearer picture than focusing on a monolithic Muslim type.[2]

It is a fact that, regardless of his geographical location, the Muslim has been used in a wide and diverse range of cinematic genres including horror (as in *The Mummy* series produced between 1999 and 2008), war, drama, historical epic and fantasy. What needs to be considered is a diverse selection of films that not only supports the deconstruction of the Muslim male on screen post-9/11, but also encompasses a wide enough scope of narrative to be indicative of the American socio-political climate of the time. The following case studies provide a reliable range of material to follow this reconstructive shift in attitude, although space restrictions limit the analysis to only some of them in detail: *House of Sand and Fog* (2003), *Ali* (2001), *Syriana* (2005), *Kingdom of Heaven* (2005), *The Kingdom* (2007), *Body of Lies* (2008), *The Kite Runner* (2007), *Hidalgo* (2004), *Sex and the City 2* (2010), *The Hurt Locker* (2008), *Rendition* (2007), *Iron Man* (2008) and *Charlie Wilson's War* (2007). The comedy genre, which has its own peculiarities, is also looked at separately with reference to *Borat: Cultural Learnings of America for Make Benefit Glorious Nation of Kazakhstan* (2006), *Jackass Number Two* (2006), *Team America: World Police* (2004), and *You Don't Mess with the Zohan* (2008).

## *Theoretical Overview*

In line with Christian Metz's (1982) assumption that the cinematic apparatus inhibits narcissism, in that the spectator identifies himself as a "kind of transcendental subject" (51), the colonial imagery of the anatomized Muslim "Other" provides a singular illustrative form. The spectator is deprived of choice and falls victim to the whim of the projected imperialist gaze. Furthermore, according to Shohat's (1997, 32) analysis and complementation of Bazin's (1967, 9) formulation of cinema in his "Mummy complex" conundrum, audiences (the spectators) are "subliminally" only given a "celluloid-preserved" cultural perspective. The deprivation of an alternative cultural existence enables the cinematic gaze to "rescue" the past and "suppress the voice of the present," and the mapping of self and "Other" becomes a means of creating imaginary boundaries, which operate homogenously with one another (Shohat 1997, 26). Most of the time, the result is the manifestation of a Euro-American ideal that favors a centralized position, which the camera accentuates in order to capture the filmmaker's perspective.

In the Muslim Arab's characterization, films have been instrumental to the thinking that a celluloid character's physical attributes signal their inner thoughts and beliefs more than their actions do. In other words, the fact that characters in films are probably evaluated in terms of their physical and linguistic features and how they look on the screen impacts the perceptions of the audience. On this point, Béla Balázs (2010), for instance, suggests that the physical aspects of a character influence the way viewers perceive them in ethical terms. The appearance and demeanor of an Arab/Muslim character in a film will help the audience draw conclusions about them; it will influence their thoughts as to whether or not this presentation is acceptable to them; and finally, it will lead them to decide if the character is a member of the in-group (i.e., "one of us") or out-group (i.e., the "Other"). This is an automatic reaction to the stage props, including sets and costumes, as the Western consciousness has been fed stereotypes for over a century in the history of cinema. Seeing only a small indicative feature will probably bring to mind all the other features associated with the same stereotype. Specifically analyzing the action film genre, Wilkins' (2009) findings suggest a common ailment in how the Arab male is perceived on screen: a dirty and ugly physical appearance with an abundance of facial hair and an unpronounceable name further justifies his "Otherness," reminding us of Shaheen's (2003a) remarks, mentioned in Chapter 1, about the image of on-screen Arabs. Equipped with such visual material, the Muslim Arab's character is expected to manifest an "infantilized," "animalized," "sexualized" or "debased" human being, as Kaplan (1997, 80) lists explaining Hollywood's character formulations of the "Other."

As pointed out earlier, American cinema has always been prejudicial towards Muslims, but the degree of prejudice has not been the same for all Muslim groups. The Arab, for instance, is cast as a manipulative mogul, evil at heart and vile in mind, and this only applies to the Middle Eastern "Other." The Indonesian character, in contrast, is unlikely to be given the same treatment, even though Indonesia is home to the largest Muslim population in the world. This indicates that the bias against Muslims of a particular geography has been stronger than the bias against "Others" from different locations, regardless of faith. The terms "Orient" or "East" are hardly used these days for China or Japan.

The image of the Muslim Arab has been through fluctuating phases, starting with the over-the-top romantic phase of the 1920s–1950s, followed by a merciless period of dehumanization that continued up to 2002, and finally going through a gradual normalization process that brings us to 2012. In connection to this "softening" attitude, a number of films have been released, showing the Arab as "one of us," and sometimes "better than some of us." In *Syriana* (2005), for instance, the good-looking, highly-educated, well-groomed prince who wants to bring liberalism to his people is killed by the CIA in favor of his younger brother, who is ready to allow the United States to administer his country's oil resources. Another example is the Middle Eastern character, Hani Salaam (Mark Strong), the head of the Jordanian special forces presented as a respectable man of professional integrity and honesty in *Body of Lies* (2008). These are not the only examples that one can cite.

In terms of their narrative content, the films appear to focus on the conspiratorial nature of power and corruption, which are offered as an alternative explanation for the threat of the Muslim male character. Morey and Yaqin (2011) claim that following 9/11, two sets of thriller genres featuring Muslims have emerged. These are, firstly, the films that offer "a fairly instrumental and unquestioning recapitulation of natural discourses and psychosocial boundaries" and, secondly, those that "begin by deploying the usual set of stereotypes only to unsettle them" (175). These films instill a universal impression of panic and threat, while at the same time offering insight into the motivations of Islamic fanaticism, which, although contaminating only a small percentage of the Muslim population at large, carries the risk of becoming a synecdoche for all the believers.

Again on the narrative side, much debate has arisen over the way the Arab has been treated as antithetical to all (cultural, economic, social, political, religious, aesthetic, and so on) views peculiar to the Western world. While Naber's (2000) work is concerned with the manner in which the parameters of the Muslim stereotype in American-mediated discourses are transgressed, so that Islamic and Arab communities are fused as one, Karim (2000) explores the Oriental framing of terrorism, which accentuates its identity. Muscati (2002), Wilkins and Downing (2002) and Tehranian (2000) can also be included within this discourse in so far as they all conclude that narratives have been devoid of historical or political contexts, thus ensuring that audiences are unable to fully grasp and comprehend the reasons leading to acts of violence. The contexts can be seen as understanding cultural relations of power and cinematic narratives, which have tended to be based on a simplistic premise whereby the centralized hero is distinguished from the villainous Arab. However, it should be noted that while these various analyses have examined the role of the Arab in cinema up to one year after 9/11, there has not been much consideration of whether a shift in mediated creative attitudes has occurred in the ten years thereafter. The present chapter undertakes this task and treats a number of films as case studies in the search for developments in the representation of the Muslim male character.

## Muslims Outside the United States

Shaheen (2008a) suggests that the number of films with a Muslim element shot in the seven-year period from 2001 to 2008 is about 100. Of these, only the following 12 take place in a non–Arab environment:

| | |
|---|---|
| TURKEY | *Around the World in 80 Days* (2004); *Out of Reach* (2004) |
| SOMALIA | *Black Hawk Down* (2002) |
| KAZAKHSTAN | *Borat: Cultural Learnings of America for Make Benefit; Glorious Nation of Kazakhstan* (2006) |
| IRAN | *Crash* (2004); *The Keeper: The Legend of Omar Khayyam* (2005); *The Terminal* (2004) |
| AFGHANISTAN | *Fire Over Afghanistan* (2003) |
| NIGERIA | *Tears of the Sun* (2003) |
| INDIA | *The Gold Bracelet* (2006); *Looking for Comedy in the Muslim World* (2005) |
| UGANDA | *The Last King of Scotland* (2006) |

To this list we can also add:

| | |
|---|---|
| AFGHANISTAN | *The Kite Runner* (2007); *Charlie Wilson's War* (2007) |
| IRAN | *House of Sand and Fog* (2003); *Prince of Persia: The Sands of Time;* (2010) |
| PAKISTAN | *Man Push Cart* (2005) |
| INDIA | *Slumdog Millionaire* (2008) |

This brings the ratio of films showing non–Arab Muslims to 20 percent, leaving 80 percent for the depiction of Arab characters, and proving that in the ten-year period post–9/11 American filmmakers continued equating Islam mainly with Arabs. However, once we come to all the films released in 2012, the following feature Muslim males, and the balance of nationalities now reverses towards non–Arab Muslims (only three films out of eight depict

Muslim Arabs), indicating that American cinema is finally giving up on the idea that Islam is the preserve of one nation/race alone:

SOMALIA *Act of Valor* (2012)
INDONESIA *The Raid* (2012)
IRAN *Argo* (2012)
TURKEY *Skyfall* (2012); *Taken 2* (2012)
ARAB COUNTRIES *Zero Dark Thirty* (2012); *The Dictator* (2012); *The Other Son* (2012)

Michalak (2010) finds that in the post–9/11 decade, the majority of Muslim-related films deal with war, which is understandable as this is the period when the audience was implicated, no matter how indirectly, in the political turmoil of Iraq and Afghanistan. Dark-skinned, grim-looking people in devastated surroundings, holding machine guns and lurking in doorways or on rooftops and street corners, are common images. Terrorist bombs make a wasteland throughout the films, even of modern city squares (*Rendition* [2007]) or self-sufficient American bases set up in Muslim countries (*The Kingdom* [2007]). In these scenes, primitive-looking individuals complement the devastation of the location. The "primitiveness" of the physical setting of the Middle East, as depicted in these movies, is congruent with the mentality it inspires in its inhabitants. The Eastern man's faith is reduced to a cinematic form of totemism, where the ritualistic action of a call to prayer acts as a contradiction within the scope of the narrative: one minute they pray to God, the next they fire their machine guns, as in *Black Hawk Down* (2002). Since the chaos of the environment is attributed to the savage-like behavior of the Muslim male, and his wild character is shaped by his impoverished surroundings, the two—his nature and his location—are implicated in constant interaction. Order is only restored during the call to prayer. By observing his cultural duties, the Muslim male is derived from an existing Islamophobic presumption that characterizes his militant behavior. Rather than being represented as a guardian of his native land, he is propelled into an extreme process of vilification that requires the justified involvement of the white protagonist and hero to try and bring order to the chaos.

The overseas Muslim male's portrayal is determined by a premise whereby the more exposure the spectator has to film and television, the more likely it is that the filmic portrayal of reality will be duplicated in their mind. Shanahan and Morgan (1999) comment that social control is seen as an extension of a cultivation theory that examines how media systems are used to build consensus—not agreement—on ideological positions, through "shared terms of discourse and assumptions about priorities and values" (15). Thus, the producers of news programs and feature films have nourished one another in terms of what has to be presented to the audience to incite interest and excitement and, in the course of doing so, they have edged away from the majority of the population and moved towards the perverse minority. Shaheen (2003a) criticizes this tendency when he makes a distinction between news reporters and filmmakers. He acknowledges that the airwaves should not cover the lives of ordinary Arabs, as this will not be "news" in the strict sense of the word, but "filmmakers have a moral obligation not to advance the news media's sins of omission and commission, not to tar an entire group of people on the basis of the crimes and the alleged crimes of a few" (29).

## *Muslims Inside the United States*

The choice of geographic region in which a film is set may dictate variations in how the Muslim is depicted. Muslims in overseas countries are viewed differently from members of the same faith resident in the United States. Similarly, those living in the United States are subject to different forms of portrayal, depending on whether they are black African American Muslims or immigrant American Muslims. Under the latter rubric, films generally underline cultural and social differences. The black Americans' rise in social respectability has had consequences for Muslim African American representations. In the pre–9/11 context, *The Siege* (1998) and *Three Kings* (1999) paved the way for black actors to take on leading and dominant roles within the scope of the narrative. *The Kingdom* (2007) and *The Hurt Locker* (2008) ensured the continuation and culmination of this trend. The black male not only took on the role of a superior in relation to his white colleagues, but also acted as an effective mediator between them and the Muslim male. In fact, this evolution has been elaborated upon through the progress from a central black protagonist to a central black Muslim protagonist. In *Traitor* (2008) and *Ali* (2001) the American lead males are not only black but also consider themselves devout Muslims, creating a complex dichotomy that reflects the changing face of a tolerant American cultural ideology. *Ali* (2001) is one of the very few examples, along with *Mooz-lum* (2010),[3] that reiterate the contrasting manner in which black Islam has been represented vis-à-vis the generalized "Arab equals Muslim" approach. In this framework, the black American Muslim male tends to act as a policing entity, being conceived as a moral harbinger of peace. Films such as *Malcolm X* (1992) and *The Greatest* (1977) remain largely impervious to the Muslim character's cultivation. This may be attributable to the lead characters having been revered figures in the Civil Rights Movement and therefore considered a part of American heritage. The black Muslim became a celebrated figure and champion of free speech and equality, whereas the Arab was tarnished as the solitary voice of Islam overseas. The differences between how the overseas Muslim male, the black African American Muslim male and the immigrant Muslim male are presented in films add a further problem to Orientalism, which is based on the notion that Islam is persistently personified in the Arab national and the Arab national in the "land of the barbarians" (Said 2003, 45), that is, the Middle East. In actuality, at least since 9/11, Islam has been portrayed globally, irrespective of nation, race, gender and age, but the most noticeable aspect of its depiction has been the setting of the narrative. Bearing in mind that some overseas characters are presented as respectable individuals (e.g., Colonel Hani in *The Body of Lies* [2008], Prince Nasir in *Syriana* [2005] and Colonel Farhi in *The Kingdom* [2007]), and others with complex personalities that can be virtuous as well as evil depending on the circumstances (Abasi Fawal in *Rendition* [2007]), it is clear that the idea of Orientalism (Said, 2003) needs expanding to make room for such novel formulations.

## *The Black African American Experience of Islam*

The African American experience of Islam has been long and arduous, recurrently going through cycles of suppression and revival since the start of the transatlantic slave trade in the eighteenth and nineteenth centuries. It is reported (Turner 2003) that a group of slaves who settled in the early 1890s in Sapelo Island, off the coast of Georgia, lived as devoted Muslims, but their isolated existence under the leadership of an ex-slave, Bilali Muhammad, fizzled out in time due to their remote location and because of the unorthodox nature of their practice. From the end of the American Civil War until the early twentieth century, there were no reported major activities concerning African American Muslims, although Turner (*ibid.*) points out that an important milestone was Wilmot Blyden's (1832–1912) criticism of Christianity on account of its racism. His ideas found followers among black people who suffered from mistreatment by white Americans. This was followed by some significant developments like the setting up of the Ahmaddiya missionary movement and the opening of the first mosque in Pittsburgh and another in New York, where the mainstream Sunni community consisted not only of black Americans, but also Turkish, Polish, Lithuanian, Russian, Indian, Albanian, Arab, Persian and Caribbean peoples. In Detroit, however, where the newly developing automobile industry attracted cheap labor, African Americans were the largest group, although the city was also home to many Arab Americans (Omanson 2013). In 1930, the Nation of Islam was founded by Elijah Muhammad in Detroit, and Turner (2003) reports that a large number of African Americans turned to Islamic practices after Malcolm X joined the organization in 1946, making it a sanctuary for black people who had been struggling for identity, freedom and equality. Some analysts indict the organization for its involvement in violence in the 1960s and 70s, but others, for instance Martha F. Lee (2011, 295), draw attention to the mitigating factors: "[T]he actual incidents of violence in which the Nation of Islam was involved have been limited both in number and intensity. This disjunction is interesting, for pre-civil rights America—and the social and political upheaval of the 1960s in particular—provided a situation that was ripe for violent conflict between African Americans and the political community that had for so long denied them equality." In 1975, Elijah's son Warith Deen took over the leadership from his father. One of the major changes he introduced was to open the door to all Muslims in America, rejecting the racial-separatist ethos of the group and adopting mainstream practices, but he was unable to prevent members from moving to other Sunni establishments. Today, black American Muslims use the mosques and masjids all over the country together with non–African Muslim immigrants. However, it is reported that there are still subtle ethnic tensions between these two groups (Omanson 2013).

The African American experience of Islam has until recently not been questioned in films for its authenticity, especially in terms of the relationship between the Nation of Islam and Islam as a whole. In HBO's mini-series *The Night Of* (2016), the character Freddy Knight comments to Nasir while in prison that Muslim African American inmates do not practice a legitimate form of the religion. This can be considered a significant moment in visual representations as it suggests that even non-practicing African Americans are able to distinguish between various practicing sects. Until the release of this show, the depiction of the African American experience of Islam tended to fixate on the discovery of the religion by individuals who had been incarcerated. Through the association of the religion with prison, cinematic characters have emerged who find salvation in their newly adopted faith and lifestyle. As Freddy Knight's words suggest, the American public differentiates between the faith of Middle Eastern immigrants who bring Islam to America as a "foreign cultural commodity" and the beliefs of African Americans who adopt the religion to free themselves from the memories of slavery. This distinction seems to be the reason why African Americans and Muslim immigrants are represented in cinema in alternative ways.

## Black African American Muslims

Considering the demography of Muslim Americans as a whole, as Dannin (2000) does, one can say that, historically, followers of the Nation of Islam have struggled to be recognized and accepted by all Islamic factions, but their failure in this can be attributed to various spatial divisions between

"New Muslims" (mostly of African descent) and "New Americans" (in this case, Middle Easterners and Asians) (215). These divisions started being scrutinized during the outbreak of the First Gulf War, when the authenticity of identity presented a collective dilemma.

It is significant that the African American Muslim male has remained outside the ongoing image formation of believers of Islam. Why has he succeeded in not becoming a part of the same monolithic representation as Eastern Muslim males? Moreover, in regard to films such as *Ali* (2001) and *Traitor* (2008), we might ask why the Afrocentric illustration of these entities have remained largely disconnected from the Orientalist approach, while in films such as *Black Hawk Down* (2002) the African Muslim is unforgivingly imagined as an anarchic savage, intent on the destruction of Western ideals as personified by their military presence.

The African Muslim, although he has not featured in many films and, even when he does appear, has not been given much screen time, does not fare any better than other characters from Africa. The screen African has gone through years of image cultivation, especially in the Tarzan films of the 1940s and 50s, but he is often reduced to an intense savage being when cross-pollinated with Islam. The African American Muslim, on the other hand, is a complex being who is not only able to traverse cultural boundaries, but also symbolically represents multicultural American ideals, without becoming victim to a stereotypical discourse. He is presented in cinema as a detached extension of entities forming part of America's historical identity in terms of the Civil Rights Movement of the 1960s but, as in the case of Muhammad Ali, he is also an iconic figure who has helped shape the present socio-political climate. Nuruddin (2000, 215) argues that the identity of the African American Muslim forms part of a "Triple Heritage, that consists of (1) Africanity, (2) Islamic Culture, and (3) Western Culture," although their spatial positioning within the whole of the Islamic sphere remains aloof. African American converts to Islam are the product of an African American demographic and have resisted being associated with immigrant activities.

The separation of American Islam into ethnic and ideological units has not been addressed in American cinema and, by this account, is testimony to the corresponding dis-unity of communal existence prevalent in American Islamic society. The black Muslim American was unceremoniously represented by filmmakers as an anomaly of an Islamic faith that was still being perceived in terms of its "Arabness." This may be because the black American Muslim male has resisted, struggled against and rejected the process pertaining to a post-colonial imperialist assumption. He has not only formed part of the historical landscape of the country, but has actively pursued an interest in asserting the right to his heritage. A drastic contrast is implemented to avoid the consummation of visual signifiers that may connect his skin color to a phobia of sorts, yet, interestingly, his character's notion of Islam is related to "freedom," and his reluctance to be absorbed by immigrant groups is understood to symbolize subservience to foreign leadership and agendas.

As affirmed in a personal communication,[4] Islam offered an alternative to the Christianity that most African Americans were raised in. This form of Christianity was rightly viewed as a means of maintaining the institution of slavery in a de facto way once the Civil War was over. Since Islam was prevalent throughout Africa in the mid-twentieth century, it became a "solution." It offered an original African religion, although it was not one, to those who wanted to reinstitute African cultural practices throughout the black American community. Islam was perhaps a less radical religious choice than, say, Yoruba, as it allowed for the existence of Christ and was thus more acceptable to people who were raised in a strongly Christian community. Black Muslims were part of a radical community, and this may be a reason why the Nation of Islam failed to engage the greater African American community. According to the Pew Research Center, American Muslims comprise only around 20 percent of the African American population.[5]

Unlike Muslim immigrants, the black American Muslim is not so much drawn to Americanization and the struggle to resist its seduction, but rather to the rejection of its imperialist culture, as illustrated in *Ali* and, much earlier, in *Malcolm X* (1992). *Ali* shows Islam as practiced by the African American Muslim, and how it remains independent from extraneous persuasions and groups. Ali's Islamic lifestyle is dictated to him by the Nation of Islam, and the film *Traitor* (2008) shows Samir Horn, a Sudanese-American Muslim, similarly experiencing conflict between his duty to faith and the special operations administration (Islamic Brotherhood) that he works for. Both characters are initially unable to register a clear understanding of their own hybrid identities, and their resolution of conflict is dependent on their personal interpretations of their faith.

Characterized by strong ideological links between Islam and pan–Africanism, the Nation of Islam represented an introspective examination of an African nation struggling to define itself in the role of self or "Other." In *Ali*, the organization is shown as a collective, and is never clearly associated with a global ideology as its extension; in fact, it manages to convey something else entirely, by exhibiting a justified means of rebellious resistance during a historical period laden with governmental and administrative corruption. *Ali* takes the opportunity to present its protagonist and the character of Malcolm X as national icons that may once have been misunderstood but are currently enjoying reverence as important manifestations of the Civil Rights Movement. Both are seen as initially struggling with the ideological dilemma between the identity of Islam as defined by its historical and geographical origins, and its Americanized interpretation, the origins of which coincide with the identity that had been given to them as slaves in the new world. The two opposing interpretations illustrate a conflict in both Muslim men, which results in an "awakening" experience. As Malcolm X begins to associate himself with the spiritual aspect of his faith and recounts this to Ali, he is ostracized not only by his friend, but also by the Nation of Islam. His eventual murder prompts Ali to revaluate the organization and his faith, and only when he is in Zaire does he endure a similar epiphany to that experienced by Malcolm X. Both men protect their identity with a historical lineage that can be traced to the times before the establishment of the American nation, and their "Muslimness" is perceived as their salvation. The narrative intention of *Ali* seems to differentiate between a personal Islam practiced by a Muslim American male and a collective interpretation that is ominously presented as corrupt, militant and misguided. Thus, both Ali and Malcolm X are portrayed as characters salvaged not by Islam, but by their own strong personalities.

## *Immigrant American Muslims*

Most migrants are likely to resist assimilation and insist on being recognized by the ethnicity and cultural features that they came with from their country of origin. Being fully integrated into the new environment and adopting new social habits is probably what the second generation achieves, rather than the first. The attachment to the past is said to be even stronger in refugees who have been forcibly dispersed from their original place of living for mainly political reasons, and made to live in "diaspora." In Chaliand's (1989, xiv) words, "born from a forced dispersion, they conscientiously strive to keep a memory of the past alive and foster the will to transmit a heritage and to survive as a diaspora." Similarly, anthropologist James Clifford (1997, 269) describes a form of diaspora as being oriented to "an axis of origin and return." Consequential to retaining the old as well as acquiring the new, we can say that immigrants in their new environment are infused with "hybridity."

The merit of the immigrant American Muslim depends on how well the individual is or is likely to be integrated into the dominant culture. Milton Gordon (1964) has identified seven dimensions of assimilation: "cultural," "structural," "marital," "identificational," "attitude receptional," "behavioral receptional" and "civic." It seems that film characters can display signs of integration not only in one of these dimensions, but in several; however, this depends on their length of stay in the host country. For instance, while Ahmad in *Man Push Cart* (2005) seems to be assimilated in the "attitude receptional" dimension, *The Kite Runner's* (2007) Amir, who arrived in the United States at the young age of seven, is fully assimilated on all fronts.

Those who have successfully integrated themselves are more inclined to dictate to those less assimilated, as we see in *Man Push Cart*. Ethnic variations of the American Muslim male are solely accounted for by the socio-economic status of the character. What differentiates the two sets of characters is the degree to which they invest themselves in an "American" version of Islam. Those who are unable to abide by the rules of Islam, as tolerated in the U.S., tend to be constructed as anti-modern, a potential threat and "un–American."

For the immigrant American Muslim male, life is not easy as he is unable to enjoy the privileges and luxuries that are bestowed upon some other ethnic groups considered as a single collective unit. The Muslim American male is shown in films as an individual rather than a group member, except for when he is in the mosque. He is rarely found living in the middle of nowhere, where his identity becomes more conspicuous to those in close proximity. Large cities like New York, Los Angeles and San Francisco provide him with the opportunity to be invisible, but the downside is that he is without protection once his identity is noticed. The character of Behrani in *House of Sand and Fog* (2003) suffers from this isolation and is victimized by a xenophobic police officer.

Immigrants persist in regarding themselves as the true authority on Islamic issues, and dialogue with African American Muslims is found to be sparse. Aminah Beverly McCloud (1994) states that the immigrant Muslim is more concerned with the injustice of communities in his country of origin than dealing with the realities that exist in America. Instead of acknowledging the priority of religious identity (as the African American does), ethnicity is of paramount concern when deciphering one's "Muslimness" (79–80). An example of this is in *House of Sand and Fog* where Nadi, a Muslim immigrant woman from Iran, shouts at her husband, "I didn't come to America to live like an Arab, a family roaming the streets like gypsies!" A racial contempt is clearly communicated by this utterance, although Iranians and Arabs are both considered to be part of the "ummah."

While the Arab was in the past associated with the Middle East, it was not until the later part of the twentieth century that the emergence of the Arab American began to be addressed in film. The economic diasporas that saw the migration and integration of the Arab into American life paved the way for presenting an alternative cinematic interpretation of this cultural identity. The conflation of Arab, Muslim and Middle Eastern communities has meant that critical and cultural differences are made indistinguishable, thus resulting in the inability of the spectator to recognize and understand variances such as Christian Arabs and non–Arab Middle Easterners. The construction of a homeland, as illustrated in the United States, sets and defines national communities, but while diasporas may exist outside of this territory, there tends to remain a sense of connection in the community with a particular area. The case of the Arab American meanwhile remains aloof since the mapping of the American Arab's space through what "we" want and what Hollywood action films assume about the "Other," systematically allows for the creation of stereotypically recognizable brackets. Past cinematic incantations are utilized and then applied in order to give a frame of reference to a community that has become ever more disconnected from the homeland nucleus.

In terms of conceptualizing Arab Americans, the identity was not acknowledged until the 1960s. Holsinger (2009, 3) attests that their role within the minority group experience was fundamental in three respects: "Racial identity, 'Human Capital' and Immigration history." While they were not recognized as an autonomous collective until much later in the century, the events of 9/11 solidified their distinctiveness in such a way that it encroached upon other cultural diasporas. Naber (2000, 37) and Cainkar (2002) have studied the sudden recognition and awareness of the Arab, whose ambiguity was preceded by the realization of their inability to become fully absorbed by and amenable to the surrounding society's politics.

## *The Economic Deprivation of Muslim Immigrants*

The success mystique has been an attraction in the American cinematic narrative. Many films have been made that concentrate on the growth of a business run by immigrants, especially of Italian and Jewish origin, perpetuating the myth that the country is a "land of opportunities." Boozer's (2002) list of films magnifying the American dream for immigrants includes *House of Strangers* (1949) and *Mississippi Masala* (1991), which showcases the increase in financial power of an Indian-run liquor store in Mississippi. Similarly, discussing Jewish immigrants' experience as reflected in Hollywood productions, Friedman (2012, 33) observes that the film *His People* (1925) "like so many others during this era (and even today)—basically equates American success with financial accomplishment." Whether one reaches this financially elevated position through legal or illegal conduct is irrelevant, as exemplified by the profit *The Godfather* (1972) and its sequels have made.

Hollywood has not been as generous in putting Muslim immigrants in the limelight as it has non–Muslim immigrants. As for the films made in the ten-year period following 9/11, the interest is not in how Muslim immigrants achieve their success like other immigrants, but in how their sweet American dreams turn into sour nightmares due to the economic difficulties they face and the harsh conditions they work in. A number of films focus on the difficulties faced by immigrants who move between locations because of globalized economies and/or sudden political changes in countries where supporters of the old regime are under threat of persecution. Economic or political migration is not restricted to the United States, but is a phenomenon experienced by several economically attractive countries. In *Sex and the City 2* (2010), for instance, as Carrie befriends her Indian manservant we gradually learn that their lavish capitalist environment is not too dissimilar to that of New York. Some of the immigrant Muslims we see here have left their families back in their home countries and are trying hard to make ends meet. In *Syriana* (2005) we are presented with two young Pakistani migrant workers in a fictitious Arab state in the Persian Gulf, where they lead a meager life. When the new owners of the oil company make them redundant, things go from bad to worse and they face hunger and deportation. In desperation, they fall victim to a conniving Islamic fundamentalist cleric who convinces them that "jihad" is the only way to salvation.

The economic difficulties immigrants face form the backbone of several films such as *House of Sand and Fog* (2003), *Man Push Cart* (2005) and *Sorry, Haters* (2005). *House of Sand and Fog*, for instance, is the story of ex-colonel Behrani and his struggles to provide a decent life for his family. Out of the opulence of the Pehlewi Dynasty's Iran and into northern California's foggy existence, he finds himself having to lead a double life—while he convinces everybody including his wife and children that he can still afford to have a lavish lifestyle, he in fact does several menial jobs during the day, including working as a laborer on a construction site and selling cigarettes at a kiosk. The celebrity status in Pakistan of Ahmad in *Man Push Cart* has already been mentioned. The common denominator in these examples is a character that leaves behind a relatively good life and comes to America with high expectations, only to be degraded in a manual job and a meager state of existence. Both characters work hard but, instead of securing better conditions, they suffer material loss (Ahmad's coffee cart disappears while he is buying something from around the corner and Behrani loses the beach house for which he had high expectations). The interesting point to note here is that, despite their different origins (Behrani from Iran and Ahmad from Pakistan), their experiences of America converge not only in lifestyle, but also in how each narrative concludes—Behrani commits suicide and Ahmad is left penniless on the streets after losing his cart. These films, therefore, project the socioeconomic realities of global migration, rather than personifying Muslim characters as the "Other" in a clash of ideologies/religions. This is a breakthrough as far as the Muslim image is concerned because, for the first time in the history of cinema, the Muslim character is presented not as a threat or an object of contempt, but as the underdog in a capitalist system, whether this is in the United States or elsewhere.

## Changes in Character Formation

One of the character types recurrently appearing in American cinema is the Muslim male aggressor, which has become a recalibration of past incantations conceived in the 1980s and 90s in films such as *Delta Force* (1986), *True Lies* (1994) or *Executive Decision* (1996). In the past, an imagined identity was used to essentialism the Muslim's cultural differences vis-à-vis a centralized imperialist ideal, as the intrinsic characteristics of an enemy who must be killed. Recently, however, Muslim's have been depicted as "Westernized" in their outward appearance in order to capture the idea of "the enemy within." The currently ongoing (at the time of writing) television show *Homeland* (the first season was premiered in the United States on 2 October 2011) and, indeed, the film *Traitor* (2008) are particular examples of portraying this kind of entity, which Morey and Yaqin (2011, 116) describe as a "post-Huntington stereotype."[6] As filmmakers have begun to implement a need to separate the connotations of Islamic visual signifiers, the Muslim male has become chastised not for the faith that he professes, but rather his racial and economic standing. Such characters in films are deprived of fiscal opportunities and are thus considered to be functioning outside the parameters of moral and acceptable behavior in American society. The Muslim American was cast aside and deprived of his basic civil rights by those who felt morally obligated to exercise an interpretational justice as they saw fit. The American cinema of the post-9/11 years has been quick to identify this situation and create a Muslim far more complex than previous Orientalist incarnations. This new character neither fits into the classic antagonist role of former years, nor is he deemed impervious enough to withstand the suspicions of an audience unable to empathize with him. As a result, the Muslim male becomes a focal point in films that examine his moral worthiness. With the exception of *Ali*, which should be treated as an anomaly, it was not until the release of *The Kite Runner* (2007) that an audience was presented with a centralized character (Amir) who personifies the "immigrant experience" as well as being deeply enriched with acceptable signifiers. This is the image of a man who is educated, well dressed, well spoken and a good family man with high moral values.

Following from the above, we can say that there has been a change in attitude in cinematic depictions. The old stereotypes have not totally disappeared but there are now examples of the Muslim male character imagined both in the United States and within his native environment overseas, satisfying a curiosity that was fuelled by the wars in Iraq and Afghanistan. It is now becoming clear that an Afghan is not a Middle Easterner and the latter is not North African. *The Kingdom* (2007), *Body of Lies* (2008), *Green Zone* (2010), *Hidalgo* (2004) and *Babel* (2006) clearly assume this stance and reposition the spectator's gaze so as to acknowledge the intrinsic nature of cultural differences. As mentioned above, the Muslim character still suffers from discriminatory representation, but the hostility is directed towards a community whose ethnic identity and cultural norms, rather than set of religious beliefs, are associated with this particular phobia. Islamism and the Muslim male character are constructed to illuminate the internal movement within Muslim communities. Furthermore, audiences also witness a change in the role distribution, when the white protagonist is cast as the object of "Othering," giving the spectator the chance to empathize with the Muslim's predicament. Examples of this are plentiful: *Sorry, Haters* (2005), *House of Sand and Fog* (2003), *Man Push Cart* (2005) and *Rendition* (2007).

## Character Types

It has already been mentioned that Shaheen (2003a, 14) lists a number of stereotypical roles that the Arab is cast in, consisting of "villains and notorious sheikhs, maidens, Egyptians and Palestinians," which is actually a mixture of descriptive terms since two of these are not character types but nationalities. One is a gender description (maidens) and the other is a tribal title (sheikh). Michalak's (2010, 1) list is not very different when he says that Arab antagonists are "villains—oversexed sheiks kidnapping white women, sword-wielding natives attacking foreign legion outposts, exotic magicians on magic carpets, mummies lumbering after screaming women, spoiled potentates in oil-rich kingdoms and, of course, terrorists killing innocent Westerners." These groupings do indeed exist in the films but they are not exhaustive as many other character types have also made their appearance on the screen, especially since 9/11. As new formulations heralding a change in the public view, they deserve a mention.

### THE ARAB TERRORIST/VILLAIN

It was not until the middle of the last century that the Arab terrorist was first realized in the film *Sirocco* (1951). In time, the framing of the stereotypical villain has evolved into the Arab terrorist character and has become part of the immediate and accepted discourse. This helped to establish a short-term rational response to terrorist activities, but the simplicity of such an approach meant that a redirection was needed in how "he" was to be conceived within the film's narrative structure. *United 93* (2007) may have been released in movie theatres towards the latter half of the last decade, but its presentation of the terrorist and implementation of a neo-realistic cinematic approach help to authenticate the narrative. The result is the echoing of a former Arab male stereotype that justifies his irrational behavior. The stereotype is, in an instance, substantiated and legitimized since it appeases viewers and maintains the trauma that has been inflicted upon an American audience. The use of a hand-held camera technique not only emphasizes the audience's sense of anxiety, but also serves as an exploitative artistic device in the manipulation and replication of recent events, orchestrated through the use of *cinéma vérité*.

In films such as *The Visitor* (2007) and *Rendition* (2007) the narrative involves innocent Muslim male characters who are assumed to be terrorists, due to a misrepresentation cast upon them. The parameters of the stereotype in American-mediated discourses are transgressed by the way in which Islam and extremism are fused as one. The consequence is a dehumanization process that affirms the animalistic nature of the antagonists.

Characters appear less human when not named and, when shown in large groups, viewers are less likely to identify with them. Hiding faces behind a black or red *shemagh* also aids this anonymity, as in *The Kingdom* (2007). Thus, Christianity and Islam are conveyed as dichotomous, representing the hero, whose righteousness is out in the open for all to see, and the villain, whose evil intentions have to be concealed. This technique is used in many films including *Hidalgo* (2004). In one scene Frank, the white protagonist, while riding on his horse, looks back to check how far behind his Arab chasers are. At that moment, the audience can easily read the worry on his face and feel empathy with him, while the pack of black-clad horsemen galloping pursuit are partly concealed amidst a cloud of dust. This clarity of the white hero and the impaired vision of his enemies increases the gravity of the threat and consequently escalates the suspense.

*Hidalgo* portrays a Muslim in the form of Sheikh Riyadh whose behavior we find tolerable, but the film also contains some of the most anti-Arab stereotypes to have been conceived on screen. Treachery, deceit, cowardice, barbarism and savagery are integral to the colonial rescue fantasy, epitomized in the role of Frank. *Hidalgo*, according to Shaheen (2008a, 31), "[r]eplenishes stale stereotypes: Arab versus American, Arab versus Arab, Arab versus African, Arab woman versus Arab man." The cinematographic shots in which the sheikh beheads an Arab raider, showing the latter's head fall to the ground while his hat remains on his shoulders, are grotesque. A man witnessing this act loses his composure and kicks the head away. The violent nature of the desert people, who will turn to terrorism in subsequent centuries, is displayed in the most graphic form. Bodies are impaled on spears, knives are in hand ready to cut culprits' testicles off, bullets are fired and the holes in the dying bodies displayed.

Male characters are usually defined according to existing paradigms of traditionalism and modernism. A significant degree of perversion is infused in the interpretation of Islam and its operations so as to convey characters that are susceptible to manipulation by others, who selfishly benefit from furthering their personal goals.

## Islamic Rage Boy

One character type is the noisy teenager, referred to by Morey and Yaqin (2011) as the "Islamic Rage Boy" on account of his unpredictable, nervous and quick-tempered behavior. His articulation is rarely controlled and consists of common expletives relating to his faith. If not presented in a group of similar youngsters, his solitary voice is broadcast as the lone voice within a chaotic environment, but his body tends to be feminized. The ethnonormative space that he is permitted to be explored in focuses the spectator's attention towards a metonymic state of cultural observation. His destruction merely seems to reduce the articulation of visual signifiers that represent the threatening presence of his faith. These can include beards, prayer beads, *keffiyahs* and attire.

The Islamic Rage Boy exemplifies a short-lived mood, which is used as the epitome of rage, but is ultimately an emotion that is unsustainable in all the actions of the character. For instance, in *Rendition* (2007), which shows these youngsters as a mob, a young Arab, Khalid, who is presented as an introvert in the flow of the narrative, brings his girlfriend Fatima (who happens to be the daughter of a hard-liner police chief) to the base where he, along with many other young Arab males, is being groomed to become a terrorist. On this occasion, the mullah's exhilarating speech ends with an invitation to all of them to chant the *Takbir*, "Allahu akbar" ("God is great"), in Arabic, over and over again, and they do this with increasing enthusiasm, as evidenced by the escalating volume of their voices, their raised arms and clinched fists, in defiance of Western imperialism. The activity is so contagious that even Fatima joins them, with her arm up in the air, shouting together with the rest. Examples of the Islamic Rage Boy have been realized in numerous other films such as *United 93* (2007), *Body of Lies* (2008), *The Kingdom* (2007), *Iron Man* (2008) and *Munich* (2005).

## The Naïve Sympathizer

A character type that surfaces in a number of films is the sympathizer of terrorism; the character who is not sufficiently trained to be involved in the action, but is used either as a pawn to enlist at a later stage or as an accomplice blowing the trumpet of hardline terrorists.

In *Syriana* (2005), several storylines converge, one of which is about two 17-year-old, naïve, Pakistani oil workers in Saudi Arabia. Wassim and his friend are sacked by the new owners of the oil company and face poverty and deportation. They try to find work but, as they do not speak the local language, their search gets them nowhere. During this desperate period, they join a school to learn Arabic, where they meet a fundamentalist Muslim preacher who provides them with food and lodgings but, at the same time, tries to increase their religious awareness. At one point in their encounter with the preacher one boy says of the other, "Wassim is still a virgin," and then adds, "I'm a virgin too." The preacher's response is "Fornication is a big problem. Abstain from sex out of wedlock," which shows the filmmaker's understanding of how such youngsters are manipulated in the name of religion even though such a dictum has no place in Islam. As in some other films, in *Syriana* (2005) Wassim and his friend easily fall victim to exploitation due to their poverty and naivety and are later coerced by the preacher into executing a suicide attack to destroy an oil refinery. The film ends when the motorboat carrying them and a large amount of explosives collides with the target, leaving the rest to the audience's imagination.

## The Victim(s) of War

The ongoing conflicts in Iraq and Afghanistan led to clear distinctions being drawn in the characterizations of Islamic militant factions and innocent victims of war. *Charlie Wilson's War* (2007) is an example that seeks solace by satirizing governmental disunity while illustrating the effects that U.S. involvement has had in Pakistan and Afghanistan. Rather than centralize a Muslim male figure, the film concentrates on the guilty conscience of an American congressman, who is only prompted into action after witnessing the after-effects of U.S. military intervention. Charlie Wilson himself is characterized as inept with no real consideration and understanding of the cultural ramifications pertaining to Islam, but his ignorance is absolved by his "humanitarian" efforts. Those Muslim male characters that he meets are either represented as aggressive military politicians or hapless victims who provide insights to educate him about the Orientalized world he inhabits. Evoking images that were broadcast on television screens in news reports on CNN or the Fox News Network, the film tries to remedy the enduring plight of refugees by differentiating their miserable existence from that of the militants. This is done through the imperialist gaze of the film's protagonist who is only stimulated by his Westernized notion of moral responsibility towards the victims that he encounters.

Another example is the film *Redacted* (2007), which depicts a 13-year-old Muslim girl who is raped by American soldiers. The scene in which the GIs charge into her house shows the adult family members crouching next to a wall in the corner of a room with terror written all over their faces.

## The Corrupt Tradesman

This is a caricature rather than a character, but it has been a recurrent feature in films about the Middle East, as has been observed by many analysts (Shaheen 2003a, Said 2003, Semmerling 2006). While the souk manages to capture the essence of the historical Orientalized space of the Muslim male trader, it has also been common to conceive a one-dimensional trader who, more often than not, is portrayed as corrupt, grotesque and conniving. When such character types are not actively involved in trading, they are shown to be lazing outside their shops or stalls, alone, in pairs or in groups, playing backgammon or drinking coffee.

Although in reality the souk, or the bazaar, in any Middle Eastern country buzzes with vitality and sociability, for some reason this space has proved to be menacing for the American filmmaker. The tendency has been to set major escape routes through such locations where the chase creates havoc among the displayed goods and the sellers, as in *Taken 2* (2012). In more tranquil conditions, the local tradesmen are projected as mysterious and ominous. In *Body of Lies* (2008), for instance, the market place is shown to be full of males who satisfy preconceived Oriental stereotypes. Similarly, in *Sex and the City 2* (2010), the crooked bag salesman's involvement reinforces the cinematic historical fantasy that has so often been presented on screen. On the other hand, the same film also features an honest trader in the form of a shoe seller. With its honest and dishonest traders, the souk as depicted in *Sex and the City 2* has the qualities of a normal market place that can be found anywhere in the world, not only in Arab lands.

## The Use Value Muslim

The name of this character type has also been coined by Morey and Yaqin (2011), and refers to characters whose existence is still structurally subordinate to the leading protagonists (131). Such characters' inclusion is usually at the level of tokenism and seldom are they seen instigating the action sequences, although they may resolve a final conflict between the protagonist and antagonist. When contrasted with the Muslim villain or terrorist, they stand for normality and are purposefully distanced from their counterparts. The scenes that they appear in with the leading protagonists are intended to bridge the gap between "us" and "them" and further distinguish and separate Islamic extremism, as envisaged by the villain. While they are prone to injury and death, they are purposeful devices that are intended to suggest an alternative, empathetic depiction to that of the Muslim male "Other." Consequently, they offer what Rogin (1992) calls a "surplus symbolic value" through which they can be made to stand for something other than their predisposed colonized image.

*Iron Man* (Jon Favreau, 2008): The inventor Tony Stark (Robert Downey, Jr., left) may be a genius, but to escape from the cave where Afghan terrorists hold him captive, he needs the help of local scientist Yinsen (Shaun Taub, right), his "Use Value Muslim."

During the post–9/11 period, the Use Value Muslim surfaces quite frequently. One example is in *Iron Man* (2008), which is notable for the ingenuity and superhero qualities of its protagonist, Tony Stark, exemplifying Western achievements in the face of adversity. When Stark is wounded and captured by terrorists, he is only able to escape by constructing a marvel of technology, which he does with primitive tools and the assistance of an educated, "liberalized" Arab scientist. Still subservient to the protagonist, the Muslim male figure consequently sacrifices himself, so that Stark can escape. The terrorists are unable to replicate Stark's technological achievements and are portrayed as mentally and physically inferior. Their persistence and irrational behavior evoke past stereotypical caricatures of the Islamic Rage Boy, while the local scientist takes on the role of the Use Value Muslim.

With extremely opposing characters in *Sex and the City 2* (2010), an intermediary is realized in the hotel manager, Mr. Safir. His role and function are to be able to negotiate and traverse a cultural landscape struggling to grasp Western imperialist influences. His existence is vital to providing a means by which a "middle" ground may be reached between opposing polemic views. He is thus the Use Value Arab in the film. He is set in the international context of a seven-star hotel, dressed immaculately in Western designer clothes—though he speaks with a heavy Middle Eastern accent—and does not appear to conservatively practice Islam.

A further well-developed character is presented in *Rendition* (2007): the police chief Abasi Fawal, whose three-dimensional portrayal is complex. He is the overseas interrogating and torturing arm of American Homeland Security. Again a well-dressed and a well-articulated character, he is a modern Use Value Arab. Given the nature of his profession, Abasi is represented as a torn individual, as a loving father at home and a torturer at work whose monstrosity is spurred by the belief that what he is doing is for the good of his country. His portrait does not involve any religious inclinations, nor is he worried about the fact that he works with and for the U.S. administration. Abasi's abuse of his professional powers allows for his character to operate without being restricted by the rules of the state or religion. He is an entity unto himself guided by his own self-righteousness, and it is his implementation of and support for the American administration's wishes that eventually make him a target for assassination.

Yet another good example of this character type is Colonel Faris al-Ghazi in *The Kingdom* (2007). As commander of the Saudi state police force, providing security for four FBI forensic experts who are sent to Saudi Arabia to investigate a terrorist attack on an American compound, he is the guide and bridge between two cultures. He has dark skin but in his uniform he appears Western and groomed and, despite his accent, speaks English well. He is shown to be tyrannical when he locks the FBI members up in the gymnasium for the night for their own security, but in another scene (where he tells the Americans, almost in tears, that he lost two of his men in the attack) he is full of emotion. When another member of his police force is suspected of a terrorist connection and tortured by the Saudi national guard in front of him, he reacts to the incident by asserting, at the risk of losing his job, that it is unnecessarily violent. His awareness of Western popular culture is evident in his references to old television serials like *The Incredible Hulk* (1978–82) and *The Six Million Dollar Man* (1974–78).

There are several very short, silent scenes inserted into the film with apparently no purpose other than to portray him as a happily married family man, playing with his son at home while his unveiled and educated wife helps his daughters at the table with their homework. When he says to Fleury (the FBI team leader), "Don't talk to me with this language," he is portrayed as a man who cannot tolerate an attitude of patronizing superiority. Towards the end of the film the FBI agents and Colonel Faris enter the terrorists' hideout, but apart from the terrorists, he is the only one shot to death. Although the Americans return home triumphantly, Colonel Faris al-Ghazi is presented as the real hero in the film. In this respect, he could even be considered within the category of the Respectable Muslim (discussed below).

## The Feminized Muslim

This is not a recurrent character type despite occasionally appearing in films. The feminization of the Arab body has become a common device used to emphasize the masculinity of the Western male. His relationship and configuration as "Other" determines his colonial subservience, which relates directly to Foucault's (1977, 25) understanding of a disciplined power within a political field. He is tortured, degraded, forced to carry out tasks and coerced into submission.

In the second half of the decade following 9/11, Muslim characters are shown falling victim to the harsh conditions operating in the name of the War on Terror. This is nowhere as evident as in *Rendition* (2007), where the unveiling of the concealed Muslim body reveals more about those doing the unveiling and their power than those who are unveiled. The sexuality and release of voyeuristic tendencies can be attributed to our need to discern and place an identity according to our own doctrines. *Rendition*'s scenes of torture in the semi-darkness of a dungeon offer further cause for examination in their ability to evoke sympathy for Anwar (Omar Metwally), a fully assimilated Arab American male. While Douglas Freeman (Jake Gyllenhaal) of Homeland Security battles with the ethics of his actions, Anwar is deliberately disassociated from his Arab heritage, so much so that he appears antithetical to our preconceived notions of the Arab male stereotype. The feminization of his hairless body, and his articulate use of the English language while begging for compassion are employed to involve and alert the spectator to his plight. Minimally used lighting, which shines on his wet body, gives a perverse quality to the scene. He is positioned between two cultural ideologies that are simultaneously in operation within the room where he is held, personified by the sinister torturer, Abasi, and the archetypal attractive American idealist, Douglas Freeman.

A similar treatment of the Muslim body is found in *Sex and the City 2*, in which a homosexual and camp waiter/servant attends to the female protagonists' needs. This seems to take its inspiration from the eunuch character who, in the past, was kept in royal households in Muslim countries as a harem servant and a guardian of women.

## The Muslim Despot

The Western audience's familiarity with The Muslim despot has continued to flourish since 2001. In *Around the World in 80 Days* (2004), the appearance of a Turkish sultan, portrayed by Arnold Schwarzenegger, is intended to evoke a proliferation of sexual imagery regarding the "Other." His visualization is intended to amuse and displace the expectations of the spectator, who is accustomed to the actor's association with the all-American action hero. The harem is an apt environment for introducing him into the course of the narrative, since Eurocentric discourse has defined the harem as a male-dominated space that acts as what Shohat (1997, 163) claims is a sign of "Eastern Oriental despotism."

Despite the fact that *Sex and the City 2* (2010) presents the Muslim male within the globalized city of Abu Dhabi, where modernity and traditionalism interrelate, the classic cinematic Arab despot appears on screen quite frequently. One of these scenes depicts an Arab husband commenting on Samantha's public display of affection for a male customer in the hotel bar while his *burka*-wearing wife is ordered by him to look elsewhere. The same despotic image is also used in the scenes set in the souk where the American women in Western clothes and with uncovered hair are surrounded by a menacing group of dark-skinned, dark-featured men.

Abasi Fawal in *Rendition* (2007), mentioned earlier in the Use Value Muslim category, can also be considered a Muslim despot because of his cruel torturing methods. He does not hide his affections for his youngest daughter, aged seven, but his rule over the rest of his womenfolk (his older daughter Fatima, his wife and his sister) is tyrannical. His strict authority at home, however, is not because he is a Muslim (in fact he is not presented as a practicing Muslim—he drinks whisky at work and also offers it to the American observer, Douglas Freeman, with no sign of shame), but because of local cultural restrictions. Of his sister, who broke free of him in the past and now leads a liberal lifestyle, he says to his wife, "She can never get married," indicating that an emancipated woman does not have many marital prospects in the society they are in. When his daughter Fatima runs away with her boyfriend Khalid, Fawal searches frantically for them to avoid her having a similar fate. He is tough and not compassionate like Douglas Freeman, whom he asks not to interfere in his torturing methods. While he has a heart of stone at work, however, he can be broken down when it comes to his family members. Later in the narrative, he is seen standing motionless, eyes closed, letting his wife silently beat his chest for being the cause of Fatima's death.

## The "Tolerable" Muslim

Since 2001, instead of the usual stereotypes, there has been a general trend in the film industry to present the Muslim and the Arab in particular in a more favorable light. One such film is *Hidalgo* (2004), where the narrative is constructed to capture the harmonious relationship between the self and the "Other," but in doing so it still offers the most perverse and Orientalized view of the Muslim male to date. *Hidalgo* evokes caricatures of not only the East, but also the West. While Frank Hopkins, a cowboy, is a symbolic representation of a past American ideal, Sheikh Riyadh is his assumed reflection. They each clarify their opposite in a manner that almost imitates the other. The more exaggerated and heroic Frank's deeds are, the more he becomes revered by the Sheikh, and it is precisely this reverence that justifies Frank's actions as the only acceptable moral outcome in the story.

The audience is acclimatized to the change from detestable to likeable taking place in the main characters, with the evolution noticeable in the surroundings. The once hostile environment, including those who inhabit in it, develops and evolves over the course of the narrative and subsequently reshapes the landscape. The setting transforms from a frightening, colorless desert full of sand storms, where individuals exist as ghost-like entities, to an oasis of vitality, filled with content inhabitants. During this transformation, the Sheikh also undergoes a change and becomes an almost likeable character. He stops calling Frank an infidel and addresses him by his first name. He also accepts his daughter's liberal ways of living. This is a remarkable portrayal, considering that the film was released three years after 9/11.

The film *Kingdom of Heaven* (2005), however, shifts the discourse towards a biblical narrative. Rather than focusing on differentiation, Christianity is allowed to coexist in a state of harmony with Islam. Despite being considerably flawed in its approach to establishing a "Muslim-friendly" account of the crusades, this religious and morally ambiguous epic merely polarizes a liberalized assumption. Conceived either as an adversary or subservient entity, the Muslim character, Sultan Saladin (Ghassan Massoud), unable to break from the shadow cast over him by a dominant ideology, is determined to justify a conciliatory stance before being accused of being wholly one-sided. The power of a religious movement, which is depicted through the series of events that lead the French crusader Balian (Orlando Bloom) to leave and return to France, simplifies complex issues and gives order to chaos in the film's attempt to entertain. Where *Kingdom of Heaven* does succeed is in its rational and sympathetic portrayal of Saladin. Not only is the film the first of its kind to correctly pronounce his name (Sah-lah-hah-Deen) as Francaviglia (2007, 80) notes, it also takes unusual steps towards justifying and empathizing with his actions, which are provoked by the murder of his sister. The scene in which Saladin respectfully restores a crucifix on top of an altar after his attack on Jerusalem is noteworthy in that it provides a unique attempt to humanize a character that has so often been vilified on the screen. In fact, Saladin's honorable actions can be interpreted as an attempt at appeasement and a reinterpretation of the Crusades as an act of aggression.

*Kingdom of Heaven* shares many common traits with the other case studies that succumb to the Orientalist whim of Islamic fatalism. Yet, here the Muslim male is fashioned as a character who openly observes "Allah's will," and the desert oasis enhances his profile as a dedicated believer. This said, it is necessary to mention that Saladin is made to visually look dark, daunting, fierce and merciless while lighter colors are chosen for the Christian soldiers and the protagonist.

## The Respectable Muslim

There have been some very positive Muslim male portraits presented in post-9/11 films. One of these characters is Prince Nasir in *Syriana* (2005). He is shown as a product of Western education as he speaks English and French fluently. He is sensible, impressionable but at the same time dignified. He is also progressive and forward thinking, and believes, with the right investment in the education of his people, in salvation for the East. His is a portrait of an idealist who falls victim to American corporate greed.

Another such character is Hani Salaam in *Body of Lies* (2008), the head of general intelligence in Jordan, who is based on a real individual. David Ignatius, the author of the book *Body of Lies* on which the film is based, describes on his own website how he created the story. Apparently, he heard from the CIA director in 2003 about the Jordanian intelligence chief who was a most helpful ally in providing the United States with intelligence. Following this, Ignatius went to Amman to meet the general in question, and the portrait of Hani Salaam was developed as a result of these interviews.[7] The character of Hani Salaam in the film is dressed impeccably, in contrast to the Americans in shabby clothes. He has an aura of respectability about him, so much so that Roger Ferris always addresses him as "Sir." He values honesty highly and asks the CIA case officer never to lie to him. With his understanding of the Arab psyche, he manipulates situations cleverly to reach his targets and gets better results than the Americans, who are more prone to killing when in difficult circumstances.

As can be seen from the examples above, the Muslim portrayals in films of the 2001–2011 period vary in terms of their presentation. The examples show ominous characters as well as likeable personalities with well-established and convincing character arcs. The above list of character types is, of course, not exhaustive but incorporates the significant cinematic Muslim male figures appearing in films during the ten-year period following 9/11. In comparison, it is noteworthy that American cinema has done away with some of its early images—the oil-rich Sheikhs in pursuit of white damsels, although the most common stereotypes in the past, do not seem to have any popularity with filmmakers anymore.

Moreover, the types that have recently been in use are not always monolithic and immutable. The same character is sometimes made up of different dimensions and sometimes moves from one dimension to another, either because the flow of the narrative necessitates it or the transformation is used as a device for surprise and revelation (e.g., in *The Kingdom* the old man with missing fingers initially looks like a victim of war but later it becomes clear that he is a terrorist who lost his fingers while making bombs).

## *The Muslim in Comedy*

Part of the function of political satire is to indict authoritative states through creative means. Comedy films, such as *Borat: Cultural Learnings of America for Make Benefit Glorious Nation of Kazakhstan* (2006), *Jackass Number Two* (2006) and *Team America: World Police* (2004) are perfect examples of cinema that ridicules the implementation of governmental policies by addressing what the acceptable social behavior of a nation is. The parody of the assumed Muslim character is not necessarily a means to mock the Muslim's image but rather to provide an illustration of how the general American population reacts to these stereotypes. These films articulate that reaction and not action is the cause for taboo and creative satirist filmmakers emphasize this point by highlighting the significance that victimization plays in American society.

As awareness develops in the manner in which each cultural identity is imagined on the screen, so too should the effect of how the self perceives itself. Perhaps only in the comedy and parody genres has there been any attempt to distinguish and identify many of the racial stereotypes that have been constructed within the realm of drama and action movies. Comedy has shown that Muslim identity is not a literal composition but an imagined entity that has been subjected to an imperialist commentary. An argument can also be assumed in the understanding that colonialist imagery, which has been rebranded in the form of humor, should also be included in this paradigm. Therefore, one should not get too carried away in the belief that social satire is an immediate guarantor of liberal multiculturalism. The effect can in itself be retrograde and, rather than being a critique on Eurocentric representations, it becomes a means of perpetuating racist views. Whether or not the Muslim males in parodies such as *Team America: World Police, You Don't Mess with the Zohan* (2008), *Looking for Comedy in the Muslim World* (2005) and *Borat: Cultural Learnings of America for Make Benefit Glorious Nation of Kazakhstan* project racist undertones remains to be questioned.

The Muslim male's demeanor and image are determined by a number of familiar creative devices that represent a current understanding of some core values set by those who project their own sense of anxiety onto the "Other." The taxi cab sketch in *Jackass Number Two* is not intended to offend and insult the object of vilification, but rather to assume an orchestrated reaction of the self, at the expense of the Orientalized Arab terrorist. In *Jackass Number Two*, the visual signifiers of an assumed Arab terrorist are blatant cognitive devices that aim to stimulate memories of a traumatic ordeal. The two actors' attire, behavior and images are devices that the filmmaker purposefully uses to mock the spectator's preconceived ideas. When a sketch concludes with a prank being orchestrated and reversed so as to victimize the pranksters, it manages to acknowledge the shortcomings and dangers of stereotyping.

The main character in *Borat: Cultural Learnings of America for Make Benefit Glorious Nation of Kazakhstan* is positioned within various politically right-wing American environments but his "Muslimness" is never directly addressed and is only presumed. In fact, Borat's staged vignettes delve right into xenophobic cultural differences without falling victim to the connotative and denotative values with which the Arab had once been cinematically portrayed. His Islamist behavior is replaced by ardent nationalism, which his American victims are only too happy to tolerate. The exclusion of his faith is designed to allow him to mingle with those he projects his parody onto. Since the actor playing the role of Borat is Jewish himself and not a native of the American society that he mocks, his disguise can only be assumed to be a post-modern, neo-realist construction.

*Team America: World Police* recognizes the effect that governmental policies have on current socio-political attitudes. Instead of creating an illustration of the effects of "Othering," puppetry is actualized to emphasize the animated nature of representation. By administering this cinematic form of character portrayal, the filmmaker transforms an assumed literal reality into a marionette. In doing so, he not only encapsulates the perverse nature of the current social environment but also reduces its importance to child-like significance. Visual Oriental signifiers of Egyptian Arabs are used widely to reinforce this point: they are portrayed with an abundance of hair, behave like militant extremists and speak incoherently as if being mimicked by an adolescent. The ridicule is not directed towards the "Other" but is intended to act as a critique of the overreaching imperialist U.S. gaze. In one notable scene in the film, the female American psychic-clairvoyant tells bemused locals, "Fear not, Muslim friends—I'm clearing your minds of all anxiety," which satirizes the aggressive manner of hegemonic orders imposing their dominance over Muslim ideologies.

*You Don't Mess with the Zohan* contrastingly explores the relationship with the immigrant "Other" without the acute xenophobic misrepresentations that *Team America: World Police* successfully scrutinizes. The Muslim is realized, along with the Israeli Jew, as a composite of the American immigrant experience. Both are recognized as having similar characteristics and sharing similar ordeals. A common thematic device to be observed here, and also in the majority of films analyzed in this section, is the motif of hybrid identity. These male characters have cast away their former lives in favor of starting afresh in New York or elsewhere in the United States but, when prompted, they revert back to a behavior that is indicative of a stereotype associated with the overseas Muslim. They are parodied and their true form, which is now considered to be that of the American immigrant, is subverted by the dominant paradigm. Middle-brow popular cultural references are incorporated into scenes, showing Muslim and Jewish immigrant males speaking like white protagonists. The effect is a reversal and deconstruction of pre-existing stereotypes, which are replaced by an alternative identification. The Islamic Rage Boy syndrome is reworked to a level of ridicule, resulting in a disruption and disorientation of a subjective condition that is imposed on the spectator.

## *Conclusion*

It is notable that in the movies released post–9/11, the dominant and subservient elements are different from those once presumed. Emphasis has been placed on presenting a diverse commonality of ideas that form the basis on which characters portraying the "Other" and the self share a deeper understanding of and respect for one another. However, the prevalent ideological discourse of opposing cultures remains at the heart of each film and although a "common ground" is established, on the whole, the Muslim male—when not an absolute villain—still remains subservient to the whim of the dominant cultural principles, in the guise of the reform and modernization that the protagonists impersonate. Most often, the role of the Muslim male is to adhere to the principle of the Western protagonist rescue fantasy and he is literalized and encapsulated by the notion that he represents part of the allegorical rescue of the "Orient" from its own instinctive destructiveness. There are also examples in which the Muslim is projected as the victim of capitalism, irrespective of the character's religious beliefs, and this is a clear departure from the established stereotypical presentations of the past. The case studies show that in the age of transnationalism, stereotype-plated Arab/Muslim characters with predictable character traits and physical features are not accepted any more as authentic representatives of their race and culture. Not only has globalization increased audiences' awareness of peculiarities pertaining to different races and cultures, movement in the modern world has also blended their idiosyncrasies with other racial features and cultural composites.

This chapter has argued that the narrative motivations of character have begun to be gradually intertwined and assimilated as part of a recognizable form of Westernized storytelling. Instead of being subservient to the central Western protagonist, the filmic version of the Muslim male has become "humanized" in a way that allows him to share similar experiences and characteristics with the white protagonist. He has become an embodiment of a construct that endorses his Islamic cultural heritage while also siding with the protagonist against their shared enemy in the form of extremism. Towards the final years of the decade, he has even become a source of respected moral authority, as in the case of Hani in *Body of Lies* (2008), while Americans themselves have become frustrated with their country's foreign policies. It is this frustration that leads the character Roger Ferris, for instance, to settle down in the Middle East.

Observations show that the interpretation of the Muslim American has taken an alternative route, providing less of a display of the excessive xenophobic behavior his overseas counterparts have been subjected to. While simultaneously exhibiting heroic and empathetic qualities, as illustrated by the African American Muslim, he equally takes on a symbolic role that suggests the re-examination and reworking of a national social and economic structure that was required to alter its preconceived understanding of Islam as a monolithic ideology. The deconstruction and reconstruction of the Muslim American immigrant has been approached in such a way as to eradicate the audience's selective historic memory of a role that had once been so prominently dominated by oil—wealthy sheikhs. Many of the current films decidedly examine the male according to his social status and mobilize a means to orchestrate his downfall. Each film makes use of various devices to bring about this consequential end.

It seems that the War on Terror has not worked to the disadvantage of the Muslim male depiction. On the contrary, while earlier cinematic stereotypes such as the Arab terrorist/villain, the corrupt tradesman and the Muslim despot have continued to invade the screen, new character types have also been created in the form of the naïve sympathizer(s) of terrorism, victim(s) of war, the Use Value Muslim, the immigrant Muslim, the feminized Muslim, the "tolerable" Muslim and the respectable Muslim. Meanwhile, the African American Muslim, whose assumed identity has yet to be universally accepted, may have incurred preconceived notions that occasionally exhibit Orientalist traits, but this has never been to the same extent as the Arab and the Middle Easterner.

When it comes to comedy, the role it has had in cinema and in the shaping of the new Muslim male character should not be underestimated. Following the passing of the Patriot Act in 2001, the Bush administration was unintentionally responsible for escalating sympathy for and interest in the Muslim, both in real life and on the screen. While political satire may derive its absolution from the principle of free speech, the production of more traditional linear comedies, as illustrated by *Looking for Comedy in the Muslim World* (2005), indicates a need to share cultural ideologies under the rubric of humanity. This humanistic approach may be what underlies the stereotyped characters of minorities being later "rehabilitated" in stages (Michalak, 2010), and we may now be witnessing the start of the same process in the depiction of the Muslim character.

The new image formation in American cinema exceeds the boundaries set by Edward Said's *Orientalism* (2003). Grotesquely wealthy womanizers have disappeared and in some cases have been replaced with dignified civil servants (*Body of Lies*) or even rulers (*Syriana*, 2005). The image of a man sexually harassing a Western female victim is either not popular anymore or has, in some cases, been reversed, with a white female character victimizing and destroying a man from the East. Western feminism flew into a passion and found its prey in the Muslim world.

# 4
# White Female and Muslim Male Characters

As social and political changes demanded different roles from individuals in the United States at the turn of the twenty-first century, and borders became endangered and needed to be protected, the protagonists in American cinematic narratives underwent a transformation. Widely televised political speeches underlined the necessity for all members of the armed forces, regardless of gender, to do their share for the protection of the nation as well as of the rest of the world.[1] In an atmosphere where so much was expected from all American citizens, it is not surprising that an aggressive female identity found in the film industry fertile ground in which to flourish.

The foundations of this identity were already laid in the 1960s with the rise in popularity of second-wave feminism, and again in the 1980s with its revival. A myriad of elements have been drawn up to create a female gender form that has not only evolved from past cinematic historical workings but has become a hybrid of feminist ideals coupled with American political and socio-ideological undertones. Consistent with the second-wave Feminists, carrying the torch inherited from their predecessors into wider areas including the workplace, women presented in the films have acquired professional skills that had hitherto been kept from them: in *Blue Steel* (1989), for instance, Jamie Lee Curtis' androgynous character works as a policewoman; in *Aliens* (1986), an intentionally plain and unsexual-looking Sigourney Weaver is influenced by U.S. Marines; and in *Terminator 2: Judgment Day* (1991), we learn that a distinctly butch and muscular looking Linda Hamilton has been trained in guerrilla warfare.[2] Equipped with such skills, the female character exercises her power over the male in the context of cultural hegemony, both psychologically and physically. The white American female representing the dominant force breaks down gender barriers and solves the problems created by a diverse selection of antagonists ranging from extraterrestrials and time-travelling cyborgs (*Terminator 2: Judgment Day*) to serial killers: *Jagged Edge*

(1985), *Blue Steel* (1989), *Eye for an Eye* (1996), *Copycat* (1995), *The Silence of the Lambs* (1991), pirates: *Cutthroat Island* (1995), spies: *The Long Kiss Goodnight* (1996) and zombies: *Resident Evil* (2002). According to the classification developed by Galbraith (1984, 14–65), protagonists exert power through all means, ranging from the "condign" (based on force) to the "compensatory" (the use of various resources), and even the "conditioned" (the use of persuasion). Galbraith contends that power derives from various sources such as "personality" (individuals), "property" (material wealth) and "organizational structure" (a hierarchy within an organization). Power acquired through all these conditions is observable in the post-9/11 films in which a formidable American female character exerts control over a weak Muslim man.

The terrorist act experienced in 2001 demanded and paved a way for a new female character who would combat the threat of Islam to the U.S. way of life. However, this time the American female character was constructed to direct her wrath, for the first time, at a passive Muslim male character. It can be argued that a film director's framing of both American female and Muslim male characters is shaped, influenced and somewhat coerced by the socio-political realities and gender arguments of the time and their impact on the public. Consequently, the filmic narrative is built around a gullible, hapless and pathetic Muslim man who has no chance of withstanding the powerful woman of the West. At this point, it is irrelevant to hypothesize about whether the filmmaker's primary concern is to break away from the conventional images of Muslim males as fear-inspiring tyrants or barbaric terrorists and to represent a true-to-nature character by suggesting that vulnerability is only human, regardless of one's geography or ethnicity. It is also futile to ponder whether a compassion-inspiring image of the Muslim man has been developed to satisfy the filmmaker's fascination with the fierce American female character, who is the by-product of successive waves of feminism. In either case, the stereotypical representation of the Eastern male seems to have undergone a remarkable transformation, which is reconcilable with the changes in the celluloid representation of different aspects of the Muslim world, as discussed in other chapters.

Although the practice in this study is to focus on one or more examples from early cinema and compare their features with examples from the post-9/11 era, movies about an innocent Muslim character and a forceful American woman do not seem to exist in the pre-9/11 context. Therefore, all the case studies in this section are films released after 2001. They will be analyzed in chronological order of the year of release, with the aim of observing how the relationship between these two character types has evolved in the span of ten years, and what implications this evolution has had for the image of the Muslim male in cinema. In the course of the analysis, the circumstances in which these movies were produced and circulated have been taken into account; as the selection is anchored to 9/11, this is almost a given. Press reviews and television news output have also proved useful in delineating the emotions of the period.

## Gender Reformulations

In order to understand the dynamics of male and female roles in films, it is helpful to observe the contextual norms of the period, as representations of gender roles usually depend on the socio-political events of the time. Recognition of the historical context in which characters are molded enables the analyst to see the links between cinematic portrayals and images created by the media through news broadcasts and other outlets. This analysis inevitably leads to a better understanding of the various distinct roles that cinematic characters have defined.

It can be assumed that a variety of problems have influenced the characterization of Muslim males and Euro/American females in the post–9/11 period, but one of these has to be the horrific events at Abu Ghraib prison in Iraq. The humiliating photos of male prisoners being subjected to maltreatment and extreme humiliation, especially at the hands of the female GI Lynndie Rana England in 2004, shook the whole world, not least Americans themselves. These images have been of particular relevance in creating a form of propaganda used by the mass media at the expense of the Muslim male. Although Lynndie England was not the first female to be capitalized on as a means of generating female military involvement in Iraq (as, too, was Jessica Lynch), it is possible to argue that her circumstances were specifically staged for propagandist reasons and that she was merely treated as a scapegoat. Seven people in total were responsible for the acts, but Lynndie England will always be the face of the crime. It can thus be hypothesized that both Jessica Lynch and Lynndie England were exploited in stories deliberately conceived by PSYOPS (Psychological Operations) in order to exacerbate a gender war that was effectively utilized to create the maximum effect of "shock and awe" on a religious enemy.[3]

Lynndie England presented a dilemma for the American media and public because, as Harp and Struckman (2010, 6) argue, with her "short, dark hair, Army fatigues, and a cigarette dangling from her lips," while jovially pointing at a hooded but naked Iraqi man's genitals, she was not a representative of the social role traditionally ascribed to females, even those working in the army. She needed therefore to be presented by the media as a "sexual deviant who existed outside the normal, accepted feminine bounds" (2). On this account, she has the kind of image that justifies third-wave feminists' struggle for intersectionality.

While the blond and pretty Jessica Lynch became the "face" of the Iraqi war when she went missing in action and was later rescued, Lynndie England became (as she was often referred to in U.S. tabloids) the "anti–Jessica Lynch." This notion of good and bad, or rather "black" and "white" propaganda, had a balancing effect in over-exemplifying the female military role in Iraq. Both accounts were intended to portray females in various guises, but their power to persuade not only lay in creating a soap-operatic narrative that would appeal to the general public, but also in playing to America's image as a stern but merciful world leader.

In trivializing and creating sensationalist narratives through factual events, these two female identities nonetheless posed the same dilemma, especially in regard to how they could be channeled into cinematic narratives. England's and Lynch's images served as polarized opposites but achieved the same ideological objectives. If Lynch portrayed the need to protect an idealized feminine from the clutches of the "backward" Muslim male, then England represented the urgency of promoting American ideals through ruthless agents as a just and moral cause. Both cases offered similar conclusions but through contrasting means by which the female image was examined, and a compromise was created, resulting in the birth of formidable female characters whose *raison d'être* was to attack the male representative of the Middle East, regardless of whether or not he deserved this treatment. As the case studies show, this newly structured and gendered dominant Western female sometimes has feminine, sexual qualities like Lynch, and at other times is asexual like England, but both crusade against a subordinated Muslim male. They have become the "soft-core" and "hard-core" female personalities dominating the new formidable American woman character types in cinema.

## *The Ascent of the Female*

In terms of role distribution, American cinema has always been inconsiderate towards women in general, irrespective of color and creed. In her essay published in the first issue of *Women and Film*, Sharon Smith (1972, 13) asserts that women, "in any fully human form, have almost completely been left out of film.... Even when a woman is the central character, she is generally shown as confused or helpless and in danger, or passive, or as a purely sexual being." The development of female characters from stereotypical "Others" to free-willed, well-rounded, convincing individuals in cinema primarily stemmed from either commercial interests that wanted to appeal to large and diverse audiences (Brunsdon 1987), or claims for equal gender rights by second-wave feminists who protested against being treated as sexual objects.

Tasker (1998, 13) argues that this strategy developed into an "articulation of 'strong women' in terms of an aggressive sexuality involving a particular kind of objectification and display." The old tradition of the "cowgirl" female in western films such as *Calamity Jane* (1953) and *Johnny Guitar* (1954) progressed into productions that promoted females to protagonist status in the form of formidable women. The action heroines of the 1980s and 90s saw the metamorphosis of the female character into an assertive force, in roles such as those played by Jane Fonda in *Klute* (1971) or Sigourney Weaver in *Alien* (1979), displaying masculine influence in terms of visual representation and behavior. Films such as *Aliens* (1986), *Blue Steel* (1989) and *Terminator 2: Judgment Day* (1991) brandished women in roles that required intense physical dexterity and a muscular body, while at the same time not overlooking their intellectual maturity, sexuality and maternal instincts. This change in female representation echoes third-wave feminism, alleging that women have the right to have both feminine and masculine qualities.

From the 1950s until the turn of the century, when problems in the Middle East troubled the United States continuously, narrative cinema focusing on the pairing of Muslim males and Euro/American females generally presented relationships deprived of affection. While libidinous Arab/Muslim characters were portrayed as being infatuated with white women, the female characters responded with hatred and loathing. It is claimed that in this unbalanced situation any kind of sexual interaction between them could only be that of rape (Bernstein and Stuller 1997, 42).

The commonly used enemy found in the movies and exemplified by the Native American, the Russian, the Vietnamese and the Nazi also underwent a change in the 2000s and was replaced with the Middle Eastern, Arab and Muslim (usually in combination) terrorist, who had to be crushed by the white centralized protagonists. However, feminist rage against law-abiding, ordinary believers in Islam is a new feature of films that emerged in the aftermath of 9/11, probably reflecting the combination of shock, bewilderment and mistrust that the nation was experiencing at the time.

The films under scrutiny in this chapter show how each female character exercises her own form of power to varying degrees over the hapless Muslim male. This new "formidable woman" character directs her authoritative power towards the Muslim male, exhibiting and promoting an ideological agenda in which the freedoms of the West triumph over the archaic lifestyle of the East. She also manifests a desire to combat Islam's long-established reputation of being oppressive and "anti-woman." Whether she appears as an "action woman," *femme fatale* or "superrat," this cinematic female character operates as a catalyst for the emergence of the Muslim man as a weak, laughable, and/or deplorable "Other." He is subjected to a process that feminizes his "inferior masculinity," and thus demoted to a despicable position in the hands of the Western female (Sjoberg 2007, 95). With the exception of *Sex and the City 2* (2010), the films in this analysis do not generally manifest signs that these formidable female characters are, in the normative sense, sexually attracted to men. Instead, the films continuously remind us of the cultural differences between two distinct patriarchies. This comparison is brought to the fore by the Muslim "Other" falling victim to the whims of a female American character, which demonstrates the effects of the political climate of the decade.

## *The Gaze*

The female character in the past was herself constructed as the "Other," resulting from a male-centered approach in classical American cinema, but her recent interaction with the Muslim male has promoted her in such a way that she has now become both the subject and object of the gaze. The concept of "the gaze" in its application to narrative cinema takes its meaning from the male perspective, that is, the female entity is perceived from the viewpoint of the male character, hence its usage as the "male gaze" (Mulvey 1975). The idea here is that the gazer (subject) is the male character and the gazed at (object) is female. The gazer may also be the spectator in the auditorium but, regardless of who he is, the gaze is a one-way activity directed from the active (gazing) male to the passive (gazed at) female. This gives the male pleasure from looking at something beautiful or something sexually attractive. Mulvey's (*ibid.*) theory would have significant traction if the majority of cinemagoers consisted of one gender only, but this is not the case. There are in general as many female viewers in the audience; in fact, depending on the genre, women spectators may be in majority. Complementary notions to Mulvey's (1975) views have developed in time, arguing that women also gaze at men for pleasure. Richard Dyer (2005), for instance, in his work on male pin-ups, remarks that male models in promotional campaigns for jeans stand out in terms of their sexual appeal, which may be gratifying for the "female gaze." The same is true for the topless male models used in male fragrance advertisements, such as those for Giorgio Armani's Acqua di Gio and David Beckham's Homme, in which masculine sexuality is on display. In the course of the theory's evolution, yet another derivative is developed in the post-colonial literature, namely the "colonial gaze" or the "imperial gaze" (Pratt 1992). In this case, the object of the gaze is an Eastern figure of either gender, and the gazer is their colonial "superior," again of either gender. The powerful ruling elite can cast their "colonial gaze" without danger of reciprocity as the subaltern is not allowed to look back. Hence, an asymmetric relation of power exists between them. What is interesting in the case of the white Western woman and Muslim man is that the female's position in inviting the "male gaze" of the audience becomes complicated. The white female protagonist, while remaining an object of male fascination and retaining her feminine qualities in that she attracts the male (spectators') gaze, simultaneously casts an "imperial gaze" on the male (Muslim) object in the film. This pleasurable and aggressive form of eroticism is rooted in psychoanalytical theory (Grossberg 1997) and can be traced in the cycle in which film narratives move from moments of melodrama or suspense to cathartic fight/action sequences (as in *The Kingdom* [2007]).

Western female characterizations are absorbed by the overreaching influence of a colonial doctrine through their centrality and relationship to the Muslim male, as pointed out by Kaplan (1997) who claims that the binary created by the white subject leads to the arrogance of looking down on the primitiveness of the "Other" being gazed at. The white female therefore becomes the signifier of this arrogance, especially in exchanges with her Muslim male counterpart. Her antagonistic responses encompass various significations, such as power, leadership, empowerment, freedom and violence. With the events of 9/11, the viewer is led on "a sliding continuum of proximal pleasure and distal discomfort as the signifier-signified relationship has become more ideologically fixed" (Graham 2007, 5). Therefore, the development of the strong female character and her imperial gaze directed at the Muslim male, both reflecting and remolding the gaze of the nation on the Muslim "Other," echoes the sensitivities and sentimentalities of the time. It is argued that the gaze, signifying the activity of the subject looking at the object, or the film director creating a Muslim character as his/her gaze dictates, is not static and ossified as claimed by Edward Said (2003), but is capable of oscillations caused by social and political resonance.

The depiction of the victimized Muslim male character as fodder for the "butch" female figure does not seem to have received as much academic attention as it deserves. The reason for this must bear some relation to the fact that the character pairing of the strong American woman and weak Muslim man is considerably recent in American cinema, developed after 9/11.

Following Mulvey's (1975) argument, we can acknowledge the existence of two simultaneous gazes in the films where the narrative is built around a relationship between a white American female character and a Muslim male character. The former casts an imperial gaze on the Muslim "Other" and the latter a male gaze on the white female character. However, we note at this point that the disparity between the pair is broken down in the sense that what was not allowed before (i.e. the colonized not gazing back) has become inoperative as both subjects can observe one another, albeit through different types of gaze. This said, the data show that the female character's imperial gaze is the dominant element in the films, regardless of whether she is presented as a *femme fatale*, action woman or superrat. A brief overview of these character types will be beneficial before specific films are analyzed.

## The Femme Fatale

The *femme fatale* character type, which was extremely prominent in European and American *noir* films of the 1940s and 50s, came back into use in the post–9/11 period. In the dyad of the Muslim male and American female, the Muslim male functions as a destructible tool for helping the *femme fatale* establish her identity. In the narrative, the Muslim male becomes an alternative means for the character to assert her manipulative power while symbolizing a "figure for projecting masculine anxiety in which she exists, principally to bring about his destruction" (Bronfen 2004, 114).

Through the *femme fatale* character in *Sorry, Haters* (2005), we can better appreciate the Muslim male's identity because his anxieties are inextricably linked to her manifestations. As Cavell (1976, 279) aptly puts it, "recognizing a person depends upon allowing oneself to be recognized by him [/her]." Therefore, through dialogic expression, self-revelation implies self-recognition as well. Bronfen (2004, 103) broadens this claim by remarking that one can never know the other but, "only acknowledge her or him as embodying precisely the limit to one's knowledge, and thus one's existence."

Much in the same way that *film noir* (and its transformation in the form of *neo noir* in the 1980s) was a response to the volatile social and economic times of the post-war period, some of the films released post–9/11 play upon the terrorist attacks, replicating this trend and transmitting a paranoid cinematic reaction replete with pessimism. The resurgence of the *femme fatale* character highlights the question of gender difference through a discussion of tragic sensibility and, in doing so, indirectly questions Islamic codes of conduct and beliefs.

The destructive female character functions as a mirror of the Muslim male victim's erotic ambivalence, resulting in what Mulvey (1996) defines as "fetishism." She says there has been a refusal to acknowledge the difference "the female body represents for the male. These complex series of turnings away, of covering over, not of the eyes but of understanding, of fixating on a substitute object to hold the gaze, leave the female body as an enigma and threat" (64). Since the *femme fatale* can be defined through her insistence on undermining the morality of humanistic values, she is frequently realized by her fall in power either through death, or, more commonly in cinema, through her visual decline. That is, she diminishes in size, suggesting a diminution of her authority, or she fades into the shadows.

The contemporary *femme fatale* has no love for any man as she has so often been abused and manipulated by men in her past. Boozer (1999/2000, 32–33) best sums up the *femmes fatale*'s rejuvenated transformation as the embodiment of the "dynamic of the overladen sign of commodity fetishism" whereby "representations of her increasingly relate to an alienated expressivity," eventually making her the apotheosis of the *femme fatale* itself.

## *The Action Woman*

Even though the action-woman character is present in only one of the case studies—Janet Mayes in *The Kingdom* (2007)—including her character is vital to this analysis since she represents the most visually visceral female of those under scrutiny. For the sake of understanding this character type better, it would help to elaborate here on the action woman in American film. Janet Mayes is used as a template and her inclusion is only to realize and appreciate the significance of the action woman as an antagonizer in the context of a Muslim environment.

Mayes is developed in a similar way to the female character Ripley in *Alien* (1979). Ripley manages, according to Hills (1999, 38, 40), to be realized as a "transformative, transgressive and heroic" female who violates "both cinematic genre codes and cultural genre codes." She represents one of the most visually active female heroines to have challenged theoretical approaches to sexual differences as well as how films have been mapped. Action women like Ripley battle with an alien monster—figurative or literal—and demand that the spectator decode the unconventional female role presented to them. Deleuze (1986) terms this a disruption in the "sensory motor-logic of genre cinema," whereby the female action character disturbs the viewer's automatic reading of her body and indulges in activities traditionally associated with the role of the male hero (205–215). In other words, the logical reading of "action woman" is of the transgression of the traditional feminine role of a highly sexualized object towards an active and destructive subject and, in some cases, a final reversion back to her original traditional form. The determining factor for her change from one form to another is her relocation from one type of environment and culture to another. Jennings (1995) claims that the status of heroine is denied to the action woman because of her ability to access traditional cinematic masculine and feminine qualities of character. However, this is contested by Tasker (1993, 152), who argues that qualities of vulnerability and strength, singly or in combination, can also be considered characteristic attributes of the hero/heroine.

In her analysis of *Alien*, Hills (1999) also defines the action woman as a female character "which breaks down the hierarchical division of active-male/passive female" (43). In this sense she becomes what Braidotti (1994,

169) terms a "post-woman woman," functioning in the middle space between male/female binaries. Yet, even in this position she is capable of being attractive to the male gaze and having maternal instincts. Ripley creates a hybrid figure that opens a new space for the action women in this particular genre of film. She needs to "reassemble" her body by covering and protecting it with weaponry and armor. Deleuze and Guattari (1987, 161) refer to this transformation as the adoption of a "body without organs," which the female requires in order to pursue a more pragmatic relationship with the company she keeps, and to escape from the gender limitations dictated by modes of binary thought.

## *The Superrat*

Although third-wave feminists are grounded in Western imperialist rhetoric in their opposition to patriarchy, they are seen to share in the common perpetuation of a male-dominated hierarchy that is prone to project its conflicts onto woman's bodies. Coined by Naomi Wolf (1991, 11), "the beauty myth" is seen as an instrument assigned by men in order to impede women's advancement within a patriarchal society. To counter-balance this suppression Paula Kamen (2000, 21) uses the term "Superrat"—also referred to as "Babe Feminism" by Anna Quindlen (1994)—to describe modern women who are "united by one common trait: The expectation of and insistence on conducting their sex lives and relationships on their own terms with a new degree of openness." This breed of predatory young woman not only disrupts the already established balance between the sexes, but also destroys the sanctity of courtship. Kamen (2000) agrees that some feminists may also take issue with the superrat type of woman because she possesses sexual values of aggression and is concerned only with self-gratification. However, the same type is nonetheless tolerated in popular culture because she "looks like she has just stepped out of the pages of *Cosmo*" (*ibid.*, 38). The entertainers, including the cast of *Sex and the City 2* (2010), she argues, "would not have attracted such a public forum (and array of corporate sponsors) to broadcast their sexual rebellions, if they did not look the way they do" (*ibid.*). This fiercely independent woman, with an aggressive sexuality we would normally associate with men, and her insistence on making decisions by herself is equated by Wolf (1993, 149) with "power feminism," which associates women's power with their success in a capitalist system. The superrats began to emerge in American cinema in the late 1980s and Kamen (2000, 32) observes that by the late 1990s, "this genre of films became noticeable as a movement." However, the appearance of this character type within a Muslim context is something that happened after 9/11.

Numerous films provide rich material in the analysis of a strong American woman praying on a Muslim man and it is beneficial to segment productions to explain various roles, devices and strategies, as well the effects that the Western female character has had vis-à-vis the Muslim male. Only by dissecting these female characters in the works under observation can one further explore the friction between the self (as represented by the female character) and the "Other" (as represented by the Muslim male character). Friction arises through interrelationships between and the choice of attire, behavior and dialogue, which not only result in cultural conflicts, but also provide insights into why they have been conceived as such. The agitations shared by the Muslim male and American female characters expose various strategies devised to provoke imperialist responses by illustrating her attempts to avoid being defined solely by sexuality and gender. What results is an underlying struggle for the recognition of identity that is not accorded and defined by patriarchal gender limitations imposed by the male. Each of the following case studies attempt to expand on this premise.

In the films made later in the decade, when the Bush administration intensified the War on Terror, the female American casts an objectifying, colonial gaze, demonstrating the unequal power exercised by a ruthless woman over a weak Muslim man. In such cases, the woman either kills the Muslim herself, tricks or ridicules him, or has him tortured to the brink of death. These acts are reminiscent of the degrading photographs of the Iraqi captives in Abu Ghraib prison suffering at the hands of Lynndie England. The excessive torture of a captive who has already lost his battle, dignity and freedom does not have a logical explanation unless it is prompted by a loss of direction, hatred or simply psychopathic hysteria; the film *Sorry, Haters* (2005) is a particularly strong case in point.

## *The Femme Fatale in* Sorry, Haters *(2005)*

Although severely criticized by critics on its theatrical release, the multilayered *Sorry, Haters* (2005), directed by Jeff Stanzler, is one of the most complex portrayals of the U.S. post–9/11 period. Questions surrounding 9/11's sociological effects on Muslim immigrants, the locals and gender roles establish a backdrop of New York under reconstruction, both as a literal context and through personal traumatic ordeals. The film tells the story of a female sociopath—Phoebe (Robin Wright Penn)—and her self-righteous crusade to find morality, truth and justice in a "new society" recovering from the attack on the World Trade Center.

*Sorry, Haters* introduces a female who acknowledges her responsibility for her fate. The transgressive Muslim male, on the other hand, is characterized as the exact opposite in attitude, unaware of his own fallibility. These two are tragically framed within a narrative that links them to one another on the basis of the law of causation. The link gets broken when the woman fails to reach her intended target, requiring her to exert a degree of authoritative power over men.

In this new society, where U.S. ideology and government have failed in their roles to uphold and protect the ideals of their people, the atmosphere of disillusionment results in nihilism. The character of Phoebe is conceived as a *femme fatale* whose life has been affected by the collapse of the American Dream and the promises once offered by the government and general society in the pre–George W. Bush era. Befriending and stalking Ashade (Abdel Kechiche), a highly educated Syrian-Muslim immigrant taxi driver, she finds motivation for revenge as a consequence of 9/11, and undertakes a personal crusade to bring chaos to his life.

The film raises questions about internal colonialization whereby Phoebe and Ashade function as figures who struggle for recognition. Both can be considered as variants of the "Other" in so far as Ashade is representative of the immigrant "Other" and Phoebe is a female who is marginalized by her career. The film requires us to view their dilemma through a post-colonial lens, in order to understand the projection of colonial assimilation. Phoebe's resistance to and disdain at being marginalized as a subordinate to an Asian employer, and Ashade's refusal to be assimilated as a consequence of his beliefs present a quandary where a *femme fatale*'s survival pattern is inextricably linked to a Muslim male's anxieties. She cannot exist without him, nor he without her. Phoebe is aware of her personal failures and misgivings, but she judges those around her in a decisive and intrusive manner. She sees herself as a voice of salvation and the last bastion of hope in a country that has not only been lied to by its authorities, but has had its ideology revealed as spurious. Her initial encounter with Ashade permits us, and him, a glimpse of the venomous manner in which she conducts her life. She asks him to take her to what we are led to believe is her ex-husband's house, where she scratches her ex's car with a rock while Ashade watches and waits for her inside the taxi. This precursor to the events that unfold later acts as a device for examining both characters' moral qualities: the passive Ashade who lives peacefully and abides by the standards of Islam, and the active and self-righteous Phoebe who spitefully and forcefully imposes herself on others in acts that lie outside the judicial boundaries of moral decency.

The irony in the depiction of characters in *Sorry, Haters* has to do with the manner in which Phoebe gradually metamorphoses from "one of us" (i.e., a white, Christian American) into the "Other." From the onset we see Ashade and various other Muslim characters praying in a mosque. Ashade is given money by his fellow Muslim friends, which we eventually learn is to be used towards his brother's legal fees in his release from prison. Their act is one of collective unity within a community that embraces them. In Ashade's world, the characters take loving care of their co-members and are not easily corrupted by the Western compulsions of capitalism and ambition. They adapt to and are absorbed by selected aspects of U.S. life, in a manner better described as a form of transnationalism. The initial gaze through which we perceive these Muslims might intentionally be twisted, distorted and perverted by imperialistic notions of Orientalism, since most of the characters in the mosque have beards and wear either *taqiyahs* (including Ashade), *keffiyahs* or a *salwar kameez*. They are the incarnation of the Oriental image engraved in the minds of those in the West. As soon as we discover that the setting of the story is New York post–9/11, we are expected to become apprehensive of these character types. The process is naturally motivated within the context of a society riddled with prejudice.

In contrast, Phoebe's appearance is that of a tall, good-looking and well-dressed businesswoman who has been visibly worn down by her career and city life. When she is refused money at a cashpoint we realize that she has financial problems, but our impression that she is "one of us" remains intact. Even the extreme act of vandalism that Phoebe commits does not sway our compassion and sympathies, as we are still able to relate to her jealousy and betrayed feelings in relation to her imaginary (as we later discover) ex-husband.

Uninvited, Phoebe forces her way into Ashade's world through lies and manipulation. He reluctantly invites her into the security of his sister-in-law's apartment and, as they discover more about each other's worlds, the positioning of characters within the low-angled camera frame is significant in that it draws attention to an Islamic male patriarchy. In this context, Ashade is authoritatively positioned in a chair and both females are left to sit on the floor with a child. Ashade's assertiveness in the scene is further accentuated by the contrasting lighting, relative depth of field and wide-angle lens that are used. The lighting underscores his supremacy in the frame, and both the depth of field and wide-angle lens emphasize impressions of the distance between genders. The camera plays to the sensitivities of feminists whose concern for Muslim men's treatment of women was at its peak at the time. Furthermore, Ashade's seemingly undeserved supremacy over the two female characters runs counter to the Western myth of gender equality and increases our initial dislike of him.

Yet, while his intentional positioning and presence command the space of the scene, he does not pass judgment on Phoebe's behavior, especially when she, in a racially motivated manner, caricatures her Chinese immigrant babysitter, who we later discover is in fact her supervisor at work. Her vulgar behavior not only creates a sense of social detachment and alienation, but also prevents us from morally empathizing with her. Her outburst gives a hint of her disdain towards immigrants who are unable to fully assimilate into her perception of U.S. life and ideology. Thus, our illusion that Phoebe is "one of us" while Ashade is the "Other" begins to diminish, and her madness stimulates the displacement of our identification of protagonist and antagonist within the narrative. The extent of her vindictive behavior in notifying immigration officials about Ashade's sister-in-law is one of the many instances that indicate the forces at play in her stormy mind. The audience is led to believe that her concept of reality is delusional and distorted.

Ashade is clearly the victim of a *femme fatale* who can dismantle and reconstruct his identity according to her interpretations of the environmental and social demands placed upon them both. His grief in watching from afar the immigration police arresting his sister-in-law Eloise (Elodie Bouchez), and his anger at Phoebe for arranging this, are used as the backdrop to his breaking into her flat. In the scuffle that follows, she invites him to rape her but he resists the invitation and explains that his uninvited entry was motivated only by his desire to seek explanation: "I have come here only to know. Why you hurt me, why you hurt my family?" The answer indicates the frustration of someone who fails to be a success in life: "I just hate me.... I don't need you to be better than me." Her mission as a *femme fatale* striving to metamorphose him is implicit in this disclosure.

By depriving Ashade of his identity, Phoebe is able to exert hegemonic control over him by objectifying his "Other-ness." Yet she can only wield her power horizontally as, according to an existing social hierarchy, they are proportionate to one another. Phoebe deprives Ashade of his former self in her need to gain female empowerment. His appearance is purposefully designed to shed any influence of this former self: he shaves his beard, polishes his shoes, does away with his *taqiyah* in favor of a business suit, imagines his detained sister-in-law is being sexually abused by immigration officials and resorts to deception in order to gain access to Phoebe's domain. However, the more he looks and acts like "us," the more we empathize with his predicament. He has lost his faith and devotion to Allah and has succumbed to the temptations that New York life offers. This is mirrored and echoed during Ashade and Phoebe's physical confrontation in Phoebe's apartment, when she says, "If you are praying, don't do it here."

The various devices that are used to emphasize Ashade's transformation and rebirth into Western capitalistic society result in his and our discovery that he has been lied to. When Ashade traces Phoebe's steps to her workplace, her attempts to hide her true identity as an introverted, mid-level account executive who has been unable to successfully climb the corporate ladder—unlike her extroverted Chinese manager—come crashing down to earth. Her delusions of grandeur, Ashade's awareness of circumstances and

## 4. White Female and Muslim Male Characters

our perceptions of character roles become clear on revelation of Phoebe's true face.

Religion, belief and ideology are prominent in *Sorry, Haters*. Since Islam is the most prevalent aspect of Ashade's existence, it is also easily identified as his weakness. Phoebe's assault on his faith creates a metaphorical dilemma of Islam versus self-righteousness, which is disseminated with religious undertones. Her constant self-mutilation, as in the scene where she has lunch with her Chinese manager, is occasionally played to shocking effect: she takes a fork and stabs her hand with it under the table cloth. It is as if her mutilation acts as a constant reminder of her failure in life, yet it also denies her tolerance for and insight into any other ideology and/or religious belief. The self-inflicted cut on her face after Ashade breaks into her flat and refuses to rape her raises the question of which character is willing to sacrifice more in terms of devotion, pain and commitment to their beliefs.

Phoebe's dominance over Ashade is illustrated in his succumbing to her will and desires. When he falls ill, her maternal instincts are aroused and she nurtures him back to health within the comfort of her lair. She cooks for him, informing him that she has not used pork in the food. The allegorical connotation of Ashade dismissing any awareness or concern as to whether pork has been used in his meal functions as a sign of his acceptance of and total assimilation into her world. He has abandoned all existence of his former self, which permits Phoebe to self-righteously pass judgment on him and condemn him to hell, realized when she pushes him down the Bank Street

*Sorry, Haters* (Jeff Stanzler, 2005): It does not occur to Ashade (Abdellatif Kechiche) that he will pay for his infatuation with the psychotic *femme fatale* Phoebe (Robin Wright) by being pushed, with a bomb, into a dark subway.

subway entrance, rigged with explosives. Her manipulation and exploitation of his trust are overshadowed by the trauma and anarchy that ensue. He is lulled into a false sense of security, only to be denied absolution from his captor, who further orchestrates his culpability by pasting pictures of him and his fellow Muslims on the street walls beside the Bank Street subway entrance.[4]

The degree to which the influence, power, glorification and omnipresence of the media is conveyed in the film is a constant reminder of how the isolated society portrayed in *Sorry, Haters* (2005) has turned into an excessive, materialistic, zombie-like nation of passive, media-obsessed citizens. The conceptualization of art imitating life and vice versa is a constant theme that runs throughout the narrative. Phoebe's final re-enactment of a music video entitled "Sorry, Haters," which is constantly referred to in the film but never shown in its entirety, is to throw her dog into the path of a moving truck. This is an act which encourages us to reconsider our evaluation of the characters and decide who is the "hater" (antagonist) and who is the "savior" (protagonist), only to reach a verdict that there is no savior in this story. The Muslim man, as the object of the colonial gaze, is destroyed, together with an innocent animal, by the hater.

In terms of characterization, the image of the Muslim male drawn here seems to be secondary to and instrumental in the portrayal of a new woman in the American society of the last decade. What we have is a female character who has failed to reach the summit in her career, and is therefore remorseful and destructive as a result. Ashade, a believer, an immigrant, an outsider, an imbecile who can be robbed, cheated, beguiled, misled and even sent easily to his death, seems to be created not for his own sake, but as an accessory in the ascendancy of this new and nihilistic *femme fatale*. She even has the audacity to call him "you camel jockey." When he changes from the religious family man that he was, minding his own business and making a decent living—but who is treated and destined to always be treated as an immigrant and an underdog—into a modern-looking, clean-shaven, mosque-evading individual in a liaison with a Christian woman, the transformation costs him his purity as well as his life. He is therefore presented as someone in a no-win situation, regardless of the lifestyle he chooses to lead. As for Phoebe, she is a psychologically disturbed woman who struggles to maintain her place within an abundantly multicultural environment. She is a representative of the nihilism caused in the minds of the American public after the attack on the twin towers, but she also displays racist tendencies. Against her psychological disorder, the Muslim male character in the film is portrayed as an individual who falls victim to seduction. Ashade is not the stereotypically rich, evil or animal-like Arab; he is simply a deplorable pawn in the hands of a disturbed *femme fatale*.

## The Formidable American Woman in Rendition (2007)

On 28 June 2005, probably as the preparations for the film *Rendition* (2007) had just got underway, President George W. Bush delivered a speech at Fort Bragg, North Carolina, broadcast to the nation on primetime network TV. In this moving speech, among other things, he said, "Our enemies are brutal, but they are no match for the United States of America, and they are no match for the men and women of the United States military."[5]

*Rendition*, released almost two years after this speech was broadcast, carries the sentiments voiced by the President and portrays a female officer of the administration trying to get to the bottom of a car bomb explosion in a north African country that kills an important American spy as well as many innocent locals.

In the narrative, Corinne Whitman (Meryl Streep) is a female politician whose purpose is to assert her authoritative power over an innocent Muslim male, Anwar El-Ibrahimi (Omar Metwally), in order to obtain information from him following the terrorist attack. Her orders for torture are implemented by two individuals under her command: North African police commissioner Abasi Fawal (Yigal Naor) and a CIA analyst Douglas Freeman (Jake Gyllenhaal).

The film is a curious blend of the uncertainty of truth and a complex web of reality in which artistic license is used far too heavy-handedly, causing misconceived judgments on the part of the viewer. As discussed by Semmerling (2006), there are four layers of truth prevailing in the film: (1) factual truth: used by the press; (2) higher truth: a form of protection from hearsay, power, emotion and zealous prosecution; (3) symbolic truth: beliefs, desires and aesthetics, and (4) a "rendition" and legal truth. Semmerling's overall conclusion is that in the film, symbolic truth triumphs over legal truth. His analysis is of the film in its entirety but his claim is also true for the character of Corinne Whitman. She is a symbolic truth that operates under the assumption that what she is doing politically is for the sake of national security. She represents the discredited and unreliable Bush administration which was in power under false pretenses and inconclusive accusations. Her actions remind us of Dick Cheney's "dark side" speech and events that occurred in both Guantanamo and Abu Ghraib prisons.[6] At one point (when responding to Douglas' sardonic remark that this is his first torture), she reprimands him with the sardonic response, "The United States does not torture," which sounds as if she is the spokesperson of President George W. Bush and his administration.

Corinne Whitman is portrayed as the modern American career woman, an individualist who completely rejects patriarchal values. She is first presented on the screen being woken by the ringing telephone, her husband asleep beside her in bed. She is not the subservient and reluctant housewife we have been accustomed to in Hollywood narratives, and doesn't explain to him why she has to go out at 3 a.m. She acts as the mother and he obediently complies: "Duty calls," and that is that. She gets out of bed and dictates her instructions to her colleagues during a terrorist crisis. She is the one who decides to step into the light, leaving her husband uninformed and in the dark. It is as if she shields her husband with ignorance of the true, corrupt nature of her work. She is aware of the politics that her administration has followed and by never giving him access to this world, she exudes power and control. When he does finally ask why someone should call so late, he is rebuked for his failure to comprehend the true nature of the situation: "I'm sure they arranged it to spite you" is Corrine's sarcastic response, demonstrating her strict authority at work and at home.

She is a formidable *femme fatale*, possessing attributes reminiscent of those cinematic female characteristics of the 1940s and also those associated with the "new Hollywood women" created in the latter half of the twentieth century, especially the 1990s. Yvonne Tasker (1998, 36) describes the qualities of the latter as follows: "The image of the New Woman, which involved the adoption of selected 'masculine' features in dress and hairstyle articulates that which it also seeks to contain, the mobility of gendered identities and behaviors.... The new woman signals a limited independence and at least the potential for transgression of gender that is aligned with lesbianism which displaces the centrality of the male subject." She also describes the attributes that this characterization encompasses: "Firstly, her seductive sexuality. Second, the power and strength (over men) that this sexuality generates for the *femme fatale*. Third, the deceptions, disguises and confusion that surrounds her, producing her as an ambiguous figure for both the audience and the hero. Fourth, as a consequence the sense of woman as 'enigma,' typically located within an investigative structure which seeks to find 'truth' amidst the deception" (*ibid.*, 120).

Corrine Whitman is never shown as anything but a calm and collected woman, whose femininity remains unemphasized throughout most of the film (except for the drinks party where she wears an *haute couture* dress). Although she has been rushed out of bed, she remains composed and capable of giving orders in a time of crisis. It is her total control not only of her emotions but of those around her that makes her antagonism seem threatening. She wears spectacles, a long trench coat and a shirt. The cinematographic framing of the scene is cautious to avoid any imagery of her attire that could associate Corrine with her feminine gender. She is shot in a medium frame from the waist up in the back of a limousine, and later in an establishing wide-angle shot standing next to a jet aircraft. As she wears trousers, the only form of feminine attire (her shoes) that may give away her true gender are purposefully obscured.

Looking for Yvonne Tasker's four attributes in Corrine Whitman, it is possible to distinguish her seductive sexuality during the drinks reception she attends. Her feminine attire is flamboyant (distinctly contrasting with her appearance earlier in the film) and her sexual influence can be observed in her male companion (who is not her husband). She is powerful in organizing and telling the men around her what to do, and it is obvious that they are subservient to her. Her experience in and understanding of the nature of torture are evident in the way she commands her male colleagues. If necessary, she can be ambiguous, deceptive and resourceful to create confusion in others and conceal her true motivations, as in the case of her discourse with Isabella Fields El-Ibrahimi (Reese Witherspoon) and the lawyer Alan Smith (Peter Sarsgaard). The fourth attribute, the "enigma," that Yvonne Tasker refers to is depicted in Corrine's ability to conceal the true nature of her work, actions and beliefs right until the end of the film.

In the same way that Corrine Whitman's gender is obscured in most of the film (reminding us of the gender obscurity attributed to Lynndie England), so is the reason she intends to obliterate Anwar El-Ibrahimi's identity. With each order she gives, a little bit of Anwar's dignity is lost. Corrine's power reverberates via the actions of the torturers, Douglas and Abasi, and Anwar's degradation provokes a reaction in us, especially in light of the manner in which he is tortured.

If Corrine Whitman is the narrative's antagonist (as far as the Muslim male characters are concerned), then Isabella Fields El-Ibrahimi and Fatima Fawal are the female protagonists who restore balance to the disruption caused in the Muslim men's lives. Janey Place (1998, 60) describes the function of this character type as opposite to that of the female archetype in *film noir*: as a redeemer she "offers the possibility of integration for the alienated, lost man into the stable world of secure values, roles and identities. She gives love, understanding (or at least forgiveness), asks very little in return ... and is generally visually passive and static." Corinne's character disrupts harmony with such ferocity that Isabella requires further female assistance (in the form of Alan Smith's secretary) to maintain a state of equilibrium, but even these combined female forces have no chance of breaking Corinne's resolution. She aggressively talks down to those who disrespect her position of authority. She addresses Alan as "Sonny" when he defies political bureaucracy and confronts her at the drinks reception on behalf of Isabella, his former sweetheart. Corinne is determined to protect national security through whatever means necessary, regardless of who may be hurt in the process.

The male characters who fall prey to Corinne's ruthless management of the case are both seemingly liberal Muslims. Anwar is a scientist attending conferences around the world and earning well over $100,000 a year. He is happily married to an American woman, and although the confusion which linked him to a well-known terrorist is never fully clarified, he leads an affluent and legitimate life in the States. There is no indication in the narrative to suggest that he is a practicing Muslim in any significant way. The north African police chief, Abasi, is also portrayed as a non-practicing, bourbon-drinking Muslim, compliant with the strict measures dictated by Corinne. They are both under the spell of the female imperialist gaze and are seen through the eyes of a ruthless American female whose vision is impaired by fears for national security. The image of the Muslim, in this case, is neither a caricature nor the traditional Arab practicing Islam, but two dark-skinned Middle Eastern men at the mercy of a powerful American female: Corinne is a woman stripped of her femininity, cool, unimpressionable and lacking in emotion; Abasi, the slave of the world power, is an autocrat and a callous torturer, and Anwar is the whipping boy of the two. Interestingly, the narrative ends with the rescue of Anwar from the north-African prison and Corrine's transformation into a discredited housewife after her callous mismanagement is publicized in the media.

## *The Action Woman in* The Kingdom *(2007)*

A secret team of U.S. counter-terrorism investigators assemble in Riyadh to search for the criminal behind a car bomb that has exploded in the middle of an American base, killing many inhabitants including women and children. The FBI agents, however, find their attempts to capture the perpetrators impeded by political bureaucracy, resulting in a cat-and-mouse investigation assisted by the local Saudi Arabian police. The team, consisting of one female and three male officers set out to accomplish their mission of hunting down those responsible in just five days. The main culprit is not revealed until the last scene of the film. It is therefore a "whodunit" scenario rather than a lengthened combat story involving an action woman and a Muslim man. The only notable female character is Janet Mayes, played by Jennifer Garner, who, as part of the FBI task force, finds herself thrown into a hostile male-orientated environment and is largely motivated by vengeful thoughts.

The film can be read as posing numerous significant questions about feminine sexuality, gender and identity. These are cross-culturally examined as differences between the FBI agents and the Saudi natives, while providing an image of an action woman with the agility, muscular strength and problem-solving skills previously associated with male characters. Janet Mayes embodies what Tasker (1998, 68) refers to as the "butch femme" as she articulates and transmits Western modernity in the form of gender equality, which is a primary concern for third-wave feminists. To understand the idiosyncrasies of the relationship between the "butch femme" and Muslim male, we need to analyze the characteristics attributed to the Janet Mayes character. Only by appreciating the governing dynamics of her role can one fully understand the manner in which she has been strategically represented as a symbol of male-orchestrated hegemony. Her representation can be read as a deliberate ploy that manifests antagonistic features similar to those accorded to the *femme fatale* and post-feminist characters.

Mayes participates in similar duties to her male counterparts, thus undermining the "patriarchal gender boundaries that separate the sexes" (Creed 1995, 96). On duty, she is made to wear masculine attire, which normally should not insinuate her sexuality. However, Aguayo (2009, 51), in her study of Mayes' character, notes the dual masculinity and femininity of her appearance: "throughout the film Mayes is dressed in military pants with a t-shirt in an attempt to masculinize her body while still showing her female curves with specific emphasis placed on her breasts." Elsewhere in her article, Aguayo (*ibid.*, 49) remarks on Mayes' "hypersexuality," indicating further that she is constructed with both feminine and masculine qualities, which alternate as the narrative situation demands. It becomes clear from this that Mayes, as an action woman, is presented to us at times as a female with sexuality, but she also has the ability to quickly take on an active phallic status for hegemonic purposes, thereby conforming to third-wave feminists' reconstruction of the female gender. Her changeability thus creates a cultural friction between the male identities who either accept or resist her transformation. In other words, Mayes embodies a character that is able to change her appearance to suit the space she occupies. She can adjust her status from that of a feisty heroine to that of a butch and muscular action woman.

This transference and capacity for cross-dressing, which further evolve into a fantasy image of physical strength (as exemplified in the climatic action scene in the film), provide her with what could be construed as an artificial identity. While, she is able to cast off the gender limitations that are imposed on her by all of her male colleagues, she still has to face the cultural restrictions established by expectations derived from a Muslim patriarchy. And, although she displays maternal instincts (which recur as motivating features in the action-woman character), she reinforces an ambiguous sense of gender identity through her attire and behavior. This poses a challenge to gendered binaries, especially in the case of the Muslim male character who, when confronted by her very existence, is troubled over how to decode her image. Consequently, a tension develops between her image of strength and the role that her gender is supposed to fulfill.

Visually, the film exemplifies Western techniques of objectification and subjugation through which the West comes to represent its actions under the guise of being just and moral. This inevitably leads to the resurrection of past Orientalist techniques that are shaped in accordance with present circumstances. According to Aguayo (*ibid.*, 49), Mayes' gender is constructed and functions as a "technology of empire" and is assessed in accordance with the "imperiled" Muslim woman. As Aguayo suggests, being in Saudi Arabia, Mayes is continuously encouraged to revoke her Euro-American appearance of individuality. In the final climatic scene, in which Mayes breaks down the gender hierarchy of the active male/passive female, she also demonstrates a further characteristic used to describe the female action hero. Displaying "power and strength over the body of the female performer" (Tasker 1998, 70), Mayes comes to represent the quality of "masculinity." When she appears in the climatic action set piece, she makes her entry through a hole in the ceiling and is flung around the room while clinging to the back of one of the kidnappers. It is only when Mayes manages to arm herself with a knife that the ultimate feminist act of defiance is performed. This is visualized in her stabbing a knife into one of the Muslim male's genitals, cementing her role as a *femme castratrice*.[7]

The depiction of the "butch" action female in cinema has often involved imposing a degree of androgyny on the character's appearance. Mayes is no exception, and the articulation of her masculinized female body associates her with potential lesbianism. Creed (1995, 88) describes "[l]esbian bodies as active and masculinised" and it is this same muscular body we commonly find in female action roles in cinema. However, Mayes' sexual persuasion is deliberately kept ambiguous, which permits her to easily enter both masculine and feminine territories, thus creating a certain degree of confusion. In contrast to the modern female action heroines in the films of the 1980s and 90s such as *Aliens* (1986), *Terminator 2: Judgment Day* (1991) and *GI Jane* (1997), Mayes' military-like aesthetics and attire allow for a sexual perversity, or rather fetishism, which is more centered on the "butch" than the feminine.

As mentioned above, *The Kingdom* (2007) is not a story of an innocent Muslim man being confronted by a formidable female character; in this respect, it differs from the other films mentioned in this chapter. It is a story of a terrorist posing as an innocent Muslim man whose identity is revealed only at the end of the film. Starting with a bomb blast in an American base where scores of families are killed, the film does not seek any compassion from the audience for the Arabs that Mayes later kills. When it becomes clear who the bomb-making terrorist is, he is startlingly killed within seconds by Mayes. The twist is that he turns out to be the least suspicious individual among the crowd—an old man with a white beard, sitting with a smiling face in the corner of a room.

Aguayo (2009) looks closely at the functional use of the Janet Mayes role and decides that this character, who has "the expertise and knowledge to catch the terrorists" (51), is used to highlight the backwardness of Islam as her gender becomes a sign of her inferiority on Muslim soil. Mayes' visual

*The Kingdom* (Peter Berg, 2007): Janet Mayes (Jennifer Garner), the action woman, enters the terrorists' den through a hole in the ceiling, castrating one of them and killing their leader.

presence is made "hypervisible," she argues, by the fact that all the other female images in the film are those of Muslim women who are made "hyper-invisible" through veiling. She further argues that ordering Janet Mayes to cover up in the presence of Saudi royalty acts as further degradation of her gender. While stating that "it is unavoidable to note that the construction of Mayes as a non-sexualized person, given her neutral clothing, represents the very small threshold within which the lecherous, dangerous Muslim man can be provoked into becoming a violent, sexual aggressor" (*ibid.*, 52). Aguayo later claims that Jennifer Garner's "hypersexual star status" off-screen must have a bearing on how she is read by the audience (52). This contradictory situation makes sense if Mayes is interpreted in the light of third-wave feminism, which objects to heteronormativity and restricted gender roles. This also helps to explain the two consecutive scenes towards the end, one showing Mayes full of motherly affection and giving the little Arab girl sweets, and the next showing her turn into a tempestuous fighter and castrating a terrorist. This duality may also appear less confusing when interpreted alongside the perceptions of Lynndie England and Jessica Lynch during America's war in Iraq, as referred to earlier.

## *The Superrats in* Sex and the City 2 *(2010)*

With Barack Obama becoming the first African American president in the United States in 2009, and his anti-war policies being publicized, changes in the representation of the ideal American woman and the way a Muslim is gazed upon were to be expected.[8] *Sex and the City 2* (2010) demonstrates the creation of four American women characters shaped in the vogue of second-wave feminism but grounded in the third wave.

Released in the United States in May 2010, this is the second feature film following from the popular HBO television show *Sex and the City* (1998–2004). Although the events of 9/11 are not even mentioned once in the film, the significance of the trauma, and the influence and omnipresence of that particular day were probably still fresh in viewers' minds. The relationship the viewer has already built with the four female New Yorkers began in 1998 when the television show's first episode was aired; each episode capturing a glimpse of Manhattan high-society life with audiences following their favorite character's development arc. The release of the 2010 motion picture arguably indirectly confronts the lingering memories of 9/11 but takes a more relaxed attitude. The leading female protagonists are placed in the setting of Abu Dhabi and the creation of a "fish-out-of-water" scenario motivates the viewer to see how Carrie Bradshaw (Sarah Jessica Parker) and friends will react in a culturally "hostile" environment that clashes with their New York City lifestyles.

The complex debate about what culture is and from which viewpoint it is perceived is a theme that runs throughout the movie's narrative. Clashes and differences as well as similarities prevail between the New York high-society cultural backgrounds of the protagonists and the Muslim environment they find themselves in. Abu Dhabi and New York City are constantly paralleled and compared with one another in the formation of a single tale encapsulating both cities. Even the title, *Sex and the City 2*, evokes an implicit reference to this duality. When these four characters arrive in the United Arab Emirates, they bring their New York lives to the new environment, which is (presumably deliberately) made to resemble their familiar Manhattan surroundings: in the opening credits we are introduced to a cinematic aerial shot of the Manhattan skyline which is later compared with the resembling skyline of Abu Dhabi. In fact, this is one of the many thematic attempts of the film to compare the UAE with the United States.

One interesting point to note here is that while *Sorry, Haters* (2005), *Rendition* (2007) and *The Kingdom* (2007) portray a Muslim male suffering at the hands of an American *femme fatale*, or a formidable new woman or an action woman, the female attack becomes less visible and less stereotypical as time goes by. The move away from one-to-one confrontations to a more general criticism is what distinguishes *Sex and the City 2*. In other words, with the exception of the angry mob deceived through the American female characters' cooperation with the local women at the end of the film, no specific Arab male character is victimized, yet we are constantly reminded of the dominant image of the Arab male, dressed in traditional attire: on posters at the airport, on a billboard in the desert and in a portrait behind the hotel manager. It is this precise provocation that attracts our attention and reminds us of the ever-present male authority that needs to be attacked in the Islamic world. In this indirect way, traditionalism is compared and contrasted with liberal/non-conformist beliefs, while the New York females debate among themselves the very same values that both of these originate from.

The film on the whole attempts to epitomize the American Orientalist gaze and the very cinematic manner of this depiction pays homage to the classical Hollywood films that portrayed a Western traditionalist and stereotypical depiction of the East. This is most evident when the female protagonists are seen absurdly walking in the desert in colorful attire that evokes quintessential representations of Orientalist or Western cinematic character depictions: Samantha (Kim Cattrall) appears wearing an asp headpiece reminiscent of Cleopatra; Miranda (Cynthia Nixon) wears a cowboy hat synonymous with the western film genre; Carrie (Sarah Jessica Parker) appears to be wearing a turban similar to that worn by Indian sikhs; and Charlotte (Kristin Davis) exhibits an oversized British colonialesque kind of trilby. Although the manner of the scene is deliberately over the top and intended to amuse, it acts as a mocking tribute to and acknowledgment of the history of Hollywood cinema's portrayal of the Orient. The intention must be to contrast and parallel modern American perceptions of Orientalism in U.S. cinema with a more traditionalist approach. This is especially apparent in the reference to the iconic movie *Lawrence of Arabia* (1962) when the four American female visitors are shown riding camels, while their contrasting modernity is emphasized through the technological gadgetry (Blackberrys and iPhones) they possess. The same is also true for later frames that show them relaxing in a Bedouin tent in the oasis, drinking champagne, while their Arab servants subserviently stand on guard. The 1962 film is referenced yet again, with contrasting effect, when Samantha's sexual awakening upon Rikard's (Max Ryan) appearance in the scene is expressed as a double entendre: "Lawrence-of-a-lay-me-a." The exuberance of the sexually liberated superrat Americans in Christian Dior clothing becomes even more conspicuous when placed in the context of the traditional East. The feministic fervor reaches its height in the Westerners' disco where the protagonists take to the stage and sing "I Am Woman."

While mocking earlier workings of Orientalist filmmaking, *Sex and the City 2* also approaches gender issues differently. Although Zine (2002, 1) claims that "[c]ontemporary feminist writing and popular culture have reproduced the colonial motifs of Muslim women, and these have regained currency in the aftermath of 9/11," *Sex and the City 2* marks a significant shift from this paradigm. The underlying narrative works to resolve the ongoing contrast between females in Eastern and Western cultures, rather than accentuating it. The main idea seems to be to underline the development of "sisterhood" by treating the Muslim men as fools. Although the film has been harshly criticized for its alleged anti-Muslim stance, the present analysis argues that such criticism is not justified. The final resolution clearly shows a collaboration between the American and Arab women in outwitting Muslim men, demonstrating how easily they can be deceived. In this sense, the Eastern women are no longer presented as the victims of male suppression, but as individuals who can be as resourceful and modern in their private lives as their Western counterparts. When they take off their *burka*s and reveal their true identity, the ultra-fashionable Arab women are hailed by the American protagonists as the "Louis Vuitton Spring collection" (uttered by Carrie). With the *burka*s provided by these women, the New Yorkers sneak out of the market place to a safe getaway, leaving behind the angry but gullible Arab men waiting in vain for them to appear.

Although, upon their arrival in Abu Dhabi, Carrie says that their presence symbolically liberates the Arab women from their "100 years of layered tradition," the exchange of identities and clothes suppresses such an argument. In fact, "who is who" becomes blurred, and the similarities between these two cultures surface in the form of male oppression of females in general. Their discussion when an Arab woman in a black *burka* looking at them in amazement is scolded by her husband and told to look elsewhere also confirms this point. At the hotel, Miranda complains about similar behavior she was subjected to at home, when she says, "It wasn't the tone of voice that my boss didn't like, it was that I had a voice. Men in the U.S. pretend they are comfortable with strong women but really a lot of them would prefer us eating French fries behind our veils." For this reason, while it will probably be remembered for its spoofing of the traditional takes of the "Orient" and its mockery of Muslim men in general, its surviving legacy will be in the echoes of the liberated voices of four superrats defying the suppression of women across the world.

## Conclusion

As the analysis has shown, all female characters in these films, in one way or another, initiate or achieve a desired act either through violence against or disdain for their Muslim male counterparts. It is noteworthy that the Muslim male characters in the films—Ashade in *Sorry, Haters*, the old bomb-maker in *The Kingdom*, Anwar in *Rendition* and the angry crowd of Muslim men in the souk in *Sex and the City 2*—either suffer under torture, meet their death or are ridiculed at the end of the narrative. Thus, the female characters are obviously created with the intention to crush or belittle Muslim male characters, but how intensely this is done seems to depend on the national politics of the time. The Muslim males are purposefully developed according to the way they react to situations instigated by these particular female character types, who are presented with mixed-gender qualities and changeable sexualities. In parallel with the times, when national security is in danger, the case studies show that the treatment of the Muslim man is rigid and unforgiving, as in the case of *The Kingdom*; however, it is more relaxed and understanding when the national threat is at an ebb, as in *Sex and the City 2*. Muslim males are portrayed as a laughing stock for their obedience, stupidity and gullible nature (*Sorry, Haters*), or as imbeciles who can be tricked into believing what women want them to believe (*Sex and the City 2*). These examples show that the mainstream stereotypes of the Orientalist approach can be modified with new forms of thought, such as those emerging from the various waves of feminism, thus making way for unprecedented formulations like the binary of strong American females and weak Muslim males.

# 5

# From Stereotype to "New" Muslim Woman

The Muslim woman for the Orientalist mind has for centuries meant either a partial existence under shape-obscuring covers, or the imagined existence of transgressive sexuality. This chapter inquires into the impact of feminism on the Muslim woman's stereotypical screen representation and shows that she is now constructed as an individual taking an active part in the flow of the narrative. The journey from the old spectacle to the image of a "new" Muslim woman enables us to see what has remained unchanged and what novel features have been woven into this character type. The idea is to find out how different filmmakers interpret and implement in their work the third-wave feminist ideals of allowing all the women in the third world the same rights that their first-world counterparts enjoy. Have their character and narrative formulations done away with the worn-out stereotypical figures of the past completely, or do new films still carry the impositions that cultural differences dictate, blended in with character modernization?

It is noticeable that, in contrast to Muslim male characters, females of the same creed are not allowed much space on the silver screen.[1] Nevertheless, a longitudinal analysis of their representation shows a striking evolution. After the films of the 1920s–1950s that were inspired by the romantic medieval stories of *One Thousand and One Nights* (otherwise known as *The Arabian Nights*), the Muslim woman frequently appeared as a stereotypical silent background presence in the majority of Hollywood films. However, she now has a fully developed character. Although her image still carries some misconceptions of the past, the way she is currently realized represents a shift away from clichéd assumptions, resulting in a fully-fledged human being with a discernible feminine body, audible voice, visible face and decipherable feelings; most importantly, she is an equal, if not stronger, partner in a relationship. This is a cinematic Muslim female character whose feelings of love and sexual behavior are on display. As such, she has become a part of the cinematic narrative, appeasing Western notions of cross-culturalism, and is not a static stereotype of the "Orient" anymore.

The current chapter analyzes past depictions of the Muslim female character, the image of the "new" Muslim woman, her physical attributes, visibility and her sexual and emotional behavior patterns. These features are evaluated by way of three films, *House of Sand and Fog* (2003), *Rendition* (2007) and *Body of Lies* (2008), which narrate the story of women from Iran, North Africa, the United States and the Middle East. This is followed by a section on the African American Muslim female character whose depiction in two films—*Malcolm X* (1992) and *Ali* (2001)—is examined.

## Past Depictions

One of the conventions in the creation of bias against Islam is to draw upon the supposed oppression of women by Muslim men, the veil and *burka* being the means through which this oppression is exercised. For those in non–Muslim cultures, the veil is "[t]he most visible marker of the differentness and inferiority of Islamic societies ... and it became the open target of colonial attack[s] and the spearhead of assault on Muslim societies" (Ahmed 1992, 152). A woman of the East is claimed to lack the autonomy of "control over her income, her body and her sexuality" (Kapur 2002, 16) and this belief was used in the eighteenth and nineteenth centuries as a pretext for justifying the invasion of her space by the colonialist, so that she could be saved from the male oppressors around her (Macey 1999). Much later, the veil also became a focal point for American feminists, who turned their attention to global issues such as forced veiling (Farrell and McDermott 2005) under the rubric of transnational feminism, but they were criticized for getting involved in matters they were ignorant about. Abu-Lughod (2013), asking rhetorically in the title of her book, *Do Muslim Women Need Saving?*, asserts that associating Muslim women's dress code only with oppression can deepen the chasm between the West and the East (6). In the same vein, Jawad and Benn (2003) defend the voluntary use of Islamic dress as the Muslim woman's effort to keep her identity, and Zeiger (2008) suggests that women in the East cover themselves up for reasons other than male tyranny, ranging from the expression of political resistance to Western colonialism to the ability to move comfortably in public spaces. Qutub (2013), while voicing her criticism of the media, in line with the sentiments of second-wave feminists, for using women's bodies and sexuality as marketing tools, defends Islam's protective approach and states that the Western "claim that Islam represses its own people, reflects a lack of understanding of Islam. In fact, Islamic traditions allow women the freedom from becoming materialized and humiliated" (147).

However, despite such defiant disapproval of equating Islamic attire solely with oppression, these objections have failed to change long-established Western views regarding Islam's coercion of women (Fernandez 2009).

The preconception in the West was that the Muslim woman had been forced by her male significant others to be invisible to the rest of the world. This assumption found its way into narrative cinema, which has until recently projected female stereotypes onto the screen, either wrapped in black cloth, or in the form of belly dancers from the harem of "lecherous men" (Said 2003, 296–297). Shaheen (2000, 23) describes a changing pattern of conventions but complains that it still carries a humiliating message regarding the Muslim woman: "Women surface either as gun toters or bumbling subservients, or as belly dancers bouncing voluptuously in palaces and erotically oscillating in slave markets." He also finds it offensive that image-makers offer Muslim women as caricatures: "covered in black from head to toe, they appear as uneducated, unattractive and enslaved beings, slowly attending to man, they follow several paces behind abusive sheiks."

De-personification with the *niqab* (veil), *burka* (a loose, generally black, garment covering the body from head to toe) or *hijab* (hair cover) has been a popular and recurrent strategy used in Hollywood films to project the Muslim female image in the public sphere. While *burka*-clad women do not often appear in panoramic desert scenes (*Lawrence of Arabia* (1962) is an exception), they are the indispensable cosmetic element of the streets in most Muslim countries projected onto the screen. These figures in black are the passersby, incidentals with no significance in how the story unfolds, and are not filmed in close-up. They prevent the audience from reading the feelings of the actors/actresses and thereby feeling empathy for them. It can be argued that the technique of filming Muslim women in the open air, using medium or long shots, simply distances them from the viewers. This is what Balázs (1970, 56), for instance, trenchantly draws attention to: "You may see a medium shot of someone sitting and conducting a conversation with icy calm. The close-up will show trembling fingers ... a sign of internal storm." Audiences of the past were never allowed to see such internal storms in filmic female pedestrians who were implicitly alleged to be victims of oppression.

Hall (1997a, 226) claims that "representation when dealing with difference, engages feelings, attitudes and emotions, and it mobilizes fears and anxieties in the viewer at deeper levels than we can explain in a simple, common sense way." Indeed, the Western man's feelings of frustration at not being able to see the face of the female, as summed up by Al-Mahadin (2013, 4), are manifold: "Fear, anxiety, trauma, sympathy, alienation, frustration, curiosity, disappointment," not forgetting "revulsion and disgust." The same attitudes are echoed in Fanon's (1965, 44) *Algeria Unveiled*: "This woman who sees without being seen frustrates the colonizer. There is no reciprocity."

Adding to these Semmerling's (2006, 106) observations that "[v]eiled Middle Eastern women are used in Western advertising, erotica, and film to support stereotypical beliefs that these women are exotic, backward, romantic, reductive, and/or oppressed," it is possible to conclude that the abundant use of disguise for Muslim women, even in contexts where liberal and Western-style dress is as common as the veil and *burka*, carries sinister cultural undertones that have been implemented for creative or ideological purposes.

When it comes to the presentation of a Muslim female character in the private sphere, it is noticeable that this was generally restricted to belly dancers and odalisques (concubines) in the period starting from the end of the 1940s. The harem with its odalisques—inaccessible even to Muslim males except the sultan, or the rich courtesans themselves—was regarded by the West as a mysterious place, fuelling the imagination of European artists since the eighteenth century. American cinema seems to have been affected by yesteryear's paintings in depicting the female household of the Eastern lands, but depictions of the private sphere in the "Orient" are just as imaginative in Hollywood productions as they are in the old works of art.

Why belly dancing has become an inseparable part of the Oriental palace setting in films is intriguing because it was not a part of the genuine royal court entertainment, at least not in the way Hollywood has imagined. According to a Turkish folklorist (Gazimihal 1991, 84), dancers in the palaces of the Ottoman Empire, which was the sovereign predecessor of many of today's Muslim countries, were all harem girls, wearing for the dancing session a velvet waistcoat over a silk blouse, and baggy trousers secured at the waistline with a metal belt. Because their type of dance required more than the shaking of the hips and belly, consisting of a variety of movements using all parts of the body, there was no reason to show a bare abdomen. The dancers entertained the viewers by smiling, acting in accordance with the words of the song, and being flirtatious but within reason. It is said that the dancers' decorum varied according to the social status of the household. As Adra (2005, 35) explains, movements vary depending on where the dance is performed: "Earthy, bawdy, or burlesque performances are not likely to take place among those of high social status. Self censorship in this form maintains accepted rules of decorum. Social class is a key factor in negotiating the appropriateness of involvement and the level of play." It is clear, therefore, that the depiction of a harem setting with dazzling but solemn-looking belly dancers in American films is a disingenuous re-creation of the Muslim royal palace, and a misrepresentation of the lively, authentic atmosphere of the exclusive entertainment of Ottoman times. Indeed, introduced to America in 1893 by a group of gypsy dancers from Egypt during the Chicago World Fair, belly dancing in film became an amalgamation of imaginative and artistic work by a variety of contributors, from flamboyant costume designers to choreographers.

Tassels, embroidery, feathered turbans and jeweler were added to the costumes in due course. Dance movements were also altered. McLean (1997, 138) claims that a choreographer, Jack Cole, who worked on a number of Oriental-themed productions, including the two *Kismet* films, made in 1944 and 1955, respectively, was determined "to deploy and manipulate the strictly gendered movements of oriental dance as a form of unmarked transvestism." The practice of using belly dancing in Middle Eastern settings has survived until recent times—for instance, in the film *Around the World in 80 Days* (2004), the Turkish sultan, played by Arnold Schwarzenegger, is shown flanked by scarcely dressed women, who move seductively with no emotion displayed on their faces, their eyes cast downward. Thus, neither the movements of the dance nor the costumes of the dancers are reflections of the original, substantiating the claims that authenticity has not been a concern for Orientalists.

Another point of interest is that, despite their nearly naked bodies and erotic dances, the celluloid girls of the "Orient" were not commonly shown in scenes of passion. Sexual behavior such as touching, kissing, making eye contact or engaging in sexual intercourse was either non-existent or rare. In the early romantic comedy genre there are examples of a Muslim girl kissing a Muslim man, such as in *The Thief of Baghdad* (1978) when Price Taj (Kabir Bedi) gently kisses Princess Yasmine (Pavla Ustinov), or in *Sinbad the Sailor* (1947) when Sinbad (Douglas Fairbanks, Jr.) kisses Shireen (Maureen O'Hara). More importantly, there are movies in which a Muslim girl is shown in physical contact with a non–Muslim man, as in *Road to Morocco* (1942) when Princess Shalmar (Dorothy Lamour) places a passionate kiss upon the white protagonist, Jeff Peters' (Bing Crosby), lips. Shaheen (2003a, 23) also names a few films in this category: "In *A Café in Cairo* (1925) and *Arabesque* (1966), actresses Priscilla Dean and Sophia Loren appear as bright and lovely Arab women" but only after they "ridicule and reject Arab suitors, does the scenario allow them to fall into the arms of Western protagonists." In a later film, *The Human Shield* (1991), the characters Lila Haddihl (Hanna Azoulay Hasfari) and Doug Matthews (Michael Dudikoff) are shown as having a romantic affair. However, the physical contact between the Muslim woman and her male partner in this and all other films referred to above, does not go beyond hugging and kissing. Scenes showing a couple falling victim to their sexual urges are non-existent.

There seems to be a change in general in Muslim stereotypes in the aftermath of 9/11. Sultana (2013, 70), for instance, notes that the old stereotypes are currently being replaced with new ones, showing some Muslims as "westernized, English speaking, comfortable with women etc.," while others are religious fanatics, "caught in the primitive idea of jihad against the infidels." Shaheen (2008a, 35) also reports that "[s]ince 9/11, screens have displayed, at times, more complex, even-handed Arab portraits" than he has seen in the past. In line with this, we are now noticing Muslim female protagonists on the screen, some indistinguishable from Western women and others in modernized, religious clothing. What this means is that the character types that filmmakers loved to use in the past do not satisfy Westerners anymore. MacDonald (2014, 30) observes: "The body of the Muslim woman is co-opted in the discourse of the veil, and flattened out: She must be veiled in order to be *seen* as Muslim and yet must be unveiled to be seen by the West as a free and autonomous individual, in the way the West sees/desires to see itself. The gaze makes demands on the body." This desire finds fulfillment when, especially after 9/11, filmmakers provide the audience with images of Muslim women whose clothes are not unfamiliar to the Western world. Yet, more striking than their attire is the fact that these female characters are shown kissing and making love, which is revolutionary in itself.

It has taken a long time for American filmmakers to display on screen a woman of the East as an equal partner in amorous encounters. Yet, one also has to remember that scenes of a sexual nature were taboo in Hollywood until recently. Kunz (2007), for instance, reports that films with sex scenes created controversy in the United States right from the start, prompting the Production Code to be introduced in 1930 with the clause, "Excessive and lustful kissing, lustful embraces, suggestive postures and gestures are not to be shown" (20). Two decades later, Elia Kazan's *A Streetcar Named Desire* (1951), featuring a rape scene, was also condemned by the Catholic Church's Legion of Decency, and Catholics were banned from watching it. Even as late as 1973, Bernardo Bertolucci's *Last Tango in Paris* (1973), depicting the sexual encounters of a couple, created an uproar and instigated a legal case between the censorship agency and the production studio. When portraying the private sexual life of an American female character in love is such a recent development in the history of cinema, the absence of similar depictions of Muslim women does not come as a surprise. What is striking, however, is that the Muslim woman is now considered worthy of a part in narrative cinema as an individual who has as much right to feel and make love as a Western woman. It is not possible to consider these love scenes as the Western filmmakers' new tool, whereby the sensuality of the belly dancer is now transferred to a modern Muslim anatomy for the same colonial gaze, because, whether Muslim or non–Muslim, belonging to any culture, the female body everywhere has the same needs and requires the same gratification of its needs.

## The "New" Muslim Woman's Love and Cura

Since 9/11, the representation of the Muslim female character has commonly been enriched with *cura*, that is, the capacity for compassion. If we are to implement Heidegger's (2008) notions of *cura* (care) and how it operates in the formation of the social subject, there appears to be a manifestation of the various forms of love, which rely upon a required *cura* as well as a demonstration of cinema's contribution to this social order. In other words, love's representation is an expression of *cura* and, in the portrayal of a social need, films are able to participate in the social construction of this ideology. Simply, *cura* is the basis on which every interpretation of *Dasein* (Heidegger's term for self-beingness) is determined, according to the extent and degree that individuals are able to demonstrate it (Heidegger 2008, 244).

The Muslim woman's current image, as projected onto the screen, is a human being who is capable of giving as much love as it is thought a Western female can. Filmmakers have started subjecting the Muslim female character to a humanizing process in which the cinematic nature of her love, lovemaking and kiss is explored for artistic reasons. In the past, it was not possible to view the Muslim female's skin and body unless her dance movements required the display of her flesh, which was treated as an object of the gaze, but recently there has been an attempt to introduce characters who reveal far more of their body than was the case in the past. The lips and voice are utilized, when speaking either in their native language or English, to mark the similarities and differences between cultures. The code of emotional states can be substantially different from film to film and the spectator is able to acknowledge the operative nature of its signs: smiling and laughter (as well as tears) have been integrated into the acting and the previously downcast eyes now lovingly look straight into the eyes of the male partner. Examples of a humanized Muslim woman as a subject, gazing at others with compassion rather than being the object of a gaze are plentiful in recent productions: Aisha in *Body of Lies* (2008) rescues Ferris from rabies as well as from disillusionment; Fatima in *Rendition* (2007) sacrifices her own life in order to save her father's; and Nadereh salvages Kathy from a suicide attempt in *House of Sand and Fog* (2003). Being liberated from social and religious restrictions is also a point deserving mention. Kollin (2015, 109), for instance, in her analysis of *Hidalgo* (2004) comments that social norms regarding the place of women are transgressed in the film: "Jazira eventually uncovers in front of the Western hero, defying her father's power and rejecting her role as the so-called oppressed Muslim woman. The uncovering is presented as a feminist move toward liberation and freedom."

## The "New" Muslim Woman's Hatred

The Muslim woman's image is rapidly under reconstruction in contemporary visual material, endowed with emotions of love and hate, albeit disproportionately. Hatred, which is also a part of the social and cultural structure like love, has not been given much coverage in the last decade or so. While a woman with love and *cura* finds room in many recent productions, a substantial character design invested with negative sentiments and hatred is reserved only for the female terrorist but, even in this form, it is scarce. The importance of the Muslim woman's part in the flow of the narrative also fluctuates, ranging from the frame filler to a character in her own right. In the foreign setting of war films, we see females covered in black in the background, radiating sinister undertones. *Black Hawk Down* (2001), *Green Zone* (2010) and *The Kingdom* (2007), for instance, reflect the overall hostility of the environment in which the protagonists find themselves. This simplistic method assumes that the Muslim female space is part and parcel of the overall world of animosity that they inhabit. They are objects of an unknown microcosm, threatening the spectator with their ability to reveal ominous signals devoid of femininity. Their presence, however, is cosmetic and not a force that carries the narrative forward.

In comparison, we see the she-terrorist in a central position, occupying the main part in the narrative of only one movie, *Day Night, Day Night* (2006), and even here we are not sure but simply suspect that she is a Muslim. The narrative of the female Muslim as the embodiment of hate evokes the centrality of an imperialist American culture. While she is still "[r]aw material for the active gaze of man," as Mulvey (1975, 208) describes, she seems to represent more than a psychoanalytical fetishistic pleasure fulfiller. Her hatred is a perversion and makes her repulsive. It is ironic that the once sexually charged Orientalist subaltern whose sexuality disrupted the basis of gender identification has now been replaced with another disruptive figure, deprived of her part of seducing the colonial male. Instead, her passion has metamorphosed into a character displaying sexual deprivation, which may be attributable to her angst and rage.

According to Kannan (2011), the unpopularity of this character type in films stems from the fact that violent women are considered to be deviant. They break the social gender norms by acting contrary to the expected roles of mother, daughter, sister and lover. Due to this, they are regarded as social outcasts whose motives are incomprehensible to the "rational" mind of the Western man. Toles-Patkin (2004, 85) argues that media representations of female terrorists consciously seek to "[a]lienate explanations behind women's participation in terror in a way that does not seem parallel in the coverage of male suicide bombers, whose official ideological statements appear to be taken at face value." Indeed, in the case of the female terrorist in *Day Night, Day Night*, any explanation of the main character's motivations is totally nonexistent.

Despite the repellent nature of the violent Muslim female's body, filmmakers started to uncover it for the voyeuristic gaze even before 9/11. Semmerling (2006), for instance, reports that Dahlia, the female terrorist in a much earlier film, *Black Sunday* (1977), is presented as a vicious and sexually uninhibited Eastern woman, despite the fact that her body is not disrobed during intimate love scenes. Dahlia was at that time a stark contrast to the West's stereotype of a withdrawn Muslim woman, but her angst and rage-driven aggressive sexuality was probably too off-putting for the male gaze. She is shown to be motivated only by violence and, in this respect, is the carbon copy of the Islamic Rage Boy, with no inkling of love or *cura*. Dahlia is not the only example of the intimidating nature of the Eastern woman's hate, and estrangement is provoked by elements that the audience are unable to make sense of. The remake of *The Manchurian Candidate* (2004), for instance, utilizes spectacles of Muslim women with Arabic writing on their faces, obviously to induce agitation in the spectator, who does not know how to interpret their appearance. In other productions, the Muslim woman's body is usually hidden under a black *burka* not because of religious restrictions, but to camouflage her hideous intentions.

The nameless female in *Day Night, Day Night* offers a striking example of how hatred is not only assumed but assessed according to one's own level of paranoia and trauma. The main character is purged of all personal identification and presented as a 19-year-old suicide bomber, while no indication is given of her name, ethnicity, religion and motivations to become a suicide bomber. In a way, she is stripped of all qualities and emotions traditionally associated with the female gender. She remains an ambiguous figure, except that she is from New Jersey, and challenges the spectators' ability to associate her with a particular trope. She is designed to act in a counter-hegemonic way through "[m]imicry, hybrid ambivalence, code switching, signifying, and zones of [an] intersubjective agency" (Foster, 1999, 174). Her hateful motivations are deliberately obscured in order to question not only her actions but also our ability to assess her within the scope of our own cultural context. Because of the degree of ambiguity woven into her identity, the spectator is forced to apply stereotypical conjecture in order to restore and establish her as a threat to the hegemonic order. The easiest way to make sense of her is to acknowledge her as an "irrational" terrorist who is purposefully presented in a nebulous fashion.

This equivocality increases the tension in *Day Night, Day Night*, where the nameless girl is additionally devoid of the expected characteristics of a she-terrorist. She possesses and displays attributes of appearance that are associated with the Westernized American woman and while her accent is not alien, it is unclassifiable. We presume from her physical features that she may be of Middle Eastern descent, and only when she appears posing for a photograph with masked males standing behind her and holding a machine gun do we identify this particular image as having an Islamic affiliation. Furthermore, she is good looking and does not have any observable hysteric or even masculine qualities. As a result, it is not possible to classify her as sexually deviant either. Donning a sporty outfit complete with a backpack (which we later learn is filled with explosives), she could be any girl on a New York street. This is probably why the tension is greater for the viewer: except for the knowledge that she is decisively heading to Times Square to detonate herself and probably many more innocent Americans, there are no answers to the questions that naturally come to mind. Why does she want to be a suicide bomber in the heart of New York City? Is she a Muslim? An Arab? Are her motivations in any way politically charged and does she have any allegiance to a jihadist movement? Her ambiguity thus creates a dilemma that viewers are not accustomed to working out and they have to search for a means by which her attributes can be deconstructed, while still gazing upon her form.

Thus, the filmmaker evokes the trauma that the viewer has experienced

*Day Night, Day Night* (Julia Loktev, 2006): A female terrorist (Louisa Williams) about whom we know nothing leads the audience through her dark journey to Times Square, where she intends to kill innocent people, showing that physical appearance is sufficient to uphold fear-inspiring stereotypes.

in life and then chooses to test the resolve of the individual gazing upon a suspicious figure that could be one of us. The idea of the "enemy within" has been presented before but never to the extent that *Day Night, Day Night* challenges the spectator's own sense of awareness and curiosity. The immediacy of their paranoia and memories of trauma are reinforced. The hegemonic discourses that construct dominant conceptions of "female terrorists" take the form of "the enemy within" or "the enemy next door" syndrome. It is probably this disturbing unpredictability that leaves the audience unsettled and makes the nameless girl in *Day Night, Day Night* the only example of her type in cinema during this period.

## Behavior Patterns

The overseas female Muslim's behavioral patterns in early films were so limited and stereotypical that the projected character could only be assessed according to non-verbal communication and non-existent expression. Ekman and Friesen's (1969) theory suggests that instinct and culture are determinable factors that can be assessed in how facial expressions and behavioral patterns are perceived. While they argue that instinct controls the link between emotion and facial expression, they also assert that culture determines what events cause emotions and what effort is made by the person to control these expressions. Since the overseas Muslim female in her earlier depiction was rarely given the opportunity to reveal her vocal and facial expressions, due to either social norms or the nature of her attire, we were left with a figure who was challenging to decipher in terms of her feelings. Especially in the case of a covered Muslim woman, the observer had to rely on their imagination and determine her emotive state as either pain, anger or remorse. In present times, however, we note that this practice has changed in the sense that an overseas Muslim female character, rather than being the silent subordinate of an authoritative order, can now exercise power over an American hero—for instance, Aisha in *Body of Lies* (2008)—or can assume leadership with her Americanized upbringing, and guide her immigrant parents as to how things need to be done, as in *Crash* (2004) and *You Don't Mess with the Zohan* (2008).

A change in her behavioral pattern can also be observed. There are two basic ways in which we interpret behavior: we either attribute it to the person's inner qualities, or to the situation that he or she is in, that is, the environmental factors. In social psychology, Attribution Theory was developed to make sense of the causal judgments people make about the behavior of others. Dispositional attribution is the assumption that an individual's behavior is influenced by their internal characteristics, whereas situational attribution analyzes a person's actions with regard to the situation (environment or culture) that he or she is placed in. This means that those with dispositional attributions deal with matters by referring to their internal resources and personality traits, whereas people with situational attributions adapt their behavior to the requirements of the situation.

The research of Bodenhausen and Wyer (1985), focusing on cultural stereotypes and their related attributions, provides some insight into the artistic reasons and motivations behind character formation in U.S. movies. Their findings show that transgressions or socially undesirable behaviors that are consistent with stereotypes are attributed by observers to dispositional factors, while those that are contrary to cultural stereotypes (the terminology they use is "stereotype non-consistent behavior") are attributed to situational factors. If their analysis is to be applied to cinematic discourse, it is expected that Muslim females who are portrayed in their overseas environment, which is alien to the American viewer, will display stereotypical behavior and are interpreted as having dispositional attributions, while those within an Americanized setting possess situational attributes. Although in the latter half of the decade following 9/11 there have been more overseas Muslim women characters on screen who are able to adjust their behavior according to the requirements of the situation, their predecessors were presented as being incapable of taking the initiative, displaying emotions and entering into various social roles, therefore exhibiting dispositional qualities.

As observed below in the case studies, *House of Sand and Fog* (2003), *Rendition* (2007) and *Body of Lies* (2008), there is now a new image of the overseas Muslim female whose behavior can be attributed to both dispositional and situational factors, similarly to the behavior of the Americanized immigrant or African American female characters. Indeed, *Crash* (2004), *You Don't Mess with the Zohan* (2008), *The Kite Runner* (2007), and *The Visitor* (2007) all present a female who does not quite fit into her perceived social community and is given rein to exert her dominance over males. In this way, the Muslim female, regardless of her geographical position, is provided with a sense of individuality that was not present in cinema before.

From a sociological perspective, a simplified form of an "interdependence control" framework exists, patterning the relational dynamics between actors, which can also be used as a matrix to demonstrate the differences between the projection of the image of the Muslim woman in the past and present. The patterns in question are *actor control* (how much each actor affects their own outcomes); *partner control* (how much each actor affects their partner's outcomes); and *joint control* (how much each actor is affected by coordinating joint responses) (Rusbult and Van Lange, 2008).

In patriarchal relationships where the character is placed in an overseas environment, the character of the Muslim woman was deprived not only of the actor-control component, but also of her joint control. Traditionally, the film portrayal of Muslim female characters was realized in terms of her interdependence with the male character (regardless of whether he was Muslim or not), and her relationship was defined according to the outcome of his actions (partner control). The films produced directly after 9/11, however, introduce a female whose interdependence has altered considerably. Although she remains visually identifiable to the Orientalist gaze—due to her physical characteristics, accent, attire, and so on—the characteristics of her personality make her function and role within a relationship less certain. She is seen to have adopted much more of the actor-control component, which results in a higher degree of satisfaction in the different activities she is shown to be engaged in. Furthermore, some character depictions within the overseas environment after 9/11 can also been seen as administering bilateral reflexive control. The only component of the character that remains unaffected by time and change in cinematic trends is actor control over each party's personal relationship with their faith.

*You Don't Mess with the Zohan* (2008), *House of Sand and Fog* and *Sex and the City 2* (2010), which all feature Muslim female characters, are just some of the examples of films that have attempted to readdress the ascendancy of female interdependency control. This is because each work constitutes an attempt to redefine the role of the Muslim woman and empower her with the prospect of emancipation, which she has long been denied under patriarchal rule. The norms and roles that she is expected to pursue within her environment have been shifted to incorporate new socio-political ideals, which were not necessarily available to her in the past. Thus, the Muslim female character on screen has given way to the realization of a new contemporary model that encapsulates current Western traits while simultaneously remaining faithful to Muslim cultural beliefs.

Recently, films have started showing a Muslim female character, whether resident in the United States or another country, breaking with tradition and manifesting her interdependence control. She protests against her subservient role and stands up for what she wants and how she wants it. We notice this behavioral pattern in *House of Sand and Fog, Rendition* and *Body of Lies*, to name but a few examples. A review of such filmic material shows that the new trend is to reconstruct Muslim female characters who are at ease with their bodies and can stand up to the pressures of their significant others and/or social rules in order to satisfy their emotional and physical needs. They are equipped with education, intellectual intensity, professional, scientific or artistic knowledge and internal power to regulate those around them. The three films under scrutiny show women believers of Islam from diverse backgrounds, such as Iran, the Middle East, North Africa and the United States. They are based either in the United States or elsewhere and are projected as "new" Muslim women, which is a breakthrough in their filmic characterization.

## Nadi in House of Sand and Fog *(2003)*

Although *House of Sand and Fog* was made when the trauma of 9/11 was still fresh in the public mind, Nadi's (Shohreh Aghdashloo) character does not seem to have been created spitefully or out of revenge, nor is it based on a stereotype. It is a balanced depiction of a secularized Muslim woman who has continued to lead the same affluent lifestyle in the United States that she was accustomed to in her own country. She is presented as a complex human being with many attributes and weaknesses. On one hand, she is seen as a soft-hearted person, which is especially evident in the way she cares for Kathy (Jennifer Connelly); on the other hand, she is shown to be authoritative, exemplified in the way she drives her husband and son out of the bathroom and forces Kathy to throw up the pills she has swallowed (in her desperate attempt at suicide).

Nadi's contradictory temperament is highlighted through close-up shots and the language she uses. When she is furious she screams insults at her husband. For example, when told by her husband, Behrani (Ben Kingsley), that they are to move to a new house he has bought at an auction, she loses her temper and shouts at him: "No! No! I didn't come to America to live like an Arab, a family roaming the streets like gypsies!" Similarly, after being threatened by Lester (Ron Eldard) with deportation she screams at her husband: "Coward! Liar! It is your fault we were forced to flee Iran. It is your fault, yours alone!" Her husband punishes her for this outburst by slapping her in the face. Even this punishment does not affect her defiance or force her into submission; she goes and locks herself in her bedroom, making Behrani sleep in an armchair for the night. At other times, however, she smiles in compliance, such as when Behrani tells her he will not sell the new house until autumn so that the family can enjoy the sea view for a while. He asks her, "Will you prefer that?" She obediently responds, "I will do as you wish."

Vadim Perelman, the director of *House of Sand and Fog*, chooses a comparative method for portraying Nadi's love life. There are two intimate scenes that take place one after the other. In the first, Kathy and Lester are on a bed lit by the lamps on the bedside tables. The camera, moving in various directions, pans to different parts of the two bodies in slow motion, from their heads, down their backs to their legs and arms. Soft piano music plays in the background and continues when the scene changes into the Behranis' sitting room. Nadi then caresses her husband and, with a suggestive look on

*House of Sand and Fog* (Vadim Perelman, 2003): Nadi (Shohreh Aghdashloo), the "new" Muslim woman, is indistinguishable from any modern, middle-class Western wife, and a far cry from earlier depictions of the Muslim woman in a burka or belly dancer's outfit.

her face, takes his hand and ushers him upstairs to the bedroom. In the next frame we see Nadi in bed with her husband, filmed in profile from the waist up, almost like two silhouettes in a semi-dark room, illuminated only by several candles on the far side of the bed. However, the heavy breathing and the words the couple utter make up for this partly restricted view. At one point during the intercourse, Nadi whispers, "Mahmoud," and when Behrani rests his body by her side, he contentedly says, "We are blessed." Both smile. Compared to the explicit details of the American couple's lovemaking, sensitivity is displayed in this context so as not to visualize the Muslim pair too overtly; yet sensuous sound effects are used to enrich the impact of the scene.

Apart from her attractive Middle Eastern features (dark hair, Mediterranean skin color, brown eyes) and her broken English (when she is angry she immediately switches to Farsi), Nadi does not display any stereotypical characteristics of a Muslim wife either in her clothes or in her behavior. She is not a religious type. In fact, the film indicates that Behrani is more of a believer than she is. As for the bedroom scene, this may be the first to show a Middle Eastern woman in an intimate activity, albeit not in as explicit terms as a Western audience is accustomed to. In short, Nadi is a successful presentation of a standard U.S. housewife who happens to be Muslim and a recent immigrant: she has the courage to stand up to her husband when her preferences are overlooked, has common sense to advise him about the course of action to take, and she has the *cura* to offer medical help and compassion to an opponent.

## *Muslim Female Types in* Rendition *(2007)*

*Rendition* takes place in an Islamic country where women's position in society is delineated by the comments of one of the Arab characters in the film: "Beat your woman every morning. If you don't know why, she does." The film has a rich repertoire of Muslim women, some with a more significant part to play in the plot than others. All types are present: young and old, traditionalist and reformist, professional and non-professional, as well as those belonging to overseas or American Muslim communities. Some of these have invited comments from analysts such as Kellner (2010, 1980) who rightly remarks that in *Rendition* we are introduced to three generations, the youngest being "represented by Halid [sic] and Fatima (who Hood [sic. The director] characterizes as the Romeo and Juliet characters)." For Boyd-Barrett et al. (2011, 150), Fatima (Zineb Oukach) stands out due to her capacity for compassion but not for her submission in love: "The movie invites sympathy not so much with Khalid but with his girl-friend Fatima ... Abasi's innocent daughter ... [who] dies in the explosion while trying to stop Khalid and save her father." No mention is made of her independent spirit, which leads her to have a sexual experience out of wedlock.

The story, recounted earlier in Chapter 4, depends on several Muslim female types to progress. *Rendition* is rich with old-fashioned female Muslim clichés as well as "normalized" and "humanized" character types. The most prominent of these is Fatima, a university student who runs away from home to avoid an arranged marriage. She escapes first to the protection of her independent businesswoman aunt, Laila (Reymonde Amsallem), and then to her boyfriend Khalid's (Moa Khouas) poverty-stricken house, where the two make love. At a later stage, she is left alone in the house, finds a diary and learns that Khalid's brother was killed by her father's henchmen and that Khalid is out to kill Abasi (Yigal Naor). She runs to the city square, where Abasi normally has his morning coffee, to stop the attack taking place but fails. Both she and Khalid die when the bomb wrapped around his body explodes.

The love scene between her and Khalid starts with him caressing her face. He smells her hair and says, "It smells like jasmine." Then comes the kiss. After this, the spectator is permitted to gaze upon her in her most revealing moments, such as when the couple are in bed. In the following sequence, she is shown sleeping innocently while her partner gazes at the ceiling, worry written all over his face. Her hand rests on his bare shoulder as an unconscious gesture, signifying her love and bodily satisfaction. In this episode the audience is given a chance to view as much of a Muslim female protagonist's body as the bed sheets allow.

While we are carried along by the struggle that Fatima faces through her defiance of her authoritarian father and her pursuit of unrequited love, she is intermittently shown as unveiled. Thus, the spectator is granted unrestricted access to her privacy, which further establishes a point of empathetic relation to character. When she ventures outside, she wears a red, transparent *hijab* that distinguishes her from the sea of monolithic black-robed entities that parade the streets in full Islamic regalia. Travelling on a motorbike behind her boyfriend, she shows no social inhibitions when enveloping him from behind. In the scene where she is shown running frantically to the city square to stop Khalid killing her father, she does not worry when her loose headscarf is blown away by the wind, and continues her journey with her long hair undulating in the air.

Douglas Freeman's (Jake Gyllenhaal) girlfriend, Safiya (Hadar Ratzon Rotem), is of Middle Eastern origin but is presented as a Western professional woman who is not afraid to take the initiative in her love life. Her enthusiasm in seducing Freeman gives the impression that she does not have any inhibitions, social or otherwise, in satisfying the needs of her own body, as well as those of her partner. The audience also sees her at her workplace. She is presented as a professional woman who knows what to do, depending on the requirements of the moment. As a second- or third-generation immigrant and a well-educated and liberated woman, Safiya embodies the type of Muslim female who has successfully integrated herself into the American way of life and work.

In contrast to Safiya, Fawal's wife is presented not as a humanized figure, but as a stereotype from North Africa, where rigid rules restrict the behavior of women, both in their private and social lives. Mrs. Fawal (Nava Ziv) is in a *hijab*, even when she is alone at home with her family. In a bedroom scene with her husband, however, she is shown with her long dark hair spread over the pillow, her eyes open, obediently waiting while Abasi reads some documents next to her. She is the embodiment of the stereotypical, passive, silent and obedient Muslim wife repeatedly used in narrative cinema to satisfy the preconceptions of a Western audience.

Another reminder from the classical period of film is the belly dancer, dancing in the background at a bar where Douglas Freeman sits alone after watching Anwar being tortured in prison and brought to breaking point. The frame captures the dancer's body from her neck down to her knees, leaving out her face and her feet. This is a cinematographic device indicating that no facial expressions would be visible and that what is seen on the screen is all that is required of this female in this context: she is a body without a soul. The opposite of this, a soul with no body, also exists in *Rendition*: Khalid's wrinkled, minute grandmother, shown momentarily in the darkness of the tattered flat, probably after Khalid has died, is all eyes and nothing else, so to speak. This old, fragile Muslim woman looks through her pain-stricken eyes at the emptiness of the room, probably seeing nothing because both are filled with tears. In this quiet position, which the camera captures for a few seconds, she speaks volumes, her message recalling the centuries-long miseries, heartaches, grief and helplessness of the East.

## *Aisha* in Body of Lies *(2008)*

This film has two Muslim female characters of interest: Aisha (Golshifteh Farahani), the woman who becomes the object of affection in the white protagonists' life, and Aisha's elder sister, who assumes the role of enforcer in the Muslim social order.

A CIA case officer in Iraq, Roger Ferris (Leonardo DiCaprio) is assigned the job of finding a terrorist organization and, while he is chasing one of the suspects, he is bitten on the leg by a wild dog and has to go to a hospital to have a series of rabies injections. There, he meets a pretty young nurse by the name of Aisha. As the two of them become more romantically involved, Aisha invites Ferris to dinner at the house of her sister, Cala (Lubna Azabal), with whom she has been living. Ferris' first encounter with Aisha's sister does not go well as Cala is too protective of Aisha and wants to save her from the possible ill intentions of an unknown American. A political discussion at the table is interrupted by Aisha who shows signs of embarrassment at Cala arguing with Ferris. She escorts him outside and apologizes for her over-protective sister's behavior. Despite this unpleasant experience, the relationship continues. Ferris is misled several times by his boss in the United States, Ed Hoffman (Russell Crowe), but he still completes his mission. The story ends with him losing his enthusiasm for continuing to fight the war. He subsequently leaves his job at the CIA and decides to stay in Amman to further his relationship with Aisha.

Constructed as a contemporary female character and a professional woman attempting to address the existence of Arab Muslim feminism, the character of Aisha offers an alternative reading to current representations. Her sister, who is ever suspicious of Roger Ferris' attempts to gain Aisha's affections, presents an alternative state within a school of Muslim feminism. Bullock (2002, xvi) defines these two classes as consisting of either liberals, who delve into "concepts of individualism, equality and oppression," recognizable in the character of Aisha, or the conservative form of a Muslim woman, who tends to avoid Western practices but at the same time is politically liberalized, using a contextual approach to rationalizing issues. This second class is presented in the character of Aisha's sister.

As it is still not desirable in Muslim countries for a Muslim girl to keep a non-Muslim boyfriend, or marry a non-Muslim unless he converts to Islam, the projection of Aisha and Ferris' romantic involvement out of wedlock probably required the filmmaker to not show disrespect to Muslim sensitivities. In one scene, when Ferris wants to hold Aisha's hand just outside her sister's house, she smiles and gently pulls her hand back. The camera then zooms in on the sister's worried face, which is visible from the window of her flat, and then travels to an upper-level balcony where two female neighbors are watching the movements of the couple downstairs. By including these onlookers in the scene, the film suggests that the rigid social codes of the local culture do not allow a relationship of this kind to be conducted in public. Yet, there is a scene in the film where Aisha and Ferris sit at a table in an open-air coffee house, full of customers, joyfully chatting and completely oblivious to the strangers around them. Her eyes never leave his while her smile shows the extent of her pleasure at being in his company. In another scene, they picnic in isolation in a meadow, Aisha lying on the ground and Ferris leaning over her, indicating that a more intimate action is about to follow. Apparently, a kiss was originally filmed but then edited out of the project. In the deleted scene, Ferris comments on his reluctance to make the first move on a Muslim woman and says, "You're gonna have to wait forever because I would never ever touch a Muslim woman first." She caresses his hand and a kiss follows. What is ultimately presented to the viewer still carries the electricity of the situation but the ensuing actions are left to the imagination of the audience. The sense of awkwardness between the couple and, in particular, Roger's vulnerability bestow Aisha with the power to orchestrate the ensuing dialogue and proceedings between the two. It is precisely this transference of power that presents Aisha with the dilemma of whether she should act on her human instincts or abide by cultural expectations of behavior.

Aisha is often framed and lit in an alluring manner that captures her beauty. The cinematic devices utilized include the regular use of soft-focus and Aisha being regularly shot in either close-up or mid shot, giving the audience the sensation of intimacy. In fact, the only characteristic remnants that contribute to her cultural identity being revealed surface through her voicing of personal political opinions, which far exceeds past attempts to illustrate similar views in comparable characters.

Aisha is presented in unassuming cultural attire and is occasionally shown as not needing a veil or *hijab*. She is identifiable as adhering to Western behavior, which involves her not having to cover herself up in the presence of men, especially when she is at work. The fact that she is seen in hospital without needing the presence of an authoritarian male figure is a motivational factor that alters Orientalist assumptions and functions as an underlying means to promote secularism. Her character is an unprecedented representation that reveals a fresh take on contemporary Muslim feminism, but also provides a justifiable contrasting ideology to that of Roger Ferris. The stereotypical image of an overseas Muslim woman—mother, faithful daughter, a woman dedicated to traditional values and obedient to the point that she does not question male authority—is not applicable in this context. Although she is doubly marginalized, firstly as a woman and secondly as a representative of an "Other" community, the character of Aisha remains impervious to the need to be accepted and respected in her journey towards self-definition. She is clearly empowered by her religion, which gives her a distinct identity and psychological support, but she does not take her faith to an extreme.

While Aisha is entertained at Ferris' expense, her behavior is never questioned, and rather than being subjected to a process of victimization, she offers emancipation, through her insight and self-awareness, to the protagonist who seems to have lost his belief and love for his country. She rescues him from death by administering a vaccine for his rabies bite and then guides him through her war-torn city to reveal another perspective that he has not been privy to in the past. This process of "unveiling," through insight and knowledge, gives her a feminine strength as an overseas "Other"—something that has not been illustrated in past cinematic incarnations of the Muslim woman. Furthermore, we as spectators become so immersed in her world and gaze that we are even afforded the wisdom of establishing Ferris as the "Other." The film administers an antidote to the narcissistic gaze of white male domination, for Ferris continuously questions his role and allegiance to his culture and country, and it is only through Aisha's *cura* that he is able to find psychological salvation.

The conflict between cultural duties and human urges has been a common theme in the history of cinema and has often been associated with religious characters, who are seen as struggling with inner conflict and repressed desires. In this particular instance, the theme is readdressed but projected onto a female who has to prioritize the consequences of a forbidden love, and love towards her personal faith and family. Although the couple do not display the kiss of erotic love, their affection for one another is carefully translated by the filmmaker using universal signs of reciprocal love such as body movements, facial expressions and looking into each other's eyes.

An analysis of *Body of Lies* from the viewpoint of cinematography is presented by Edelman (2013), who comments on the way Ridley Scott contrasts spatial differences between the United States and Iraq by accentuating them through the use of lighting and sound: "As the action cuts back and forth between the two, it is obvious that a cold gray and blue tone used for the West remains in stark contrast to a warmer earth-colored, golden, and brownish 'toast' ... that is used for the Middle East" (102). As for the sound effects, he comments that the "opposition of dramatic and loud background sounds and music for Ferris and a calmer soundscape (and in part even the absence of such) for Hoffman" accentuates Ferris' location as Iraq and Hoffman's as the United States (105).

In conclusion, it can be said that *House of Sand and Fog*, *Rendition* and *Body of Lies* are replete with realistically drawn portraits of Muslim female characters, in contrast to the stereotypical images that have been persistently fed to us for nearly a century of cinematic history. A handful of films is not enough to crush the fixed spectacles of the past, but it at least heralds the birth of a new approach.

## *The Black African American Muslim Female*

McCloud (1991) describes the African American Muslim woman as a conundrum in so far as she is depicted with all the strict traits of an Islamic existence but at the same time displays the individualistic qualities that are upheld in the Western world, which celebrates "somebodiness" (181). Being "somebody" incorporates the attributes of a loving wife, compassionate mother and confident participant in the social structure, among many other merits, and African American Muslim women are shown in films to enjoy such attributes. Yet, there is a price to pay: "These women have to establish their 'women's world' because they have been made acutely aware of the closed-door policy of other Muslim women. They are also aware of the ambivalent nature of their existence in the Islamic world as a whole" (*ibid.*, 185–186).

According to Thompson (2009, 6), "The idea of being both black and a 'lady' is a dichotomy that continues to haunt African American women," but observations of *Malcolm X* (1992) and *Ali* (2001), featuring African American Muslim women, do not support this claim. In each case, the Muslim woman is represented as an admirable individual despite her indirect connection with the radical Nation of Islam. Being an ardent preacher, Malcolm X was initially useful for the Nation of Islam, promoting views about the supremacy and self-determination of black people, but after his visit to Mecca, where he was introduced to Sunni Islam and Pan-Africanism, he distanced himself from the organization and as a result was assassinated in New York by its members. Tischler (2016) tells us that Ali's connection with the organization was also short-lived and ended in disappointment. It is therefore reasonable to assume that because Malcolm X and Mohammed Ali were iconic personalities, each resisting violence as practiced by the Nation of Islam, the filmic portraits of women associated with them have also been painted by the respective filmmakers with great reverence.

African Muslim women living in their indigenous territory, as presented in *Tears of the Sun* (2003) and *Black Hawk Down* (2001), are the set props used to accentuate the authenticity of the chaotic environment they exist in. In contrast, Malcolm X's and Ali's Muslim partners are envisaged as the voice of common sense and a guide to a dignified family life. One may assume that the creative decision to portray the voiceless African Muslim women in *Tears of the Sun* and *Black Hawk Down* was meant to evoke xenophobic conjecture because the women are positioned within the camera frame to intensify and detail the chaotic nature of their environment. Their Muslim space is measured by the way they are able to effectively replicate and contribute to a stereotyped portrayal of their location, and they are frequently found in the background of a given landscape. They are deprived of the affirmative attributes that the African American woman has been empowered with, since the choice of identifying her as a Muslim is not motivated by political reasons. The African American woman in film is revered for her stance of rejecting Western feminism in favor of pursuing a monotheistic religion, and her filmic portrayal concedes her the right to freely choose her lifestyle. Despite the similarities between Muslim and African American Muslim women in their religious affiliations, there are stark contrasts in the means by which they are apotheosized within a given socio-political and economic environment.

In *Malcolm X* (1992), the focus is on Malcolm X's (Denzel Washington) conversion to Islam and the ensuing rise of his popularity within the Nation of Islam as one of Elijah Mohammad's disciples, rather than on his marital life. For this reason, the role of Betty Shabazz (Angela Bassett), whom he marries, is of secondary importance within the overall progress of the narrative. *Ali* (2001), on the other hand, features the portrayal of two Muslim wives, Sonji Roi (Jada Pinkett Smith) and Belinda Ali (Nona Gaye). In Sonji we see an ex-playgirl whose carefree lifestyle and exhibitionist behavior make it impossible for her to fit into the traditional mold of a Muslim wife and, as a result, the marriage fails. In contrast, Belinda conducts herself gravely and satisfies the requirements of her masochistic environment. The film was released shortly after 9/11, on 25 December 2001 and, just like *Malcolm X*, further indicates the evolving nature of the Muslim female character type in American society.

Betty Shabazz, as the wife of Malcolm X, is represented as a dignified, respectable individual, always dressed in public in austere clothing fit for a nurse, which she was in real life. The projection is that of a powerful figure with firm principles, strong resolution and wise words. At one point, she says,

"I'm not made of glass and I won't break," referring to the risks involved in falling out with the Nation of Islam. There are no scenes in the film that are sexual or romantic in nature. Even Malcolm X's marriage proposal is conducted like a business deal, him asking her the relevant question and her abruptly saying "yes" before both smile, stand up and continue with their walk. When she is shown in private with her husband several years into their marriage, her words display *cura* in that she tries to protect him from the malice that is blossoming within the Nation of Islam as a result of his increasing popularity. She remains his moral support until the end of his life. In some respects, Betty fits the description of the African American Muslim female role summarized by Moxley Rouse (2004), who says that a Muslim woman residing in the United States has several priorities for achievement in her community. These achievements, which are not much different from the expectations of an upper-middle-class white Christian woman in the United States, except for the religious affiliation, are listed by Moxley Rouse (*ibid.*, 128): "'Promoting Islam,' 'fostering family and community,' 'supporting general and Islamic education,' 'expanding and creating services for the poor' and 'developing an economically viable community.'"

These priorities, applicable to Betty Shabazz to some extent, are exemplified particularly well in the realization of Belinda Ali. Belinda is presented as a companion who brings stability, at least for a while, to Ali's (Will Smith) unstable emotional life. Meeting him at a shop where she works as a young salesgirl, she is shown naïvely laughing at his childish pranks. As their relationship develops, she agrees to convert to Islam, supports the basic characteristics of universal gender equality and rejects the prioritization of gender over race and class.

While the portrayal of Malcolm X and Betty is not charged with emotions, Michael Mann, the director of *Ali*, decides to include some romance and sensuality in portraying Ali and Belinda. In one of the earlier sequences, they are shown standing side-by-side at a Nation of Islam meeting while their hands search for and find one another in secret, giving the sequence a sensual electricity. Yet Belinda is also shown to be a betrayed woman at a later stage in their relationship, when she walks into a hotel room in Zaire, having flown from the States to confront her husband about his infidelity. She attends his last fight for the World Heavyweight Championship against George Foreman, sitting in a seat far away from the ring, wearing a bright yellow dress and matching head cover, loosely thrown over her dark hair, with worry and compassion written all over her face. This is the last frame that features Belinda, although the film continues for another half hour, switching the viewer's attention to his next love interest.

Both female characters in these two films are created with respect, demonstrating domestically acceptable female Muslim types who conform to U.S. ideals of diversity in belief, and equality. The intervening ten years between them is significant only in terms of how much sensuality is portrayed. While Betty is merely an unbending support for Malcolm X, Belinda provides the same strength plus romanticism and physical satisfaction in marriage. Neither character is comparable to their African counterparts who are simply silent fixtures in a ravaged setting.

## *Conclusion*

This section has been about the change in the Muslim female character in films from the veiled figure or the exotic dancer of the past to the current normalized (humanized) figure, reflecting how she exists in her authentic environment or in relocation. In the earlier samples of American cinema, the audience had to make do with stereotypical images that became fixtures in the Western mind. Renderings of the female character in her harem existence were manifestations of a Western man's overworked imagination, yet in recent character portrayals the barriers seem to have fallen, revealing the Muslim woman's human qualities. Overseas women are now shown in a variety of attire from the *burka* and *hijab* to Western-style clothes, presenting a spectacle that exists in many Muslim countries. Female characters in a U.S. setting, for their part, conform to Hollywood ideals of appearance. While the Americanized female of Middle Eastern origin is almost always publicly devoid of her identifiable Islamic attire, as exemplified by Safiya in *Rendition* (2007), and Nadi in *House of Sand and Fog* (2003), her counterpart in another part of the world may enjoy personalized variations in the style and color of the garments imposed by her culture. Aisha's (*Body of Lies* [2008]) medical cap covers only a small section of her hair, and her medical uniform is figure hugging; while wearing jeans, Fatima (*Rendition*) still dons a scarf as required by the social norms of her north African country, but it is loosely tied over her hair, showing that, as an individual, she courageously bends the rules as she likes. We see the same independent spirit when the scarf flies away in the wind while she is running, and she continues regardless. This and similar examples display filmmakers' current sensitivities towards representing female Muslims as characters exercising individual preferences while not being totally disrespectful to the norms of their own culture.

Irrespective of the location in which Muslim female characters are depicted and how they are dressed, we notice that there is an enrichment of their domesticity, caring attitude and even their desire for sex. This can be described as a metamorphosis, in which the Muslim female character is changed from a monolithic existence to an entity with a body and soul; from being the object of the gaze to being a subject gazing at others; and from a submissive follower to an individual who recognizes her own importance and is someone to be reckoned with. There is currently a tendency to show Muslim females not as illiterate and oppressed members of a patriarchal society, but as individuals whose personal identity is enriched by education. Although Fatima in *Rendition* is still a university student, Nadi in *House of Sand and Fog* is a sophisticated representative of her liberalized culture. The same quality of mind can also be observed in Aisha in *Body of Lies* (2008)— she is not only a practicing nurse, but also capable of conversing about both domestic matters and world politics. These female characters are emancipated from their previously prescribed domestic roles and duties. In their behavior, they exhibit actor control and/or joint control, either deciding what course of action they have to take and/or making mutual decisions with their partner. Partner control over their actions is shown to be minimal and, in cases where this exists, the "new" Muslim woman is shown to have the courage to object to, instead of accept, the pressure to behave subserviently, as Nadi does in *House of Sand and Fog*.

A section on the representation of the Muslim female would have been incomplete if no attention was paid to the African American Muslim woman as depicted in films. While the African Muslim female has been widely used as a silent Orientalist trope in narratives set in Africa, her American counterpart is available only in two films. In each case, the story is about an iconic figure of outstanding achievement in the U.S. Black Muslim movement, one an orator and the other a world-class boxer. The female characters associated with them are constructed as respectable individuals who still look colorful and attractive in their Islamic clothing. They are not frightened to say what they think, despite the fact that they live in a male-dominated milieu. Their resoluteness reflects an altogether different approach to character composition. It is as if the makers of these films project them as "one of us trying to be like Others," whereas the overseas or immigrant Muslim women appear to be "one of the Others trying to be like us." This distinction is important, for it demonstrates that if there is any discrimination implicitly communicated at present through the art form of cinema, its focus is not the religion itself, but the place where it is practiced and the cultural pressures regarding how it is practiced.

It is reasonable to conclude that current trends favor the portrayal of Muslim female characters, both in the United States and elsewhere, with universally recognizable emotions, using their bodies as these emotions dictate as much as their cultural norms allow, or sometimes in contravention of such norms. Whether the changes noted here in the filmic depiction of Muslim women since 9/11 are to remain with us permanently—or even be extended in terms of more screen time and larger speaking roles or whether this is just a passing phase inspired by current socio-political conjectures, destined to change yet again, only time will show. For the time being, filmmakers seem to have come to the realization that, especially in some parts of the Middle East and north Africa, women are not as submissive as originally thought when they were being fought for by American feminists. Whatever the future holds, it is still reasonable to think that there is no going back from the current fully-developed character types to the flimsy female tropes of the past. The Muslim female character with body and soul is now closer to reality and should continue to be more convincing than past presentations of absurd Orientalist stereotypes.

# 6
# Muslim Children

With the exception of a recent publication (Bayraktaroğlu, 2015), the image of Muslim minors in American cinema in the pre–9/11 period has received almost no scholarly attention, probably because children appeared in films less often than adults. Nor did the cinematography in the past allowed the audience to see the world through Muslim children's eyes. Those films that used youngsters had some recurrent features. Firstly, young boys were framed more often than young girls. Secondly, these children either did not speak at all or spoke like an intelligent (American) adult, which gives the impression that the scriptwriters and filmmakers did not have a clear notion of the communicative idiosyncrasies of these minors. A further noticeable fact is that in a number of films, a Muslim child was used as a "rescue agent," to help the (usually American) protagonist(s) out of a difficult situation. At the comparative level, the portrayal of the Muslim juvenile has not followed the same path of change as the depiction of other minority youngsters from African and Latino communities in the United States. The situation, however, has changed significantly since 9/11 in the sense that Muslim female minors now appear in films as frequently as their male counterparts but, on the whole, there is a noticeable geographical distinction in terms of the Muslim child's portrayal. The character depiction is not the same for those Muslim children living in the United States and those living in their country of origin. For minors resident in the United States, a new generation of immigrant characters has been developed in the form of Muslim children who have recently been assimilated, are indoctrinated in and loyal to U.S. ideologies, but still have an allegiance to their cultural heritage and past. Films usually underline the conflict caused by this dual pressure on child characters, who fight for recognition of their hybrid identity. The films *Crossing Over* (2009), *Pretty Persuasion* (2005), *Towelhead*, also known as *Nothing Is Private* (2007), and *House of Sand and Fog* (2003) fall into this category. On the other hand, the Muslim child who is depicted as a native of another country, although still carrying some American Orientalist features, is delineated with universal qualities of childhood. The films in this category are *The Kingdom* (2007), *The Hurt Locker* (2008), *Babel* (2006), and *Traitor* (2008). Meanwhile, *The Kite Runner* (2007), with its child characters in both Afghanistan and the United States, falls into both categories.

Clarification regarding the use of the terms "child" and "adolescent" may be beneficial for the reader. In dealing with the projection of a minor in cinema, a distinction between "child" and "teenager" is usually made so as to properly evaluate their "rites of passage." The 1997 *Moving Image Genre-Form Guide* defines "Youth" cinema as [f]ictional work portraying aspects of the trajectory through adolescence,' including high school years, peer pressure, first love, beach parties and initial attempts at adulthood, along with strains in the relationship with family. Teenage years are usually emphasized, although younger characters may also be included in a mix of ages or the work may cover the transition from pre-teen to teenager, depicting a coming-of-age. A frequent emphasis is on a school setting including these ages.[1] The report goes on to detail movies with minor characters aged 12 years and younger classified as "children." Adolescents over 12 are termed "teenagers." However, looking at recent film productions, we notice that filmmakers do not apply as strict a yardstick to distinguish between minors aged eight and 15 (i.e., the range that most of the child characters fall under in the present selection of films) as they do to delineate the location where the child lives, i.e., in the United States or elsewhere, as mentioned above. For this reason, the terms child, adolescent, juvenile, minor, youth and youngster are used interchangeably in this book.

## *Theoretical Background*

Said (2003, 286–287) asserts that in the Western world Islam is equated with the Arab national whose image, as presented in the visual arts, carries nothing but negative connotations. Although his references do not make a distinction in terms of age, the images he mentions seem to cover all Arabs, old and young. Similarly, Shaheen (2003a), criticizing the productions of the American film industry from 1896 to 2001 for showing Muslim Arabs as only stereotypes, complains that real individuals are not reflected on the screen; an observation which is also valid for the portrayal of children. Indeed, he (*ibid.*, 13) goes on to say, "[n]or should you expect to encounter friendly children, those real Arab youths who participate in sporting events, or who are Boy Scouts and Girl Scouts." Although these claims by Shaheen appear in a book published in 2003, he must have been in the process of evaluating films of the pre–9/11 period at the time of writing and his comments therefore do not cover the depiction of Muslim children thereafter.

The image of the child in U.S. cinema has gone through several transformations over the past century and, in the analysis of a particular group of children, such as those of a Muslim background, it is useful to remember the tendencies developed in filming minors in general. The historic progression of the child's portrayal is attributed to two separate viewpoints in the United States. Jackson (1986) argues that the cinematic child is either wild and requires taming, or is tender or innocent, the latter viewpoint being influenced by the Christian doctrine of sin (14). This categorization may be feasible as long as the white child is set within the social nucleus of U.S. family life. Unfortunately, as is the case in many of the films discussed in this chapter, such a viewpoint is too restricted to absorb the complexities that are associated with immigrant children from cultures other than that of the United States. When a 14-year-old girl is extradited for speaking her mind freely but in contradiction to the state politics, as in the film *Crossing Over* (2009), do we group her with "wild" youngsters or classify her as a "tender and innocent" adolescent? A crude division like this is too narrow to encompass the majority of Muslim child characters in narrative cinema.

Another viewpoint, as developed by Sinyard (1992) in his extensive analysis of minors in films, is also based on the portrayal of American children. He says that filmmakers have three approaches to the portrayal of children. Firstly, there is the "aesthetic exploration of nostalgia," in which adults may feel that events define the characteristics of a child. Secondly, "a romantic outlook: Where childhood is the site of innocent understanding of an instinctive imagination." This romantic approach aligns the child with nature and the environment. Thirdly, a "Freudian approach where the roots of the adult mind are attributed to childhood consciousness and experience" (*ibid.*, 7). However, a tripartite explanation like this, based on personal memory and imagination, does help with regard to the creation of Muslim child characters in American cinema, for the simple reason that the culture in question is alien to many filmmakers and they cannot rely on their own childhood memories in the making of unfamiliar character types. If the producers cannot draw on their personal experiences, where would they get their inspiration from? From the collective but second-hand repertoire of the times? Regarding the evolution of filmic child images, Considine (1985) suggests that this is affected by the socio-political and socio-economic changes experienced by the country before or during a film's creation. Similarly, Featherstone (1974, 357) comments: "Images of childhood fashioned by artists and writers are important sources because they sometimes influence and reflect popular thought and because they often constitute profound imaginative explorations of unacknowledged cultural dilemmas and tensions." While this viewpoint is valid for the creation of a child character modeled on the filmmaker's own childhood, considering that most filmmakers in America do not have a Muslim heritage, it does not answer the question of whether or not the adult mind can create an authentic child from an alien culture. The Muslim child character, usually developed by a non–Muslim adult scriptwriter, and performed by children but directed by adults for the purpose of a mainly adult audience, cannot be anything but a creation of the adults' imagination influenced by the ongoing ideologies at the time of production. The current entertainment needs of the public are also a factor influencing the way films are designed. For example, in the remake of *Arabian Nights* (1942), the screenwriter was Michael Hogan and the director was John Rawlins, and the purpose was to provide escapism for the entertainment-hungry wartime population rather than produce art-house material enriched with authentic childhood behavior. With regard to the perfect formula for exotic melodramas such as this and its sequels, with their "wholesome family appeal," Jeffrey Richards (2015, 97–98) writes: "For the women, there was handsome, dashing hero Jon Hall; for the men, glamorous Latin beauty, Maria Montez; and as an identification figure for the children, the resourceful teenage sidekick." In the later movies although a child character appeared "as the loyal, energetic, quick-witted friend of the hero, the difference was that the emphasis now was not on the boy but on the glamorous adult couple."

The projection of the child onto the screen was used as a vehicle for and a consequence of the adult gaze, which was not a completely legitimate reflection of a child's true self. The transparency of the adult's imaginary state with regard to what the child must or should be like conjures up "child-like" features that allow the audience to empathize with these artificial qualities which they themselves are never able to relate to. Yet this "child-like" presence should not be confused with "childish" behavior, since the overall performance of the character's "child-like" actions is predetermined by adults. When a child on film is able to emulate adult-like qualities in their ability to mimic/perform child-like behavior, a contradiction occurs, as our preconceived notions of how a child is supposed to conduct themselves becomes subverted.

According to Sokoloff (1986, 239), children are "the objects on whom adults foist their highest hopes and deepest fears and insecurities," and, by virtue of their constant growth and change, they challenge adults' fixed attitudes. Therefore, "children figures in narrative may serve to put into relief with special acuity the limited understandings, feelings, and perceptions of those who attempt to describe them." When applied to the process of filmmaking, the child image amounts to what Ledesma (2012, 153) refers to as a "colonising practice" that entails a forceful adult identification through the narrative and with the character. The collapsing of adult and child perspectives erases the child's subjectivity and the characteristics that distinguish the two. This process merely acts as a filter, whether subconscious or not, since the empathetic adult spectator is unable to become a child again and relies merely on his instinctive recollections that are aroused on seeing a child character in the film. If the image cannot be built on one's childhood recollections, however, then it is assumed to be based on the "Other." That is, the interpretation of the child character takes its inspiration from the imaginary state of the adult's mind. In the case of a Muslim child character, the challenge for the creator and the interpreter increases because, apart from the difference between the adult and the child, cultural differences between the two also come into play.

Cultural differences have proved to be an area where "Otherness" can be explained in post-colonial terms. One of the most influential theorists in this field, Homi Bhabha (1994 and 1996) proposes that no identity or culture can be described in essentialist terms as these mutate the indigenous properties of the colonized. These indigenous properties form the "first space" and the structures provided by the colonizer the "second space" and, as a result of the two, a "third space" develops. Within this "third space," individuals and cultures stand as "hybrid" entities. Films such as *The Kite Runner*, *Pretty Persuasion*, *Crossing Over* and *House of Sand and Fog* depict examples of colonized Muslim children who exist within the "third space." Indeed, the U.S.-based Muslim children in these films are presented as U.S. subjects who manage to preserve their hereditary cultural ties and survive within an alien environment that not only influences their everyday actions, but becomes a part of their cultural DNA. They are neither their indigenous selves nor do they reflect only the identity of the colonial structures that are imposed on them. Instead, they have an in-between identity—in other words "hybridity"—a fusion of the two. In this way, they become the elements of transnational cinema, which cannot be confined within the boundaries of any one nation-state.

The crisis of image and identity is not simply a recognizable model of "Otherness" between an adult and a child/teenager, as is the case with the white American child and adult, but, as mentioned above, derives from a broader amalgamation of "Otherness" between cultures. In addition, as these children are usually confronted by authoritarian figures (the police, soldiers, civil servants, teachers, and so on), the division between civil and official life also becomes a consideration. Such collective "Otherness" results in the formation of what we can term "hybrid Otherness," referring to not only the Muslim American youth, but the offspring of almost all immigrants. This hybrid status may additionally involve other deep-seated cultural assertions, an example of which is cited by Ledesma (2012). He refers to the "radical Otherness" of a Latino child, who is perceived as a "double Other" because s/he invokes simultaneously the categories of "adolescent" and "criminality" (157). Interested in a comparable dynamic, Ledesma is concerned with the duality of character traits. How much this duality, or even multiplicity, applies to the depiction of the child can be looked at during the analysis of each case study, but so far our concern has been on the techniques available to the filmmaker to present a culturally alien minor to the audience, seeking their understanding and empathy. Naturally, with the change in times, circumstances and techniques evolve. Different cultural worlds are not as distanced from one another today as they were in the earlier days of cinema, and there has been an increase in general awareness of other lands and their people, provided by easy travelling and the proliferation of visual material through electronic media. As a consequence of this modernization of life, the problems inherent in the representation of a child character from a different location and culture have been minimized. The proof of this is in the use of a cinematographic and narrative technique called "focalization," which has become fashionable in the representation of celluloid Muslim minors. This style, although at times utilized in the projection of male and female Muslim adults in action, is more useful in making sense of child characters. This is because adult spectators can better understand adult "Others," despite cultural differences, with the help of shared attributes of "adulthood." However, in the case of children, focalization significantly helps the American viewer decode an enigmatic and alien entity, and feel sympathy for it.

## *Focalization*

Since the Muslim child is perceived as a threat to the fabric of the American way of life, they are rarely given the opportunity to display child-like or even childish qualities. Instead, they are usually considered a means of abstaining from integration, which further fuels their alienated status. In order to avoid exploiting the child portrayal but at the same time engage the spectator politically, cinematic devices are employed to bring the adult spectator's perception closer to a child's subjective worldview and experience. To this effect, internal or external focalization techniques are implemented.

Bal (1996, 116) defines focalization as a means of creating a vision which is "seen" and being "perceived." The filmmaker can either frame the figure of the child in close proximity, displaying his or her physical, psychological or emotional state, or choose to deprive these figures of inner subjectivity and render them from afar. Bal (*ibid.*, 119) summarizes these framing techniques as follows: "When focalization lies within one character which participates in the *fabula* [story] as an actor, we can refer to *internal* focalization. We can then indicate by means of the term *external* focalization that an anonymous agent, situated outside the *fabula*, is functioning as focalizer." The child focalized internally thus serves to present the adult spectator with the youth's subjectivity, while in external focalization the child becomes less directly identifiable. As a consequence, the spectator is forced to observe from the position of a distanced but protective sympathizer.

Along similar lines, Rimmon-Kenan (1983, 74), in a study of narratology, explains that an "external focalizer" is external to the story and can also be called the "narrator-focalizer" because the focus of perception is that of the narrator. An "internal focalizer," on the other hand, is a character through whose focus of perception the story is told, and is thus also called a "character focalizer." If we apply this distinction to the analysis of a film, we sometimes come up with a situation where the filmmaker is the external focalizer as s/he is articulating a story from their point of view. Nonetheless, more often the filmmaker allows the story to develop from the viewpoint of a film character who then becomes the internal focalizer. This technique has been in use for a long time in depicting adult Muslims on screen. Two examples, among many, are *The Message* (1976), which narrates the birth of Islam from the viewpoint of the Prophet Muhammad, and *The 13th Warrior* (1999) in which the story develops as the main Muslim character, Ahmed ibn Fadian (Antonio Banderas), adapts himself to Nordic culture.

The start of internal focalization in films featuring children in general goes back to the 1960s. The following example from the film *Oliver!* (1968), explained by an anonymous author, clarifies the technique[2]:

> At first the camera presents an overall perspective, a point of view that hovers above the scene and the audience is able to see the entire scene all at once. Then the perspective changes (as Oliver ducks under the man's arm) and the camera reproduces Oliver's perceptions, the quick passing of surroundings as he is running, even the loss of consciousness when he is knocked out and the screen momentarily goes black. As the camera changes perspective the audience adopts Oliver's point of view and sees and experiences events as he sees and experiences them, Oliver becomes the focaliser.

The same technique starts being utilized in Muslim child representations after 9/11, with the camera capturing the world through the eyes of a minor.

In the pre–9/11 context, American cinema rarely gave the viewer the opportunity to empathetically view the adolescent from a standpoint different from their own. The character Ali Bin Ali in *Arabian Nights* (1942), for instance, is hardly an authentic character in appearance or behavior. Other child characters in later films are not convincing either. This highlights the dramatic variation in films such as *The Kite Runner, Babel, Towelhead* and *House and Sand and Fog*, all of which were released in the years post–9/11 and offer an insightful and introspective look at the Muslim adolescent, whom the spectator had never been privileged to see in the past.

The choice to represent the Muslim child in American cinema through internal or external focalization depends on whether or not the film's intention is to subject the spectator to empathetic identification. Usually, this means of examination enables the American spectator to scrutinize sociopolitical circumstances and question existing administrative policies in a post–9/11 context. *Crossing Over* (2009) is a particularly notable example, in which the child character Taslima poses a question about Homeland Security's treatment of American Muslim children and the way in which immigration policies are implemented in light of the Patriot Act 2001. The inherent criticism of current politics, however, is insinuated through Taslima's struggle with the law enforcers who are judged from her point of view. The Muslim American child here serves as a medium for probing into domestic American policies and is therefore a strong example of internal focalization.

While Muslim youth in America tend to become a means of internal focalization, the Muslim overseas has until recently been portrayed through external focalization, with no inner subjective qualities. *The Kite Runner* and *Babel*, however, give the American spectator the chance to examine foreign spaces from a simplified, child-like point of view. This exploitative means of self-identification through the child overseas has tended to function as a bridge across which universal themes of childhood innocence (and innocence lost) are made available to American spectators. Such themes are not new because, for many years, they provided the backbone of films about white American youngsters; however, Muslim children being placed in contexts where their innocence (and innocence-lost) are observed is a novelty.

## *Historical Progress of the African American and Hispanic Child*

A Muslim child living in the United States is categorized as an "immigrant," as opposed to a "native." However, there are differences in the way the depiction of the Muslim child has progressed in comparison to that of, say, the Hispanic or African American child. While the portrayal of the Muslim child has also changed over time, the pace of this transformation has not been as pleasing as that of the portrayal of African American and Hispanic child characters.

On the evolution of the film image of African American children, Rhines (1996) reports that, as early as the turn of the twentieth century, they were used in silent films to underline white American racism. Taking his example from *Ten Pickaninnies* (1904), produced by Thomas Edison, he observes that "a group of nameless Negro children romped and ran about while being referred to as snowballs, cherubs, coons, bad chillun, inky kids, smoky kids, black lambs, cute ebonies, and chubby ebonies" (14). In the next decade, settlers in the south reiterated their justifications for white dominance over African Americans with films like *The Birth of a Nation* (1915), which consolidated the degrading stereotypes of African Americans who were depicted as unruly and inherently wicked. A famous character from this era is Topsy in *Uncle Tom's Cabin* (1927), who seems completely perverse and corrupt. As a thief and a liar, she is endowed with abominable qualities which presumably were exacerbated by the horrible conditions in which African slaves were forced to live in those days. Her creator, the nineteenth-century novelist Harriet Beecher Stowe, was an abolitionist and it is probable that Topsy, the despicable child character of African origin, was the author's way of showing the world the effects of the transatlantic slave trade contaminating the American south.[3] However, things started changing in the 1930s and 40s when economic depression became a universal problem, regardless of skin color. In *Our Gang* (1938–1944), a series of short films released by MGM, white and black boys and girls were presented together in a frame for the first time (Lury 2010).

The cinematic scene was dominated in the 1950s and 60s by westerns, and issues that related to African Americans and/or slavery did not feature much on the theatrical screen. From the 1970s to the 1990s, however, child images came back, but this time in a more realistic form, reflecting individuals engulfed in intercity gang culture as interpreted by African American directors. One of the important films of this era is *Boyz n the Hood* (1991), which portrays the rites of passage of three African American boys growing up on the rough streets of Compton, Los Angeles.

Horton, Price and Brown (1999), drawing on Lichter and Amundson (1997), report that, over the years, repulsive stereotypes of African American children in films have gradually decreased.[4] The tide turned decisively to the benefit of African Americans with the start of *The Cosby Show* in 1984, with its sensible parents and amiable youngsters. In the 1990s, well-groomed African American youngsters, such as Troy in Spike Lee's *Crooklyn* (1994), Mary Shuttleworth in *He Got Game* (1998) and Jaden Smith in *The Karate Kid* (2010), became popular movie characters. With no drug lords around them, these children are featured in loving homes with encouraging parents guiding them to reach those goals that are highly regarded in society.

Films about Hispanics have taken a similar route. Initially, they were based on stereotypes, showing Hispanics as social failures. Early silent films presented Mexicans as the most violent, wretched and evil characters in their stories. As Figueroa (2009, 64) puts it, "[t]hey cheated, robbed, raped and killed without hesitation.[5] These 'Despicable' Mexican characters were named *greasers*, alluding to the degraded social status of Mexicans in American society." Hispanic children's intransigent behavioral patterns were attributed in some films to their social or family conditions. However, some analysts probed deeper into the issues. It is, for instance, claimed by Wolfenstein and Leites (1950) that the generation gap presented in the movies addresses the diversion of the cultures in contact. They see most films converging on the point where immigrant children try to escape from "protracted involvement with their parents" (105). This is an inter-family uprising whereby adolescents protest against the old culture that their parents brought from their land of origin, and fight to emancipate themselves from its grip (105–108).

In the 1980s, however, the image of the Hispanic child began to underline positive aspects, and has recently been presented favorably, for example by the Chicano boy in *Once Upon a Time in Mexico* (2003), Pita in *Man on Fire* (2004) and Carmen and Juni Cortex in *Spy Kids* (2001). In the latter, the strong family bond is accentuated, Carmen saying at one point, "Spywork: that's easy. Keeping a family together: that's difficult and that's a mission worth fighting for."

Thus, while Hispanic and black African American children are now generally considered to be assimilated into the mainstream American way of life, the Muslim child is not afforded the same tolerance, immunity, freedom of expression and understanding that other children in the country have benefited from, regardless of skin color. The Muslim child does not feature in films these days as part of a happy family, nor do the majority of these films end happily. There is still a long way to go to normalize the depiction of Muslim child's family and social life, but long strides have been taken since the days when s/he was either non-existent in films or existent on a superficial level, carrying the nuances of either romanticism or utter hostility.

## *The Muslim Child Before 9/11*

In terms of the ways in which the Muslim child has been depicted in a pre–9/11 context, there seems to be little material to consider. In the past, this child was often seen encapsulated in an Orientalist setting, where actors playing the characters were either from a Euro-American background or were selected according to their indigenous geographic approximation to a Muslim country. The development of the Muslim child image in American cinema has fluctuated in line with American foreign policies over the years. Until roughly the start of problems in Palestine in 1948, this was a positive image, enriched with imaginative but fairly positive material. What was projected on the screen, however, was as unreal as the rest of the Muslim space portrayed in standard Orientalism, with its colorful environment and cheerful Arab adults falling in love, singing English songs and becoming strangers not only in paradise but even in their own environment. An example from this period is the film *Arabian Nights* (1942), in which the child character Ali Ben Ali is presented as the centerpiece of the narrative, an ingenious matchmaker in the love story involving a Khalif and a beautiful singer. Ali is a 15-year-old acrobat and magician, a dexterous all-rounder with no stereotypical characteristics associated with the Orient. He is well versed and a quick thinker. When he is stopped at the palace gates by the guards because "men can't enter here," he responds, "I'm not a man, I'm a boy." Despite his tender age, he talks sense into his singer friend, Scheherazade (Maria Montez), when she acts unwisely and always provides the ruler, the khalif, with solutions at difficult moments. "You are a very old one for someone so young," says the khalif at one point. Despite his age, Ali rides a horse and is a swordsman and is therefore not an Arab who needs a "savior." He himself is that "savior," helping others. The character is played by a young and good-looking Indian actor, Sabu, who became so popular in this archetypal role that he appeared in many similar movies in succession.[6] The first Turkish actor in Hollywood, a young Turhan Bey, took up the reins when Sabu became too grown-up in looks to fit the part.

The American fascination with Arabian-themed fairy tales declined towards the end of the 1950s and, in the following decades, Muslim child characters were used in the movies only occasionally, if at all. When they appeared, they were either silent minors helping the adult protagonist(s), or youngsters behaving like American children. The prime example of this period can be seen in the third section of *Invitation to the Dance* (1956). The section is entitled *Sinbad the Sailor*, although Gene Kelly does not impersonate the *Arabian Nights* character. He is simply an American sailor visiting Arabia and wearing the traditional white, military uniform and a white cap. When he rubs a lamp that he bought in the souk, out pops a 12-year-old child genie (David Kasday) clad in an oriental vest and pantaloons, with a fez on his head. As soon as he appears, he starts imitating the dance movements of the American sailor. The sailor wants the genie to discard his Eastern clothing and replace it with a U.S. sailor's outfit. This way, the genie becomes his lookalike, the alter-ego of Gene Kelly's character. As the film is all music and dance, neither character speaks, and the tradition of a "mute" Arab child is thus kept unbroken. Additionally, the genie disguised as a minor helps the sailor get rid of an animated dragon and two animated henchmen in the Emir's palace, fulfilling the "rescue-agent" role that is recurrently played by Muslim child characters of the period. The film also takes Americanization to the extreme by showing a little boy from the East, dressed in American sailors' clothing, tap dancing with the main character.

A similar attempt to Americanize Muslim minors can be observed in the five-year-old character Mahtob (Sheila Rosenthal) in *Not Without My Daughter* (1991). However, while this may be more credible, especially as the narrative tells us that she has been raised in the States by her American mother, the same cannot be said for Walt Disney's animated feature film *Aladdin* (1992). *Aladdin* has a controversial history. It is one of the studio's most successful productions ever, and received two Academy Awards. However it has also attracted criticism for the way it portrays Arabs. A noteworthy feature is that Aladdin and Princess Jasmine are presented like American characters rather than children from the East.[7] Shaheen (2003a, 52) writes: "Aladdin doesn't have a big nose, he has a small nose. He doesn't have a beard or a turban. He doesn't have an accent. What makes him nice is they've given him this American character." Shaheen's criticism of the animated child not having a beard or wearing a turban is unfounded, but there is no denial that the character, with the cherub-like facial features that are Disney's trademark, does not look Arabian. We can add to this the fact that Aladdin talks in the film not like an inexperienced youngster, but like a grown-up, a feature which we also saw in *Arabian Nights* in the character of Ali. However, while the latter is a good-hearted "wise man" in the body of a youngster, in *Aladdin* this grown-up talk is seasoned with racial remarks. The much-quoted opening song sung by Aladdin about his homeland sets the tone of what follows.

In contrast to child characters with exceptional linguistic skills, there is also the image of the mute Arab child recurrently appearing in films. These urchins lack witty conversational techniques, but are still pivotal helpers for the protagonist in overcoming obstacles. One example is the little desert boy wearing an orange kaftan in *Sahara* (1983). He appears at times of desperation in the desert to help the American female racer (Brooke Shields) and the sheikh's English valet, Cambridge (John Mills), continuously smiling but never exchanging any words with them. Strangely enough, he does not break his silence in the presence of Arab characters either. This convention of using a mute Arab boy as a "rescue agent" has survived until recent times; indeed, in *Hidalgo* (2004), a similar black African youngster in the desert camp pretends that he does not understand English when Frank Hopkins (Viggo Mortensen) asks him to bring some water for his thirsty horse, but then comes back later with a bucket of water in his hand and a smile on his face.

Shaheen (2003a, 238) refers to a group of ragged Algerian children in a souk scene in *The Hell with Heroes* (1968), hustling newly arrived tourists who throw the youth some coins, grumbling "Come on, get away, get away!" Despite their initial presentation as a social nuisance, these child characters become an indispensable element later in the narrative. The main character, Byrnie Mackay (Rod Taylor), cares for these homeless youngsters and they in return hunt down Mackay's enemies and save him from a certain death. There is no mention in Shaheen's (2003a) catalogue description of the film as to whether these Arab boys are shown to be conversant with Mackay and whether they sound as "childish" as they should, but it is clear that they are again in this film given the role of protectors of the principal white hero.

The only exception to these repeated characteristics associated with the Muslim child is the behavior of the ungrateful Palestinian girl in *Double Edge* (1992). The film is about an American journalist/photographer (Faye Dunaway) visiting the Middle East and witnessing a student riot in the garden of a girls' secondary school in East Jerusalem. She follows one of the girls who breaks away from the crowd and disappears into a side road, with a police officer in pursuit. There, the journalist finds the officer beating the girl on the ground with his truncheon and intervenes to save the youngster. Once the officer departs and the journalist starts gently stroking the girl's hair, asking "Are you all right?" the girl, without responding or showing any appreciation, spits in the journalist's face, gets up, and runs away. This non-conformist attitude is probably injected into the sequence to signpost the Palestinian hostility towards the West for making them live under Israeli rule.

Not counting the last example, it is clear that the Muslim child was frequently used by U.S. filmmakers in the past as a "rescue agent" who would control or prevent disasters developing in the storyline, and would do this either while displaying adult-like eloquence or in complete silence. It can be observed that, until the 1980s, the Muslim child did not carry hostile feelings, as did the Muslim adult characters, but this positive approach may have either been the result of the West not feeling as intimidated by children as they did by adult Muslims, or due to a widespread ignorance about these minors, leading to an inability to deliver a more convincing and authentic portrayal. The earlier depiction of the Muslim child changed in tone in the last two decades before the millennium and, just before 9/11, the child was represented as a composite of the Muslim terrorist. Considering that the Muslim male image has been reconstructed with increasingly negative undertones since the 1950s, the representation of Muslim children as a threat to America was a relatively delayed act, probably resulting from the sudden surge in numbers of child soldiers and suicide bombers in Islamic countries. The practice first started during the Iran-Iraq war in the 1980s and spread quickly to the war zones in Afghanistan and the rest of the Middle East. The drafting of youngsters, sometimes as young as 13, urged Hollywood to catch up with this change in the conventions of warfare and to utilize child terrorist images in films (Singer 2006).[8] A case in point is the film *Rules of Engagement* (2000), which, although it hardly features fully developed Muslim child characters, shows multiple images of children bearing military weapons who, of course, are again deprived of a voice. These striking visuals not only reinforce a vilified stereotype, but also remind the spectator of the Westernized monolithic approach in which all Muslims share a common characteristic infused with hatred and aggression towards Europe and the United States.

## *The Muslim Child After 9/11*

An analysis of the Muslim child character in films after 9/11 yields interesting results, as the character has been created during the historic period of the American government's War on Terror and extreme Islamic fundamentalism. As Jackson (1986, 36) claims, "[i]mages of children in film provide a cultural shorthand for determining attitudes toward childhood; they transmit some of the important social values, fears, and concerns that Americans have regarding their children." However, instead of concentrating on themes of racial prejudice and hatred between cultures, which would have been expected during this period, these films narrate experiences of American Muslim youngsters who are persecuted by authoritative governmental bodies. The implied justification for such treatment is the child's claim to his or her cultural heritage. These child characters define an ideological struggle between the officially promoted U.S. identity and the Muslim child identity, which is a complex composition of a diasporic existence.

## Muslim Minors in Diaspora

Muslim minors living in the United States are reflected in films as the offspring of de-territorialized individuals who have left their country of origin to settle down elsewhere, either voluntarily so that they can recreate their life in more affluent surroundings, or to escape persecution. As such, they can be regarded as "transnational," indicating their personal identity and allegiances over and beyond the confines of any one nation-state, and incorporating national characteristics of both the country of origin and country of settlement. At this point, it is worth mentioning the distinction made by Dunphy (2001) between the "emigrant perspective" of the migrant who focuses mainly on the country left behind, and the "immigrant perspective" of the migrant reconciled with the culture of the country of arrival. The celluloid Muslim child characters are neither emigrants nor immigrants, but placed in between these two, in a Janus-like position, exhibiting a status of "hybrid Otherness," a term mentioned earlier to indicate the multicultural restraints on the immigrant Muslim child.

The large number of films under observation is a testament to various degrees of "hybrid Otherness," expressed either in their production set-up or in the nature of the narrative. Such films create local impressions of Islam through the manner in which they portray Muslim characters. Diasporic and/or hybrid individuals become shaped by their location and participation in a multicultural environment. On the other hand, their relationship and connection to their host country acts as a contrast to an immigrant discourse that emphasizes assimilation, and an emigrant discourse accentuating segregation. Guided by such facts, transnational cinema has explored common universal themes for the sake of multilingual and multicultural audiences alike, yet elements are intermittently derivative of U.S. filmmaking sensibilities with careful implementation in the storyline. The characters' multicultural existence may be an indication of the current socio-political times, but they also share a converging similarity (with the child image in film) in how they are cinematically realized. This has been presented through contrasting artistic devices that have either favored a romantic Orientalist approach (like the little silent boy from the desert in *Hidalgo*) or a neo-socio-realist application (as in *Babel*).

The alienation that hybrid "Other" characters are subjected to in the narrative pushes them into loneliness, and the growing dysfunction can be attributed to the failure of each adolescent's understanding of the adult society he or she lives in. A striking example is the adolescent in *House of Sand and Fog* (2003), Ismail, who is presented as an adolescent conveying passive symptoms of alienation, skateboarding alone, never being seen with any friends and playing the dutiful son to his overbearing father. But outside his comfort zone, he yearns to be socially accepted and recognized with his transnational identity, so much so that he snaps at the end and falls victim to a color-sensitive police officer who does not take his tender age into consideration. This psycho-social/Oedipal model was an especially popular standard, formulated and applied in the 1960s by the likes of Erik Erikson, Bruno Bettleheim, S.N. Eisenstadt, Talcott Parsons, Ruel Denney and Kenneth Keniston. They treated the disillusionment of youth as the fault of adults, who had difficulty in representing their own culture as inviting and exciting.

In addition to the family circle, the social environment is also shown in these films to be responsible for the disillusionment that Muslim youngsters face in the host country. At the heart of each adolescent's predicament lies the malevolence and non-conformist attitudes displayed by their elders. On this subject, Keniston (1965, 191) tries to rationalize and understand adolescents' disenchantment with life by claiming that a young person "desires to find in adulthood the qualities of warmth, communion, acceptedness, dependence and intimacy which existed in childhood, and one reason this desire leads to alienation from adulthood is because adult life in America offers so few of these qualities." He also elaborates that the genesis of alienation "is a response of individuals especially sensitized to reject American culture ... and it is in part a response to social stresses, historical loss, and collective estrangements in our shared existence" (*ibid.*). The alienation that each Muslim child character experiences differs dramatically from film to film, as does the intensity of their resistance to being indoctrinated. Some are persuaded, in the end, by one particular cultural ideology, and some are discarded as a result of their abstinence. By and large, the overseas Muslim child tends to be the victim of or participant in the physicality that war and conflict have brought upon them, but in the case of the U.S. inhabitant, the violence that they are subjected to is administered by their prejudicial peers or by governmental policy-enforcing agents. This shared concurrence may be attributable to the level of resistance to assimilation that each character is shown to display. Whenever the child asserts their resistance to authoritative demands, whether from a teacher, the police or Homeland Security, they are either killed or separated from their family and/or home. Bulman (2005, 37) claims: "Adolescence today is marked by two distinct social processes. First, the adolescent must search for an identity.... Second, the adolescent must search for independence."

In line with this, we can see the emergence of a pattern, in terms of representation, in the films under scrutiny. Each Muslim child strives to be unique and accepted with their hybrid qualities, as they challenge authorities in order to discover or protect their identities, which are fundamental to their ethos and wellbeing. On the other hand, the aggressive and hostile behavior that adults exhibit towards them reveals a further displacement within the American social hierarchy. If, as Tocqueville (1836, 202) observes, "adolescence is a manifestation of a social construction," then the Muslim hybrid youth should be a by-product of this particular categorization.

Although Stewen (2012, 280) describes the child as a "liminal being [that] mediates general doubts and fears of contemporary society," this rationale does not seem to be wholly applicable to Muslim child representations post–9/11. These representations show that the child is rarely given the same considerations and challenges that are the result of deeply held convictions about the naturalness of childhood; the Muslim child is quite often deprived of a childish mentality. In comparison, the non–Muslim American adolescent is regarded as vulnerable, dependent and, most importantly, innocent. The relationship between an American youth and an American adult and a Muslim youth and an American adult is not the same, which can be read in the way the adult's actions and reactions are coordinated. American adult characters in films display a protective and nurturing stance towards the American child. For instance, in the majority of John Hughes' films, the white American youngsters question their identity in the face of adversity and/or under adult pressure. The youngsters' non-conformist attitudes lead to an inevitable clash with adults. However, in each of his films the unanswerable question arises as to whether these youngsters are hopeless delinquents or rightful claimants of their own identity. Most of these films end with the child character coming out of trouble without much to lose, either physically or emotionally, and making up with their immediate circle of adults. In comparison, the Muslim child is treated with sinister undertones that pertain to an adult hostility, which indicates that the child is no longer considered an innocent being. The dialogue and physical interactions convey a much more mature level of interplay, one closely resembling traits of behavior adults would display.

There has also been some difference between youngsters in the type of focalization used, depending on the character's racial background, but luckily this difference started getting less obvious towards the middle of the decade. The indigenous American child used to be treated with internal focalization and the adult spectator could easily find comfort in identifying with him or her. In comparison, the objectified Muslim American child was not given much consideration and was realized in an externally focalized manner. As mentioned earlier, there might have been reasons for this. Firstly, the American Muslim child functioned as a symbolic figure through which current administrative polices, directed towards immigrant "Others" could be questioned. Secondly, they might have undergone a process of objectification in which the centralized white American characters' point of view was favored. Thirdly, their "hybrid Otherness" (whether evoked through attire or cultural behavior) might have been be taken as justification for the ill-treatment they received. While some films made in the middle of this decade (e.g., *The Hurt Locker*, 2008) have raised questions about our ideas of subjectivity and objectivity, the majority of commercial U.S. films released during the period have shied away from this altogether. They may still question our ways of perception and open up new reflective spaces so as to mediate meaning, but the cultural "Otherness" ascribed to a Muslim child character all too often impedes our ability to view them in the same way as we do their white, mainstream, centrist equivalents. *Pretty Persuasion* (2005) and *The Kite Runner* (2007) are two of the period's films that display these characteristics most vividly. The former in particular force viewers to witness the social dangers awaiting a Muslim schoolgirl in a white neighborhood.

### Randa in Pretty Persuasion (2005)

This film concerns high-school students from wealthy families in California. A new student, a Muslim girl named Randa (Adi Schnall), enters a racist environment rife with a questionable demeanor and scandalous behavior. On her first day at school, Randa is accepted into her schoolmate Kimberly's (Evan Rachel Wood) clique, involving one more white girl, Brittany (Elisabeth Harnois). Yet, even under the protection of these two friends, she becomes the source of ridicule among other students. Her non-conformist image, her dark skin and Muslim headscarf, provoke hostile responses from other students and even Kimberly remarks, "What's that thing on your head? You haven't tried to bomb anybody, have you?" Another girl shows fake empathy: "I know all about the immigrant experience, how hard it can be. I'm a Canadian." As the audience is all too familiar with the predictability of high-school clique genre films, such as *Heathers* (1989), Randa's mere presence verifies that socio-political events have suddenly become ingrained within an all too familiar setting. She is positioned in the center of groups as a "mute" participant with almost no facial expressions, encouraging Kimberly to

*Pretty Persuasion* (Marcos Siega, 2005): The inclusion in the frame of an Orientalist element can disrupt an all-too-familiar scene, and conveys the message that something is out of place, as is the case in the line-up (left to right) of Kimberly (Evan Rachel Wood), Randa (Adi Schnall) and Brittany (Elisabeth Harnois).

explain to the other girls that "Randa doesn't speak much." Her knowledge of this new world is limited to rudimentary popular culture. When asked what she likes the most in America, she responds, "Sylvester Stallone."

In one particular scene where the three girls have a sleepover and watch television, lying chest down on the floor, elbows resting on a pillow, Randa is strategically placed in between the other two. The American girls are wearing vests and shorts and smoking cigars but Randa is the center of focus, not only as a result of her placement in the line-up, but also because of her Islamic attire which covers her from head to toe. Her image has an incongruous look in a typical scene that we know well. Her inclusion disrupts our feeling of familiarity and adds an awkward, comical effect to the common set-up.

As with some other culturally hybrid youth characters in films, Randa is torn between the expectations placed upon her by the people of two different worlds and the cultures pertaining to these worlds. Her predicament is further aggravated by her teacher's criticism of her poor writing skills, for which she is threatened with expulsion unless she improves herself. While her parents, who are practicing Muslims, expect her to speak only the truth, her loyalty to her close school friends requires her to make false accusations against the teacher. Her need for others to accept her for what she is and her desire for belongingness leave her unprotected against exploitation. Committing perjury becomes too much for her to live with. The psychological torture that she experiences is vividly shown on her face and in her actions when she goes into an empty classroom, throws away her headscarf and writes on the blackboard the words "We are all sinners" in Arabic before she shoots herself.

Throughout the film we observe Randa in the same way that the other white girls at school (and of course the audience) see her: an awkward object that does not fit when placed in a very familiar Western school context. This external focalization changes only in the last scene when she commits suicide. In this scene the viewers become a fly on the wall, so to speak, and they enter the empty classroom together with Randa (observing her while she writes on the board, witnessing her private moments when she removes her headscarf and releases her hair and finally takes the pistol from her pocket). The internal focalization ends here when her hand moves up to her head; the audience's viewpoint is transferred at this point to the area outside the classroom where the noise of the gunshot is heard.

Although all three youngsters commit perjury, the consequences are shown to be different for each of them. Kimberley attracts media attention and is invited back by the film people who had rejected her in her first audition. Brittany's dreams are shattered but she manages to cope with her guilty conscience. It is the Muslim girl who pays the greatest price out of the three, taking her own life instead of living with shame.

### *Sohrab in* **The Kite Runner** *(2007)*

A large portion of this film deals with events leading up to the Soviet Union's invasion of Afghanistan in 1979 and a significant amount of time is spent exploring the aftermath of the war and how it affected Muslim children. There are two youngsters aged about ten, a rich man's son Amir (Zekeria Ebrahimi) and his servant's son Hassan (Ahmad Khan Mahmidzada), who later turns out to be Amir's half-brother. These two youngsters are portrayed as close friends in a world with colorful kites and a bustling city. In this section, the film misleads the audience into believing that they are watching the Middle Eastern form of romantic narrative expression they are familiar with; the projection remains inherently American in its stylized visual and fictional content.

As the danger of a Soviet invasion looms, Amir migrates to the United States with his father, but his childhood in the United States is not further explored. After his escape from war-torn Afghanistan, the film cuts to his university graduation ceremony, symbolizing his acceptance of American cultural ideals. This enables the Western audience to relate to a protagonist who has been speaking in a language other than English for nearly half the duration of the film. Once he settles down to a comfortable life with his wife, also an Afghan refugee, Amir hears that his childhood friend Hassan has died, leaving a young son, Sohrab (Ali Danish Bakhtaran), unprotected in an environment terrorized by the Taliban. Amir rescues Sohrab and brings him to the United States to start a new life.

When Sohrab is shown in the context of the United States, his past experiences in Afghanistan could have worked to his advantage, inviting sympathy for the abuse he suffered. However, his apparent distance, isolation and alienation give him a negative aura. Instead, one feels more affinity with Amir, who has by now become indoctrinated with ideals that the audience can share. Amir is shown as trying hard to integrate Sohrab into this new life but failing to get positive results. Devices used to alienate the character of Sohrab in America include his silence—he acts as if all of a sudden he has become deaf and dumb—his absence from the dinner table during a family dinner, his lack of interest in making friends, and his reluctance to participate in the kite-flying towards the end of the film. Even when he is first shown to his attractive room in Amir's house, Sohrab's lack of communicative skills is designed to portray alienation, although he is now safe within the confines of an American family. His distinct show of disinterest in his comfortable bedroom, the equivalent of which he has never had in his life, and his critical attitude when given the chance to indulge in the most popular pastime of his country of origin (kite flying) seem to suggest that he is not happy being in America and that he is definitely an "emigrant" seeking to go back home. This is despite the fact that earlier in the film, when the audience was first introduced to Sohrab at a compound in Afghanistan, they were invited to feel compassion for him because he was dressed like a girl and forced to entertain Taliban soldiers by dancing for them.

Unlike any of its contemporary films, *The Kite Runner* gives us the opportunity to see the first impressions of a Muslim child immigrant arriving in the United States. The lack of explanation of the character's situation is probably deliberately constructed to further alienate the American audience. He is shaped as a potential threat which resonates with the realities of the spectators' everyday existence. As the film received its U.S. theatrical release during a period of American involvement in Afghanistan, a critical Afghan face on the screen possibly acts as a reminder of the ongoing political hostilities. Equally, the suspicion evoked by watching Sohrab's reluctance to integrate socially, in view of the contrasting lifestyles that he has experienced, triggers a sense of superiority in the Western viewer. The harsh conditions of the Taliban-ruled life in Afghanistan and the character's maltreatment at the hands of Afghan adults, are contrasted with the comforts, opportunities, safety and love that the United States is able to provide. The pessimism that Sohrab is portrayed with slightly changes when Amir shows him how his father, Hassan, used to cut the string of the kites flown by other runners, which brings a shadow of a smile to the child's face. The technique of kite flying that his father mastered builds a bridge between the life left behind and the life found anew, opening up a new possibility of becoming a "'hybrid Other" in this new environment. The film ends with a positive sign—a child's smile—promising that life in America will be more enjoyable for Sohrab in the future.

The Afghan child in this part of *The Kite Runner* has no subjectivity demonstrated through either verbal or non-verbal means. He is simply in the scene as an aloof object. Except for that faint smile right at the end of the film, his feelings are buried behind an inexpressive face through external focalization. This is in contrast to the first part of the film, where the world was reflected through the eyes of two little Afghan boys whose perspectives made them internal focalizers.

## Muslim Minors in Their Country of Origin

Most films in this category reflect either a war-torn environment or places where hostility towards the United States is common, and the child/adolescent characters are active participants in or victims of the conflict. Those minors who are not at arms are used as spectators or bystanders, having an insignificant influence on the film's white American protagonist character.

The contradiction between innocence and war plays out like an oxymoronic element in which a child's innocence is thrust into the reality of conflict, in order to exemplify and exaggerate the chaos and disorder. The youth is no longer a "child" as, in war, the qualities they once possessed have become perverted character traits and the distinction between adult and child has become blurred. Their exposure to war and the lack of adult protection results in a loss of innocence, and what remains is their ability to identify themselves within their environment with simplistic reasoning and action. They remain aesthetically child-like and their analytical judgments are hindered by their lack of crucial skills, which only experience can provide. Their inability to properly grasp and adopt adult-like qualities such as rationality, logic and analysis is predominant in the films used here as case studies.

Each film concentrates either on the effects of local Islamic extremism on the child or deals with Muslim children bearing arms. For example, in *Redacted*, *The Kingdom* and *The Hurt Locker* each child character is portrayed in their natural habitat as it is torn apart by conflict, whether as a consequence of terrorist activities or war between nations. In some cases where the child becomes a device for exploitative gains, they may be utilized in order to establish a link to wider suffering or to generate insight into the current nature of extremist Islamism.

While each child is perceived from the viewpoint of the white centralized American protagonist, he or she remains distinctly ingrained as a figure that is externally focalized. However, in notable films such as *Babel* and *The Kite Runner*, a unique and refreshing dilemma is presented in that the centralized Muslim child character has much more flexibility and depth in the way they are inwardly focalized. Both films differ from *Redacted* and *The Hurt Locker* which tend to depict youth as metonyms, as is evident in the deliberate underdevelopment of character. The death of a child in *The Hurt Locker* and the insertion of a live bomb into his corpse provokes an act of retaliation from the protagonist, Sergeant William James (Jeremy Renner), who deems the atrocity a barbaric act committed against the innocence of youth. A teenage girl is raped in *Redacted*, and children wandering in the war-torn streets of Iraq are conveyed as either vermin or helpless victims. This form of animalization of the ethnic "Other" has been a common theme that Western cinema has been unable to relinquish. The productions still emphasize America's cultural hegemony through imperialist discourse.

Again, in *Redacted* and *The Kingdom* (2007) children are used as a means to antagonize and distract American officials or soldiers from their duties. Especially in *Redacted* and *The Hurt Locker*, Muslim children use the war as a playground in which they are seen playing football with either each other or U.S. soldiers. Their form of pastime, except for playing football, is also out of the ordinary. The two brothers in *Babel* stroll or run about in the hostile wilderness, or try their hands at guns, an activity which is encouraged by their father. At other times, the younger of the boys in the same film finds entertainment by peeping through a crack in the wall at his sister of a similar age getting undressed in her room. His inner focalization and first sexual awakening is incestuously suggested and conveyed at her expense.

Children in *The Kingdom* play with marbles, the innocent-looking and attractively cultured playthings that later turn out to be the containers for explosives used by terrorists to kill the residents of a civilian compound. In *Redacted*, they chase a chicken and in other films they run about like a flock of chickens themselves. They are armed with primitive weapons such as stones, as in *The Stoning of Soraya M.* (2008), or catapults as in *The Kite Runner*. These child characters are projected as uncultivated, uneducated and undisciplined little savages with no morals or future aspirations. They are a permanent fixture of the streets or house windows, mostly watching the American artillery with no expression on their faces. Yet, they are also presented as imitations of Muslim adults, described by an African American officer in *Redacted* as "Midget Ali Babas." The comment necessitates a symbolic reaction as it references a method of storytelling that Lury (2010, 141) claims is present in stories where children are portrayed as victims as well as "resourceful agents who often find their way home, richer and wiser than before." However, since Muslim children are portrayed as thieves or exploiters of a naïve soldier's generosity, they can hardly be the "resourceful agents" that Lury refers to. Intentionally, the children displayed in such large groups are not given a voice but, through their actions, are made to look like scavengers and corrupt products of their environment.

Children in war zones are pictured imitating adult bravura to cope with the circumstances that have been inflicted upon them. A good example of this comes from *The Hurt Locker*, in which a dialogue between a ten-year-old Muslim streetwise boy nicknamed Beckham (Christopher Sayeg) and Sergeant William James (Jeremy Renner) of the U.S. Army shows the audience a child who has lost his innocence through war. Lury (*ibid.*), in her analysis of child characters in war movies, claims that Beckham participates in a prosopopoeial form of expression, mirroring the actions and conduct of adults in an attempt to construct his identity. Here, James (WJ) is complaining about the quality of the DVD Beckham (B) sold him a couple of days earlier:

> WJ: Hey, wait a minute. Look who it is. Give me back my five bucks, buddy.
> B: Five dollars? For what, man? You're crazy enough?
> WJ: The DVD you sold me was a crap.
> B: You're crazy, man? That's impossible. It's Hollywood's special best.
> WJ: It was shaky, it was out of focus, buddy.
> B: What do you want? Donkey porn?
> WJ: It's crap.
> B: Guys on dogs? Gay sex? Man, anything you want.
> WJ: (laughs) OK, all right. What's your name?
> B: Beckham.
> WJ: Beckham like the soccer player?
> B: Yeah, man, like the soccer player. Give me my ball back.
> WJ: You're a soccer player?
> B: Yeah, man, best of the best. I'm better than that.

Black or immigrant children talking in Ebonics is not a novelty in films, but in this case the child is speaking in the midst of blasting bombs, roaring tanks and firing guns. He is singled out as an existentialist mind in the body of a child, using machismo as his survival kit.

The decaying environment seems to be instrumental in the conversion into adulthood and death, and is also seen in *Redacted* and *The Kingdom*. All these films can be categorized within the *Trümmerfilm* genre, which was hugely popular after World War II. The *Trümmerfilm*, otherwise known as the "rubble film," narratively dealt with the harsh realities of civilians having to survive within the confines of an annihilated city in the aftermath of war. The style was mostly adopted by filmmakers in the rebuilding of the film industries of Eastern Europe, Italy and the former Nazi Germany, but has evolved in the process of being incorporated into the U.S. filmmaking sensibility to resonate a more urbanesque feel for environment.

Whether in the form of the persecution that is directed towards them in their American environment or due to a landscape of conflict, hostile environments seem to dominate and affect the children in many of the films mentioned in this chapter. Each child functions within a heterotopian space, but in the particular case of the Muslim war child, it can be argued that they feature in large geographical peripheries or "spaces of abjection where those displaced by poverty, drugs, and armed conflict are to be found" (Ledesma 2012, 153).

*Babel* and *The Kite Runner* are only two of the examples presenting such "spaces of abjection," where Muslim children are subjected to extreme poverty, inhuman treatment and cruelty.

### *Yousef in* Babel *(2006)*

Iñárritu's *Babel* is composed of the intertwined stories of several families, one in Morocco, another in Japan, another in the United States and, finally, one in Mexico. The present analysis is concerned with only the two Moroccan brothers, Yousef (Boubker Ait El Caid), aged ten, and Ahmed (Said Tarchani), aged 12.

Regarding the Muslim setting in *Babel*, Elouardaoui (2011, 6) observes the "the film reinforces a number of regional stereotypes. For instance, the whole story about the Moroccan family is shot in a small village, exposing the miserable life of the locals." However, his observations do not cover the impact of the environmental barrenness on the actions of the two brothers. These actions are primitive and dangerous partly because there is nothing in the area, other than wild nature, to effect a change in their lifestyles.

In comparison, Jackson (2014) suggests that alienation is purposefully worked into the film *Babel*, in which the little mountain boy, Yousef, critically wounds an American woman while playing with a rifle. She suggests that the filmmaker uses themes of "taboos, poverty, and ultimately pain and imprisonment of the Moroccan boy, creating a critical distance between him and the audience" (68). However, the guilt felt by Yousef and his efforts towards redemption, although central themes in the Moroccan segment of the story, go unnoticed by Jackson.

Being the offspring of a poor farmer, they live in the most primitive conditions in a rough-cut limestone house in the mountainous wastes of southern Morocco. They don't go to school but help their father in tending the herd of goats and carrying brushwood bundles to other settlements in the scarcely inhabited landscape. They are projected as uncultivated, uneducated and undisciplined little savages with no future aspirations. Intentionally, these children are not given much of a voice but, through their actions, are portrayed as scavengers and corrupt products of their environment. When they talk, they are at ease lying to their father and, at a later stage, to the security forces. Yousef is presented as the more sophisticated and worldly-wise of the two, always trying to beat his brother at everything. He shoots better, talks more sense, secretly watches his sister through a hole in the wall while she is getting undressed and lies more convincingly. He also wears Western clothes and does not don the white *thobe* as his brother does. Their pastimes are of a simple nature: strolling or running about in the hostile wilderness, always with Yousef in the lead, followed by Ahmed. When their goats are grazing, the boys' idle existence is communicated through cinematographic long shots, showing them running against the sunny yet partly cloudy sky. Their location, however, is the arid, rugged, rocky, yellow mountains instead of green pastures.

An exciting element is introduced to their otherwise dull lives when their father buys a rifle from a neighbor. They have it with them the next day on the mountain and Yousef shoots and hits an approaching bus on the road below, wounding by mistake an American woman tourist on board. The national police, under pressure from the American Embassy, hold an investigation to catch the culprits. In the last scene, the boys and their father are shown running away from the security forces, hurriedly jumping over the barren rocks trying to reach safety. Yousef's animal instincts awake again when his brother Ahmed is shot by the officers. He takes aim at a police officer and wounds him in the arm while his father tries to restrain him. As Ahmed is shot for the second time, Yousef finally gives up, kneels down in front of the police officers and begs for mercy, continuously repeating himself as if he has by now lost any common sense that he might have once had.

The parts of the film concentrating on the Moroccan boys have many scenes of internal focalization. One example is when Ahmed watches Yousef's face light up after their father praises him for being a better marksman. This smile may not mean anything to the adults present, but to Ahmed it is yet another instance of falling behind his younger brother. A further illustration of internal focalization is when Yousef peeps through the hole in the wall to see his sister Zohra (Wahiba Sahmi) undressing. The technique used here is point-of-view (POV) editing. The girl appears through a hole in the wall, seen through Yousef's eyes. The camera then cuts to Ahmed approaching and telling Yousef off for secretly peeping at their sister.

*Babel* demonstrates the behavior of a child when frightened to face the consequences of an offence that he has committed. In this instance, Yousef accuses his brother, who is the person closest to him, of a crime in order to escape punishment. However, his character is molded realistically with depth as there is also a scene of remorse at the end. The section in Morocco closes with him falling on his knees in front of the security team and imploring: "I killed the American, I was the only one who shot at you. They did nothing ... nothing. Kill me, but save my brother, he did nothing ... nothing. Save my brother ... he did nothing. I killed the American."

It is noteworthy that a similar false accusation followed by remorse is a theme in our next case study, *The Kite Runner*.

### Amir in The Kite Runner (2007)

*The Kite Runner* is probably the most memorable film among the present case studies for its depiction of loyalty, betrayal and remorse in childhood friendships. The Afghanistan part of the film starts with a high-angled perspective shot of Kabul in 1978. The aerial views of the city show a striking contrast between the few mansions of the rich in the center and miles of mud-bricked houses with flat roofs in the poor suburbs. The coexistence of extremes is displayed in affluent abodes accommodating lavish garden parties with fireworks, and not-so-affluent quarters where dogs fight next to the food vendors. However, the citizens converge in the main square on the day of the children's kite fight to see who will win this exciting traditional competition. Kites of different patterns and bright colors float in the sky and groups of shrieking children run in all directions to pick up the fallen kites whose strings have been cut by other kites, demonstrating that the place is still happy and vibrant despite the unfair distribution of wealth and the looming Soviet invasion.

Two child characters are at the center of the narrative. They are ten-year-old Amir, the son of a rich philanthropist Agha Sahib, and eight-year-old Hassan, whose father is Agha Sahib's servant. There is a strong bond between the boys and they spend time together chatting on the outskirts of the city under a pomegranate tree, which is the only living thing in a vast arid expanse occupied by a graveyard.

During one of their meetings, Amir carves something in Pashto on the tree; subtitles in English translate the carving: "Amir and Hassan, Sultans of Kabul." Amir does not have any other friends but Hassan is always conscious of the class distinction between them; he looks up to and respects Amir and at one point says, "I would eat dirt for you if you asked." The difference in their personalities is voiced by Agha Sahib in a confidential conversation with a family friend, when he complains about Amir being too placid and not standing up for himself: "Amir never fights back. Hassan steps in and fends them [the bullies] off." Indeed, one day Hassan, with his catapult, scares off some streetwise boys who are about to bully Amir. The same boys, however, corner Hassan on another occasion and rape him in an isolated back street. While this is happening, Amir stands behind a staircase, watching the atrocious incident and not doing anything to save Hassan. Sometime after the boys leave the scene, Hassan comes out of the alley where he lost all dignity and his virginity, stumbling along the road while blood drips from his trousers, leaving a red trail on the snowy ground. Unable to cope with his own cowardice, Amir accuses Hassan of stealing money and his watch and thus tries to throw him out of his sight and life. Agha Sahib confronts Hassan, who, rather than calling Amir a liar, falsely accepts the guilt. After this, Hassan and his father leave Amir's house, which is later abandoned when Russian troops enter Afghanistan. Agha Sahib flees to Pakistan with Amir before the Communists arrive in Kabul.

The camera transmits Amir's feelings by capturing his facial expressions. The expressions of shock and helplessness on his face while he watches Hassan's ordeal with the street boys are especially effective. The close-up spectacle of his eyes in between the steps of the ladder, behind which he is hiding, conveys the anguish he is experiencing. The way Amir destroys the future of his only friend who has given him so much should invoke a feeling of disgust in the audience, but by displaying his emotional turmoil with the help of close-ups, the technique of internal focalization seeks understanding and empathy from the viewer. Amir stands out as a child forced to betray a loved one and make a false accusation but, unlike Yousef in Babel (2006), he defers his redemption to much later in life. As an adult, he returns to his home country to take Hassan's son with him to America. In switching between different types of focalization on a Muslim child—external on Sohrab in the States, and internal on Amir in Afghanistan—the filmmaker makes Amir the "eyes" of the narrative and the audience watches the film from the viewpoint of this tormented individual.

*The Kite Runner* is extensively analyzed by Dong (2013) as a "war zone children's film." He regards the time spent as a minor in Afghanistan, even before the Russian invasion, as a mixture of carefree and happy moments frequently interrupted by lies, discrimination and violence. Two sexually disturbing scenes, one which indicates that Hassan is being raped by an older boy in a quiet alley, and another showing his son becoming a dancing boy for the same rapist, are only two of the instances that collectively show the detrimental effects of poverty and war on children. Dong (*ibid.*, 196) observes that the film represents the "atrocities of war through the lens of Afghan children with virtually no direct portrayal of the battle scenes." Explaining the film's storyline over several pages, he draws attention to the reason why Amir had to take Hassan's son Sohrab to America: "Portrayed as another victim, Sohrab now provides Amir with the opportunity for redemption" (*ibid.*, 204). Although most of the critical positions in Dong's article are consistent with the current analysis, Amir's keen sense of guilt, which is the binding force between his childhood and adult life (and leads him to redeem his early disloyalty by rescuing Hassan's son from Afghanistan), is not the focal point of this study.

## Conclusion

The historical development of the cinematic coverage of children in general has been looked at in this chapter to assist the comparison and to introduce relevant concepts in transnationalism, such as diaspora, focalization and post-colonial studies, which are key for analytical purposes. The most notable point to surface is that in the second half of the last century, Muslim child portraits were either under the influence of Orientalist romanticism or used the character as a silent entity, who could help eradicate the problems that challenge the protagonist. In other examples, an Eastern youngster looked or talked like an American, becoming the mouthpiece for current ideologies. In either case, these underdeveloped and one-dimensional character types, with the exception of *Aladdin* (1992), were of secondary importance in the overall progress of the narrative, being situated outside the *fabula*, and focalized externally.

Starting with the new century and intensifying in the course of the following ten years, the Muslim child image has undergone significant changes, depending on where they are presented in the film. Regardless of their location, a fully developed character arc is established while the child becomes a central component in the narrative, with embedded behavioral, psychological and/or emotional features. These features have been mentioned in reference to a number of films and presented in a more focused way in the analysis of *Pretty Persuasion* (2005), *Babel* (2006) and *The Kite Runner* (2007). In the two, additional thematic similarities are noticed, such as betrayal and redemption, and the loss of childhood after being subjected to crimes of a sexual nature.

The effects of international confrontations in Muslim countries have generated child characters whose representation raises ambiguities about whether they are children-at-arms or victims of war. In war-torn country settings, they are also portrayed as a part of the tragedy developing around them. Both in appearance and behavior, they are presented as being harmonious with the apparent decadence and devastation in their landscape. They talk and act in excessively macho ways, in contradiction to their obviously tender age; they are children with no childish qualities.

As for those characters portrayed as living in the United States, the issue at hand is identity recognition. Because a large proportion of the existing theoretical work on children in the movies is related to American youth, if not to black or Hispanic youth, it does not fully account for the Muslim child characters' striving for identity. This struggle is better explained by the concept of "hybrid Otherness," which is a development on Bhabha's (1996) notion of hybridity. In light of this theory, celluloid youngsters appear to be coerced or manipulated by family or elders into embracing their cultural responsibilities and their duty to (Islamic) law or social norms. They are shown to be totally determined in their quest for recognition, even if the route takes them to a dead end, resulting in loneliness, separation from family or death. They receive no compassion from law enforcers and even a 15-year-old can be shot at and killed in cold blood if he is too persistent in claiming his identity.

Equally important is the manner in which the Muslim child is focalized externally compared to internally focalized youth. While there are exceptions to this claim, it seems that past filmic incarnations favored external focalization, although in the decade under observation more and more films have presented their Muslim youngsters through internal focalization. The internally focalized child has achieved something that was never accomplished in American cinema prior to 9/11: s/he provides viewing knowledge through his/her point of view so that the position-dependent spectator can gain the ability to imagine a unique standpoint different from their own.

If American cinema continues with a fair depiction of the Muslim child, the filmmakers could do no better than adopt Jones' (2008) stance, which offers a remedy to the dilemma of the adult's agenda colonizing children's spaces on the screen. He comments that before we can begin to do children justice we must "first acknowledge the otherness of children and the great asymmetries of body, knowledge, emotion, imagination which exist between adulthood and childhood" (206). But more important than the physical differences, which are easy to replicate, cultural idiosyncrasies need to be apprehended well so that the depiction will be of the substance, not the fantasy.

# 7
# The Normalization of the Muslim World

In the history of American cinema, the image of Islam and the portrayal of Muslims have changed many times, with varying degrees of negative undertones in each phase of this evolution. Ramji (2016, 1) explains that American cinema has "used images to construct sentiment, to strengthen attachment, and to promote replication, and it has reproduced its relationship to the Orient in an ever-changing progression." With the aim of investigating the current stage in this progression, each chapter in this study has focused on a different aspect of the world of Islam and how it is represented, but while the findings can answer the question "What are the most noticeable changes in the depiction of this alternative world?" they do not throw much light on the reasons *why* these changes have taken place. Unlike earlier periods in film history, regarding which there is a consensus that representation was influenced by America's politics towards the Middle East, for the post–9/11 period, apart from such political and economic affairs, analysts propose additional reasons for the way the East has come to be perceived. However, in the course of the current study no single text incorporating all possible causes for the changes has come to light. For this reason, this chapter collates the views expressed by different scholars so that a more collective pool of motives is made available.

Two main rationales for the emergence and maintenance of stereotypes—the psychologists' explanation that stereotypes ease the cognition process, and the sociologists' interpretation that stereotypes boost the feeling of superiority among in-group members—provide convincing reasons for the presence of stereotypes in general but do not satisfactorily explain why stereotypes change. The fluctuations in the use of stereotypes indicate that they have further, fine-grained purposes, which may tell us more about what instigates their modification at certain points in time.

Morey and Yaqin (2011, 31) mention three overlapping functions, two of which are the "social causal" function, "where the stereotyped group is seen as the cause of an event (such as economic recession or acts of terrorism)," and the "social justificatory" function, where "stereotypes are created to justify behavior towards a given group (as in the denigration of the Other in colonialism, slavery or in official rhetoric about the detainees at Guantanamo)." In these examples it is noticeable that socio-political and economic events are the milestones for such functional aspects of stereotypes. Similarly, Arti (2007) attributes the continuation of the negative typology of Muslim characters in film to a number of political events.[1] Shaheen (2003a, 29) also comments that "[r]ight through the 1980s and the 1990s, and into the twenty-first century, the 'bad people' image prevailed, especially during the Palestinian intifada and the Israeli invasion of Lebanon." With regard to the reasons for the intensified anti–Arab feeling and more damaging film representations, he also refers to the Iranian hostage crisis in the 1970s, the Iraqi invasion of Kuwait leading to the Gulf War in 1990s, and the destruction of the World Trade Center in 2001. Almost all these factors are in fact originally mentioned by Said (1997) in *Covering Islam: How the Media and the Experts Determine How We See the Rest of the World*. What follows from all this is that after events that threaten national security, interests or values, stereotypes are either developed or enriched with new characteristics, or they undergo a change. These fluctuations in the nature of stereotypes seem to depend on the escalation of, or reduction in, tensions between the United States and the national groups being depicted. We can deduce from this correlation between the political situation and celluloid image formation that the more strained the relationship between a nation and the United States, the more repulsive the image of its nationals in films. This was the equation during the Cold War, the Vietnam War and the war in Afghanistan. In the latter case, for instance, the same group had contrasting images at different times depending on where it stood in terms of America's changing interests: *Rambo 3* (1988) depicts the Taliban as a useful ally when Russia had to be driven out of the country, but in *The Kite Runner* (2007) the Taliban is the enemy and the filmic presentation of its members is hateful.

As the shock caused by the 9/11 disaster was unlike anything America had ever experienced, it was bound to cause significant changes in all areas of social and political life.[2] Representing Muslims in films by intensifying their vilification and demonization would have been meaningful as a form of figurative retribution and reprisal, or manifestation of fear (Michalak 2010, Semmerling 2006), but quite the contrary happened, with Muslim terrorists disappearing from the theatre screens for several years and narrative cinema projecting some normalized, ordinary Muslim characters thereafter. This unprecedented situation requires an explanation other than, or at least in addition to, the one based on politics that we have been accustomed to. The effects of third-wave feminism and transnational cinema mentioned earlier appear to be further reasons contributing to the softening attitude.

The avoidance of making films about terrorism during the period 2001–2005 was apparently due to the film industry's respect for public sensitivities. When the public went through a quiet period, nursing its psychological wounds, it was spared the disturbing images of the incident or anything resembling it. It seems the media and the film industry decided not to release films thought to be too traumatic for the victimized public. As Cettl (2009, 14) mentions, "[t]hose films already in progress were completed and released, some of them modified beforehand, but terrorism as a subject was considered off-limits." Ten years later, on 8 September 2011, Bradshaw reported in *The Guardian*'s Film blog: "For years after the attacks, a kind of willed blindness set in. Due to an unacknowledged understanding among broadcasters, only the most distant shots of the plane's impacts were shown on TV screens.... It wasn't until YouTube was launched two years afterwards that people could see these blackly horrifying images." After this recuperation period, however, the action movies returned and some of them involved normalized Muslim characters. At the same time, TV programs were packed with "hate crimes, workplace discrimination, bias incidents, and airline discrimination targeting Arab and Muslim Americans," aiming to attract sympathy for the hardships they were subjected to in an atmosphere where all Muslims were held responsible for the disaster (Alsultany 2013, 161). The imagined Muslim space, bulging with Orientalist elements and clichés pre–9/11, has gradually been replaced with true-to-life locations, and the human element in this space has similarly evolved to such an extent that while the undeveloped, flat, "only good" and "only bad" characters of the past remain to cause nuisance in the storyline, they have been eclipsed by the newly developed complex characters with multifaceted personality traits, as we have seen in the analytical sections in this book. This is, indeed, a transformation noticed by a number of analysts, including Sultana (2013) who divides the current filmic portraits into "radicals" and "moderates" in the same way that Yenigün (2004, 46) does:

> The mainstream American media stopped essentializing the Muslim world as a monolithic bloc whose basic character of Islam overrode all of its inner differences and proved that these differences were irrelevant. Instead, a differentiation strategy between two types of Muslims was pursued: Fundamentalists (i.e., Muslim extremists, Islamists, Islamic radicals) vs. moderate Muslims. The mainstream media, following the government, was careful to maintain a fine line between these two groups. While moderate Muslims were not considered a threat to American interests, fundamentalists/extremists were considered enemies.[3]

Some analysts have preferred to categorize these contrasting character types not from the viewpoint of terrorism, but by using general qualifiers like "positive" and "negative." For instance, Alsultany (2013, 161) considers it strange that after 9/11, "[i]f a TV drama or Hollywood film represented an Arab or Muslim as a terrorist, then the story line usually included a 'positive' representation of an Arab or Muslim to offset the negative depiction."

Similarly, Michalak (2010) defines the fresh introductions as "positive portrayals," as opposed to "negative portrayals." In his analysis of 23 American films produced between 1999 and 2010, Michalak (*ibid.*) finds that 11 of these (in other words, almost half) project Arab, Muslim or Middle Eastern characters in a favorable light. Of the remaining productions, five reiterate the old stereotypes (though three of these were made before but released after 9/11, so are technically pre–9/11 productions), and eight represent the Muslim character neutrally.

There are similarities in the way different analysts have interpreted these portrayals. In Sultana's (2013, 69) reasoning, "The good Muslim is westernized, English speaking, comfortable with women etc. while the bad Muslim is religious—when reversed all religious Muslims are potential threats." This definition is almost the same as that attempted by Bradshaw (2011, 4): "The good Muslim character in Hollywood films is the westernized Muslim." A similar critical stance is exhibited by Alsultany (2013, 162): "[P]ositive representations of Arabs and Muslims have helped form a new kind of racism, one that projects antiracism and multiculturalism on the surface but simultaneously produces the logics and affects necessary to legitimize racist policies and practices." These views, however, do not take into account the recent changes in narrative construction, where the Muslim characters are assigned the role of a protagonist who is central to how the story unfolds. Nor do they give due attention to the way Muslim space is nowadays represented not as a static location where "evil" Arabs do their dirty work, but as an environment to which both the East and the West contribute. It may be the city of Baghdad seen through the Americans' green surveillance monitors, or the city of New York gazed upon by a disillusioned Muslim immigrant. Unless the whole picture is evaluated in its entirety, in which this study claims originality, the changes in national/cultural representations cannot be correctly identified.

Favorable portraits also include those character types termed "Use Value Muslims" by Morey and Yaqin (2011). The origins of this character type may be found in America's reluctance to employ ground forces in modern-age conflicts. Regarding this, we can refer to Zizek (2002) who says finding local friends to fight local enemies is what America needs to be doing while policing the world. Mokdad (2013, 88) expresses reservations about the use of this character type and wonders if their inclusion in the films is "just another way of stifling or thwarting dissent," a point which she claims deserves further investigation.

There is certainly a need for further investigation into the reasons why the Muslim world is presently depicted in a less monolithic and more realistic way because no single factor on its own adequately explains this, although the following are some of the possible motives.

## Political Atmosphere 2001–2011

The way the War on Terror was conducted by the Bush administration attracted serious criticism with respect to many issues including civil liberties, the cost of newly implemented security measures, the invasion of Iraq and Afghanistan on unjustified grounds, and the treatment of suspects gathered at Guantanamo Bay prison. Cettl (2009, 16) writes:

> That is what the Bush years amounted to: a wave of patriotism replaced by a moral consideration of just what Bush et al. had turned America into during the War on Terror, just what compromises to democracy and the Constitution were made. And although the films were exciting, immediate and tense in a way they were not before, the cinema of terrorism became the primary means for the political criticism and assessment of America's War on Terror legacy. Terrorists were clearly defined as religiously inspired (as were their adversaries in the Bush government…) and a new concern for religious and cultural sensitivity to the Muslim world infiltrated films such as *Body of Lies* and *Traitor*.

It is therefore possible that an inclination developed in the United States, after the planes acted as missiles attacking the World Trade Center and the Pentagon, to learn how Muslims and Arabs think, feel and might act when pressed, rather than employ the brutal force that the Bush administration preferred, as a solution in the Middle East. Knowing Muslims better and representing them in the media more favorably might be the outcome of this need.

## Turning Disaster into Opportunity

Some public view makers have argued that the experience of 9/11 could be turned into an opportunity for the United States to raise its profile in the world arena, and have advocated that a sympathetic approach should be adopted in the way Muslims are envisaged. Judith Butler (2004), for instance, views the post-attack period as a gateway for America to form better relations with the rest of the world by showing a unified front. For Alsultany (2013, 162) too, "the production and circulation of 'positive' representations of the 'enemy' have become essential to projecting the United States as benevolent, especially in its declaration of war and passage of racist policies." She also remarks that "[i]t is no longer the case that the other is explicitly demonized to justify war or injustice. Now the other is portrayed sympathetically in order to project the United States as an enlightened country that has entered a postrace era" (*ibid.*, 162). Although contradicted by some other observers, she alleges that TV programs after the attack started begging for sympathy towards Muslim Americans by showing them as either (1) patriotic Muslim American characters, (2) Muslim Americans who are subjected to hatred, racism and hardship, or (3) Muslim males driven to terrorism because of their experience of past misfortunes.[4]

## *The Communications Revolution and Easy Access to Knowledge*

With the advent of the communications revolution, the world has rapidly emerged from the analogue era and proceeded into a digital landscape which, by access to and exposure through social media and news outlets, has provided people with opportunities to explore and exchange thoughts and ideas with others from all walks of life. The increasing awareness of global affairs—including those concerning the Muslim world—resulting from easy access to all parts of the world, either in actuality or virtually, has kept curiosity levels high regarding any changes happening in other nations and their cultures. Although propaganda and the flow of information had been controlled and centralized by government regimes, the communications revolution has aided a better understanding of the global landscape. Orientalism has been affected as a consequence, as we are now furnished with facilities to reach others with different beliefs, viewpoints and doctrines and can make up our own minds about these variables instead of relying on unsubstantiated information. Regarding the importance of information technology for self-education on foreign nations and cultures, Yenigün (2004, 44), who has investigated the "Muslim discourse" developed in American media after 9/11, proposes that "[i]t is easy to find many Muslim organizations, along with their press releases, on the web. Given this fact, focusing on the Internet media seems to be a far more appropriate way to approach this whole issue. More importantly, thanks to the Internet's development, news stories in the printed and visual media can now be accessed, thereby making the Internet an all-encompassing media source." Consequently, websites, among other kinds of media, have been used by Muslim Americans who "have become interested in establishing interfaith dialogue, [and] engaging with Christians and Jews" (el-Aswad 2013, 50).

## *Experts and NGOs Helping Muslims Raise Their Profile*

Understanding the world of Islam better rather than dealing with it as a form of fantasy is the kind of enthusiasm spurred by 9/11. The violent attacks have incited "[p]rofessionals from both the academia and the media industry in the United States to approach the Arab-Islamic culture with an inquisitive and unbiased mind, aiming at a better understanding of its main tenets and principles. This might be in part the reason behind the shift that has taken place in regards to the representation of Arabs in several post–9/11 Hollywood films" (Elouardaoui 2011, 11). Similarly, el-Aswad (2013, 48) reports that in order to educate the public on Islam, "public lectures, sermons, conferences, workshops and media programs have ... been made by Muslim scholars and media activists to present Muslims positively at both national and global levels."

Developing familiarity with the East has been possible as a result of reduced airfares, increased mobility and curiosity. Salazer (2004) and Wilkins (2009, 29–41) have separately observed and collated data from random American focus groups and have come to similar conclusions. They have found that people's response towards favorable and unfavorable film portrayals have been dependent on their experiences in Arab countries and on having Arab friends. el-Aswad (2013, 49) reports that a recent survey conducted by Pew Research Center found "modest increases in Americans' familiarity with Islam compared with the months following the 9/11 attacks." Those people who know a Muslim are found to be less likely to see Islam and Muslims as encouraging violence.

There is also a marked increase in the number of NGOs complaining about the vilification of Arabs in films. Elouardaoui (2011, 11) additionally draws attention to the usefulness of, for instance, the "interfaith activities led by the Public Affairs Council situated in Southern California in order to help shatter the old stereotypes about the Arab-Islamic culture." In addition to existing NGOs, new ones have been established to rid people's minds of unfounded views against Muslims. el-Aswad (2013, 48) gives the examples of the Council on American-Islamic Relations (CAIR), the Islamic Society of North America (ISNA), the American Moslem Society (AMS), the American-Arab Anti-Discrimination Committee (ADC) and many others, which have been set up and are active for this purpose.

## Increased Input from Muslim Professionals in the Film Industry

The changes observed in the post–9/11 films are attributed by some to professional Muslims holding more positions in the creative sector. Ramji (2016, 11), for instance, reports that the "normal" Muslim character has made a comeback in independent films written or directed mostly by Muslims, and cites as an example *Towelhead* (2007), starring Aaron Eckhart and Toni

Collette, adapted from a novel originally written by Arab-American, Alicia Erian. Similarly, Shaheen (2008a, 8) notes that there are now a number of Arab-American or Muslim American directors working in the film industry and contributing works like *Man Push Cart* (2005), *Salt of this Sea* (2008), *Slingshot Hip Hop* (2008), *Three Veils* (2009), *David and Fatima* (2008), *American East* (2008), and *Amreeka* (2009). These writers and directors have brought a new perspective into the film industry, offering the public at large the view that the majority of Muslims should be distinguished from a handful of fundamentalists.

## *New Finance from Arab Countries for the U.S. Film Industry*

Since the latter half of the twentieth century, there has been a rising trend of foreign wealth and investment in the West, none more so than Arab investment in global economic hubs such as London, New York and Los Angeles. The film sector in the United States has been of particular significance as the rise of Middle Eastern investments has resulted in unofficial bilateral arrangements, with film schools and festivals (such as the NYU Abu Dhabi University and College, and the Doha Tribeca Film Festival) being initiated with the intent of training up-and-coming Arab Muslim artists in the ways of American filmmaking. In return, Middle Eastern investments in U.S. cinema have come from notable sources such as the Beirut based FFA Private Bank and Abu Dhabi's Image Nation. As this commerce has affected cultural representations through an exchange of ideas and finance, it has made a difference not only to Orientalist, but also Occidental perceptions. With future plans underway to build upon this successful union, it may be possible to conceive that the shift in Orientalist representations will be further developed to a point where Islam and its radical off-shoots will be clearly defined in contrast to their current tendency to be monolithically conceived as the "Other."

Finally, to summarize this section on the reasons why the Muslim world has been constructed favorably after 9/11, this citation from Meiloud (2007, 26) is informative:

> Despite Hollywood's long history of presenting Arabs as the embodiment of the dark side of human nature, the last five years witnessed a significant positive shift in Arabs' image in Hollywood films. It is ironic that after the terrorist attack of 9/11, which has reinforced among considerable sections of American population the image that has been fed to them for quite some time, such change would emerge. Americans were shocked by 9/11, and they might perhaps for the large part have felt that the clock was ticking for revenge. This was a quite understandable feeling under such circumstances.

Simultaneously, however, they were eager to know what were the motives of those who carried out the attack and who they represented. This questioning mood left the door ajar to myriads of possible answers, a phenomenon you would anticipate in a democratic society.

The list of reasons collated above to answer the question "Why?" is definitely not exhaustive and has much room for expansion but, even as it stands, it provides adequate evidence that not one but many factors have affected the surprising change in the representation of Muslims in films after 9/11. Research into the following ten years, covering 2011 to 2021 may add further factors affecting the image improvements that have been the subject matter of the current work. It may also show us whether the global conjectures of the new decade will have necessitated even further changes in how the Muslim world is perceived by both the makers and viewers of films.

# 8
# "Be sincere, be brief, be seated"[1]

This study has demonstrated that the celluloid depiction of the Muslim world in American cinema has changed after 9/11 in line with the tendency among the public to view the East in a more pragmatic way than they did before. It has made evident that the old-fashioned Orientalist stereotyping is no longer adequate for securing credibility with audiences whose awareness of other cultures and peoples has developed through increased exposure to the media and internet, and greater global mobility. America's extensive policing presence in the world and, hence, its firsthand experience in many countries have also been factors that have helped the public increase their knowledge of different peoples and cultures, and subsequently become dissatisfied with delusive depictions based on fossilized tropes.

One of the areas of interest in this study has been whether new forms of thought, tendencies and trends, such as those which have developed from successive waves of feminism and transnational cinema, have taken precedence over the old-fashioned Orientalist heritage and, hence, made its essentialist approach to the "Orient" less conspicuous in films. The study has approached the subject comparatively to find out how Muslim space and Muslim people were depicted in the past and how they are formulated now. This unique panoramic view has shown that the cinematic depictions of the world of Islam until the 1950s bore Hollywood's hallmark of spectacular scenes adorned with dance, color, music, sparkling costumes and jewelry. The tone changed noticeably from the 1970s, when films depicted the Muslim world with menacing men and tormented women, not to mention the uncontrolled children in war-torn cities with dilapidated buildings. The effect of the formation of the state of Israel in 1948 introduced a vilified cinematic Muslim character, bent on the fanatical destruction of U.S. interests abroad. During this period, America's military might was suspended over the followers of Islam and their lands like the sword of Damocles, and the repercussions were felt in cinema. The Muslim overseas was subjected to a continuous process of "Othering" that offered little else than xenophobic conjecture. The Arab became associated with a particular role that homogenized all Arabs (indeed, sometimes non-Arabs or non-Muslims as well) into one monolithic spectacle which has served as "a cultural warehouse from which stock images and narratives can be wheeled out to explain international events or to justify foreign and domestic policies" (Teo, 2012, 9).[2] The aftermath of the 9/11 terrorist attack, on the other hand, demanded a revisionist approach to how the West perceived Islam and the locations where it is revered. This revision has benefited the Muslim world, which has come to be represented in more favorable terms, contrary to what one might have expected during the War on Terror period. While old-school stereotypes and forms of "Othering" still appear on the screens, a more convincing Muslim world has begun to be illustrated. Some of the changes may have started taking shape even before the events of 9/11, but such sporadic modifications have become more constant in American cinema in the years following the Al-Qaida attack. As well as a variety of other factors affecting this evolution, ideas and arguments developed under the rubric of feminism and transnational cinema are also found to be responsible for this partial departure from the traditional Orientalist approach.

It has been argued that in the pre-9/11 period Muslim space (Chapter 2) was simply a setting where the tropes indicative of the Muslim world were placed in abundance, with an underlying sentiment of contempt for, or fascination with, the exotic. One type of Muslim space, the desert, was used in the classical period as a battleground for primitive tribes to settle their scores, while love stories flourished in the colorful environment of the nearby exotic city. In its past depiction, with its ever-changing physical conditions, the desert terrified even the locals themselves, casting an impeding cloud of doom and fear. In comparison, in the second half of the last century, it turned into an expansive void, the natural movements of which helped narrative events to develop. In both cases, though, the desert did not have a part to play in the film, nor did it interact with the humans living in or passing through it. In the post-9/11 period, however, the desert is treated differently, as though life has been injected into it, so that it can become a character in its own right in the narrative, in reciprocity with its inhabitants, influencing and also being influenced by them. A device previously implemented in *Lawrence of Arabia* (1962) and later used in *Hidalgo* is the projection of space interacting with the characters' psychological state—natural changes in the space being reflected in the protagonist's mood and vice versa. In this way, due to the angle at which the camera is positioned, abundant wilderness is used as a means to foretell the narrative's dramatic developments. The desert is now a changeable force which, despite its opaque, monumental sand dunes, is able to dramatically assert its conditional power over those who inhabit it. It is a landscape invested with ideology, expressing a condition of excitement but also of fear. Those who inhabit the desert are considered a naturalized part of its landscape. Occasionally, as in the case of *Sex and the City 2* (2010), the desert is also an illusory entity that plays to romantic Orientalist assumptions about a geographic region filled with mysticism and promise. At other times, it is a mercilessly battered living being, too devastated to strike back (*Three Kings*), or a mighty fighter that uses all its weapons on the hero, testing its power and his resilience (*Hidalgo*). With the transnational character imposed on it by other visitors, however, it is not a space indicative only of one race and one culture anymore. It is currently presented as carrying the imprints of Muslims as well as non–Muslims, whom it treats equally.

In the latter part of the twentieth century, the Middle Eastern city was similarly given new meaning as a dilapidated ruin. Its congregation points, streets and souks moved down the ladder, from being a place of color, Eastern mysticism and vitality to providing a hiding place for fundamentalists and terrorists. The present analysis has highlighted the fact that while Lamont's 1949 production, *Bagdad*, presents a city radiant with all the Eastern tropes, Post, the director of *The Human Shield* (1991), creates a drab, partly demolished location with no history or drive to excite its inhabitants, visitors or spectators. Both are imagined spaces with no resemblance to how the city actually was at the time. In neither film is there any interaction between the population and the location, nor is the city looked at from the viewpoint of its inhabitants/visitors. A change, however, is noticeable in the period of our concern with the destruction of Baghdad taking place right in front of the audience's eyes, through the night images captured by CNN cameras. What is projected onto the screen draws the spectator back to March 2003 to relive the bomb shells blasting like fireworks on and around the river Tigris (*Green Zone*). This is the depiction of a city being punished mercilessly for reasons unknown even to the Americans themselves. While the slow motion of a shell shattering a wall creates a contrast with the hysterical commotion of the people, the make-do cafeteria set up for the foreigners in the stately hall of the presidential palace provides another example of incongruity. This and other films made in the 2001–2011 period prove that the person–environment transactions create convincing, realistic spectacles and make the narrative move forward.

A further observation is the change in our habit of correlating a place with a certain set of people. We presently see in American cinema that this correlation has been disturbed. The wilderness is up for grabs now and can be conquered by an American cowboy (and his horse) as easily as the city of New York can provide a desolate Muslim space to an immigrant. The desert might be harboring not only the evil Arabs, but also the evil colonial antagonists, just like the city of Baghdad, which is transformed into a no-man's land by the heavy military technology of the United States and the hysteria of the locals. The national and cultural boundaries for any space are not as boldly drawn as before.

This study has also found improvements in character formation. Looking back, we notice that the male Muslim character had always been monolithic (until recently) and essentialized, although it must be said that the nature of the stereotypes employed had not always been of the same kind (Chapter 3). A mixture of "only good" and "only bad" Arabs of the earlier periods was replaced in the 1950s by the "only bad" fundamentalist, in response to the political and economic pressures of the time. This tendency persisted for several decades, with the Muslim character being an antagonist at worst and the hero's helper at best, but always remaining in a supporting role. In the post–9/11 period, however, some male and female Muslim characters have been promoted to the lead role, while white characters provide support in the narrative development. At the time when this reformulation was taking shape, U.S. cinema was simultaneously creating a hybrid Muslim character who comprised a balance of both Western ideology and Islamic beliefs. As a result, more respect-inspiring representations of the Muslim "Other" have started to populate the screen, alongside acceptable figures like the naïve accomplices and "Use Value Arabs" (Morey and Yaqin 2011). We now witness the stereotypical "evil" Arab existing in the same frame as an idealistic ruler who nurtures respectable aspirations (like the two prince brothers in *Syriana*, 2005), demonstrating that new images are being developed to exist alongside old clichés. During this period, we even see a complex character formulation whereby the stereotypical tyrant figure of the East is blended with the loving father figure of the West (Abbasi Fawal in *Rendition* and Sheikh Riyadh in *Hidalgo*), illustrating that the fixation with "only good" and "only bad" Arabs is becoming an anomaly of the past.

A further noticeable fact is that while there has been an increase in celluloid African American characters in prominent positions—*The Kingdom* (2007); *House of Sand and Fog* (2003); *The Hurt Locker* (2008)—Muslim black Americans only appear in two films: *Malcolm X* (1992) and *Ali* (2001). Both were produced before 9/11 and represent the main characters with great reverence.

With critics raising their voice against vilifying representations, a more objective approach is called for. In response, Hollywood has developed an ability to reformulate the narratives and characters that it had been so hesitant to reconsider for nearly 90 years. The preference for the familiarity of a stereotype over a more complex, "ordinary" Muslim has been in the process of changing, so much so that in some productions the recognizable tropes do not exist at all.³ Another striking novelty is the projection of the Eastern man not as a practicing Muslim, but simply an immigrant whose dreams of prosperity have been shattered by the ruthless conditions of capitalism and the pressures of a metropol in the United States (*Man Push Cart*) or a Gulf kingdom (*Syriana*).

It is noteworthy that the formulation of the terrorist has evolved in the post–9/11 era. Productions such as *Body of Lies* and *Syriana* offer a balanced analysis of the emergence of a Muslim reactionary while simultaneously faulting the national ideology that is based on alienation. These films question the means by which governmental administrations conduct their activities in dealing with the East, and implicitly blame American policies for the upsurge in terrorism. It is during the same period that terrorism has even become a comedic topic. A case in point is the satirical portrayal of Muslims in *Team America: World Police* (2004), which parodies the reconstruction of fundamentalism. It manages to satirize Hollywood's essentialization of the Arab terrorist, who is projected as muttering incomprehensible, monolithic words, some of which sound like "Jihad" or "Mohammad."

Resulting partly from the need to develop a counter-image to the female Muslim terrorist of the 1990s, and partly from the impact of the feminist movement on popular culture, the Muslim male image has suffered a blow to its masculinity at the hands of the white woman of formidable strength (Chapter 4). In the development of this strong and superior female character, the film narrative is progressively built around gullible, hapless and pathetic Muslim men who have no chance against the invincible superwoman of the West. Films such as *Sorry, Haters*, *The Kingdom*, and *Sex and the City 2* introduce this female character and a pitiful Muslim male opponent as reflections of third-wave feminism's crusade against male tyranny. Furthermore, the incidents at Abu Ghraib related to Lynndie England, and the story of Jessica Lynch, resonated around the world and consequently filtered into cinematic narratives in the form of a strong female personality in which both feminine and masculine attributes are amalgamated, reflecting feminists' assertions of intersectionality and individualist identity. Resulting from the reformulation of genders, the Muslim man is pushed into a humiliating position and represented as a victim destined to lose out in the struggle.⁴

This study has also noted a significant change in the way the Muslim woman is depicted pre- and post–9/11 (Chapter 5). In the exoticized and romanticized historical approach of the past, the Muslim female figure was used as a symbolic token, metaphorically embodying the cultural clash of opposing ideologies. She complemented the oriental space by ornamenting the projected cinematic frame as an insignificant figure in background scenes, her veil reinforcing stereotypical beliefs that she was oppressed. Alternatively, her sensuality was foregrounded when she was presented in the role of a belly dancer or odalisque (concubine). Her indelible figure, capable of seduction, exoticism and romanticism, additionally offered a quasi-fetishistic device onto which the post-colonial male was able to project his sexual fantasies by disrobing her.

Artistically, the *burka* and *niqab* have required revision with regard to how the female is to be conceptualized in a post–9/11 context. While the obscuring of the female form through cultural attire frustrated Westernized interpretations of gender roles in the latter part of the last century, former apparels have been replaced by the *hijab*. Head-to-toe cover of the Muslim female form has been used only to amplify the contrast she provides to a Western woman, or to assist the turns of surprise in the narrative. We see this surprise element in *Sex and the City 2* when a group of unidentifiable Arab women discard their robes to reveal their outfits of the latest Western fashion and amaze their trendy American counterparts. We also see it in *Rules of Engagement* when the innocent looking *burka* conceals female terrorists. The use of this ploy aside, the identity of the Muslim woman has been revealed by degrees in recent films, the degree again being dependent on local constraints. Exposing her body as a spectacle does not invite the male gaze as intensely as it did in the past because her sensuality is now only a small part of a large package consisting of developed identity, education, professional standing, political awareness, situational attributions, and in some cases, partner control. She is presently a complex figure by way of which themes of love, lovemaking and the kiss can be explored. While feelings of hate and her rage are limited to depictions of the female terrorist, which is not a widely employed character type, films such as *House of Sand and Fog*, *Body of Lies* and *Rendition* present a female who not only displays tenacious characteristics, but also introduces active traits that affect the course of the narrative. The code of her emotional state can differ substantially from film to film, but gone are the days when she was considered inept and in need of rescue. This is the filmic emancipation of the Muslim woman whose inner strength is now out in the open for everyone to see. Third-wave feminists' expedition to liberate the women of the East is likely to have influenced the development of this new female Muslim's image.

Meanwhile, it is noticeable that the black African American Muslim woman has not been treated in the same way as other Muslim female characters resident in the United States or elsewhere. The use in *Tears of the Sun* and *Black Hawk Down* of African female figures are still stereotypical and ineffective in terms of narrative development, whereas in films made even before 9/11, such as *Malcolm X* (1992) and *Ali* (2001), Muslim black American females are envisaged as the voice of common sense and the custodians of a dignified family life. One may assume that the creative decision to portray voiceless African Muslim women in *Tears of the Sun* and *Black*

*Hawk Down* is intentional in order to alienate and distance any compassion that the spectator may have towards their plight. They are positioned within the camera frame as devices to intensify the chaotic nature of their environment. They are also deprived of the affirmative attributes of the African American woman, as their choice of identifying themselves as Muslim has not been politically motivated. Why they remain an Orientalist stereotype may be connected to the fact that protests in the United States against the vilification of Muslims in cinema have been voiced by professionals and corporate bodies of Arabic origin, as discussed in Chapter 7. Institutions that were set up before and after 9/11, such as those listed in el-Aswad (2013), have challenged the unrealistic creations nurtured by Orientalism in general, but not enough voices have been raised on behalf of African Muslim women.

Another previously overlooked area that the current study taps into is the depiction of Muslim children in films of the pre- and post-9/11 periods (Chapter 6). The analysis suggests that a considerable change has taken place over the years, with representations evolving from the caricatures of the earlier period to more developed character types. However, even in the present day the formulation of the Muslim child character has predictable features and serves as a dramatic element in the narrative, at the end of which s/he either dies, or is arrested or deported. While child characters in the African American or Hispanic contexts, for instance, have been reformulated over time and can now be projected as likeable and well-groomed youngsters carrying the film to a happy conclusion, the same positive perspective has not yet been adopted in full for the Muslim child. In many of the pre-9/11 films, where the overseas child was represented as a caricature or a stereotype, s/he was either silenced completely or made to speak like an American adult. Whether mute or eloquent, the child's role in the narrative was limited to being the hero's helper, if not a background filler. In films made after 9/11, geographical differences are observable in the exertion of control over children. Youngsters from city families in overseas countries are shown to be under strict parental control (for instance, the viewer witnesses Aisha's two nephews in *Body of Lies* being forced to eat their food by their authoritarian mother, and Colonel Faris' wife helping her children with their homework in *The Kingdom*), but in war zones they are left to fend for themselves in a chaotic environment, or they fall victim to the evil practices of their compatriots (e.g., Beckham in *The Hurt Locker* and Sohrab in *The Kite Runner*). Yet, through all turmoil and strife, some Muslim children in the war and conflict genre are still shown to be playing as children normally do, oblivious to the violent world of adults. The neglect of these children by their parents is a common theme. Instead, they are cared for by the Americans. In *The Kingdom*, for example, it is Janet Mayes who acts on her maternal instincts and shields the Muslim children from the conflict during the climactic fight scene, while in *The Hurt Locker* the death of Beckham prompts William James to seek retribution.

In American contexts, depiction is influenced by the child's cultural hybridity. The Muslim child is represented as a youth whose inability to establish a respected identity results in their social ostracization and subsequent downfall. From a Marxist perspective, for instance, American infants can be defined according to how characters, their families and their environments are represented in terms of social class, but in the case of immigrant Muslim children this rationale is inapplicable. Control in their case is in the hands of educational establishments rather than parents.

However, because such institutions promote only the state doctrines, there is no system in place to protect the non-conforming children from estrangement. In *Pretty Persuasion* and *Crossing Over*, both female children are used as scapegoats in a manipulative process that denies them their civil rights as American citizens. While their characters form the basis of a social commentary, they are used as thematic tools to describe the current immigrant condition. They are considered as threats whose removal from the narrative, either through deportation or death, is required in order to reverse the imbalance that their preceding actions have caused. In this way, identity is found to be a crucial concern in the manner in which a child is presented within an American environment. Their duality of character and ability to traverse both Muslim and American cultures make their circumstances unique. They are neither fully registered "Others" nor fully accepted American natives and, thus, their unstable existence becomes an attractive base on which examples of transnational cinema are built.

The loss of innocence is an ingredient that is constantly reworked regardless of where the story takes place. Children's persecution by authoritarian figures (soldiers, teachers, the police, and so on) who show no reservation in mistreating, abusing or even killing them, is also a recurrent feature. For instance, Ismail in *House of Sand and Fog* is shot by a Californian police officer; Taslima in *Crossing Over* is deported to Bangladesh by Homeland Security personnel; Ahmed in *Babel* is gunned down by a member of the north African security forces while his brother Yousef is arrested; Beckham in *The Hurt Locker* is killed by Islamic insurgents; and Sohrab in *The Kite Runner* is physically abused by Taliban soldiers.

The themes of friendship, loyalty, disloyalty and redemption are also popular in the representation of Muslim minors, both at home and abroad. Yousef in *Babel* laying the blame on his brother for wounding an American tourist but later repenting vehemently, and Amir in *The Kite Runner* accusing Hassan of stealing his watch and money but later rescuing Hassan's son Sohrab from Afghanistan are just two such examples. While childhood disloyalty and redemption are popular themes in children's films in general, exemplified, for instance, by the lies of the character Edmund about Lucy in *The Chronicles of Narnia: The Lion, the Witch, and the Wardrobe* (2005), in the case of the Muslim children the act of disloyalty verges on criminality.

Themes such as fear, death, divorce, sexuality and violence find a way of being presented through the characterization and imagery of the Muslim child, whose role is defined by their lost childhood in society. Sexual repression features as one of the factors leading youngsters to a tragic end. The way two Pakistani boys boast about being virgins at the age of 15 (*Syriana*) foretells that, with no attachment in life, they will easily fall prey to the imam who is trying to recruit them to a group of Jihadist activists. In *The Kite Runner*, the young bully who rapes Hassan grows up to be a Taliban commander. Differences in location also influence the sexual politics that apply to females. In *Babel*, the Muslim girl sexually manipulates her brother who observes her getting undressed through the cracks of a wall at home, for which both get a beating from their father.

This study has offered an evaluation of the pre- and post-9/11 cinematic landscape and has assessed whether changes in narratives, characterizations and social attitudes have affected the way the Muslim world has been constructed in the first ten years following the terrorist attacks. While the focus has been on how a range of devices are artistically implemented to fulfill various political or doctrinal agendas, the study is in no way complete. This process seems to be constantly moving into new areas of representation. Although the first ten years in cinema following 9/11 can be evaluated in terms of civic affairs, we have to make room for the fact that political and social attitudes are continuously evolving. There is no denying that as the Middle East, in particular Qatar, the UAE and Jordan, or even India and China, are financially contributing to mainstream American cinema, cultural representations have to go through not only a natural change but a forced one as well. Added to this are the effects of social media, globalized markets, diasporas, relative ease of travel, the entrance of Muslims into the film industry, and pro–Arab groups raising their voices against unjust vilification. Cultural representations today may be inspired by Orientalism, feminism and transnationalism, but new coordinates may be needed in future, given evolving social theories, political conjectures, world order aspirations and economic conditions. With all these factors generating, stimulating and contributing to a change, the durability of stereotypes in cultural representations is bound to be fragile. Whether fresh reformulations will displace stale tropes and clichés in totality is something that scholars will need to observe. It will be interesting to assess the representation of the Muslim world in films in the ten years following 2011. The Islamic sectarian struggles that have disrupted Iraq and especially Syria have not yet been mirrored in American cinema. The views attributed to "the new Orientalists," influenced by historian Patricia Crone's (1980) analysis, suggesting that Islamic countries have never had an effective civil society and are therefore destined to stay non-democratic, unstable and at war with one another, may also hit the screens in the second decade after 9/11. Or, will the reports of the Middle East and the Kingdom of Saudi Arabia now turning towards "Liberal Islam" affect the representation of the Muslim world in American cinema? These are all questions which arouse curiosity but need to be answered at the end of the second decade.

The analysis in the present study has highlighted many areas that point to the presence of new forms of Orientalism. The exact bearings of these forms and how they correspond with other movements like feminism and transnationalism need further research. The present findings, coupled with any fresh evidence regarding the changeability and demobilization of stereotypes in depicting "Other" groups in American cinema, will be a significant contribution to the discipline of Humanities.

# Filmography

Titles in **_bold italics_** are analyzed in the text.

*Act of Valor*. Mike McJoy, Scott Waugh. Relativity Media, 2012.
*Adventure in Iraq*. D. Ross Lederman. Warner Bros, 1943.
***Aladdin***. **Ron Clements. John Musker. Buena Vista Pictures, 1992.**
***Ali***. **Michael Mann. Columbia Pictures, 2001.**
*Alien*. Ridley Scott. Twentieth Century–Fox Film Corporation, 1979.
*Aliens*. James Cameron. Twentieth Century–Fox Film Corporation, 1986.
*America America*. Elia Kazan. Warner Bros., 1963.
*American East*. Hesham Issawi. Distant Horizons, 2008.
*Amreeka*. Cherien Dabis. Virgil Films & Entertainment, 2009.
*Anna Ascends*. Victor Fleming. Famous Players-Lasky Corporation, 1922.
*Arabesque*. Stanley Donen. Universal Pictures, 1966.
***Arabian Nights***. **John Rawlins. Universal Pictures, 1942.**
*Argo*. Ben Affleck. Warner Bros., 2012.
*Around the World in 80 Days*. Frank Coraci. Buena Vista Pictures, 2004.
***Babel***. **Alejandro Gonzalez Iñárritu. Paramount Vantage, 2006.**
*Bagdad*. Charles Lamont. Universal Pictures, 1949.
*Bicycle Thieves*. Vittorio de Sica. Arthur Mayer & Joseph Burstyn, 1948.
*The Birth of a Nation*. D.W. Griffith. Epoch Producing Corporation, 1915.
*Black Hawk Down*. Ridley Scott. Columbia Pictures, 2001.
*Black Sunday*. John Frankenheimer. Paramount Pictures, 2007.
*Blue Steel*. Kathryn Bigelow. MGM/UA Distribution Company, 1989.
***Body of Lies***. **Ridley Scott. Warner Bros., 2008.**
***Borat: Cultural Learnings of America for Make Benefit Glorious Nation of Kazakhstan***. **Larry Charles. Twentieth Century–Fox Film Corporation, 2006.**
*Boyz 'N the Hood*. John Singleton. Columbia Pictures, 1991.
*Breakfast at Tiffany's*. Blake Edwards. Paramount Pictures, 1961.
*A Café in Cairo*. Chester Withey. Producers Distributing Corporation. (PDC), 1925.
*Calamity Jane*. David Butler. Warner Bros., 1953.
***Charlie Wilson's War***. **Mike Nichols. Universal Pictures, 2007.**

*The Chronicles of Narnia: The Lion, the Witch, and the Wardrobe.* Andrew Adamson. Buena Vista Pictures, 2005.
*Cobra Woman.* Robert Siodmak. Universal Pictures, 1944.
*Copycat.* Jon Amiel. Warner Brothers, 1995.
*The Cosby Show.* NBC, 1984–1992.
*Crash.* Paul Haggis. Lions Gate Films, 2004.
*Crooklyn.* Spike Lee. Universal Pictures, 1994.
*Crossing Over.* Wayne Kramer. The Weinstein Company, 2009.
*Cutthroat Island.* Renny Harlin. MGM, 1995.
*Dances with Wolves.* Kevin Costner. Orion Pictures, 1990.
*David and Fatima.* Alain Zaloum. Kari Bian, 2008.
*Day Night, Day Night.* Julia Loktev. IFC First Take, 2006.
*Dead Man.* Jim Jarmusch. Miramax, 1996.
*Death of a Princess.* Antony Thomas. ITV and BFI, 1980.
*Delta Force.* Menahem Golan. Cannon Film Distributors, 1986.
*The Desert Song.* Roy Del Ruth. Warner Bros., 1929.
*The Desert Song.* Robert Florey. Warner Bros., 1943.
*The Desert Song.* H. Bruce Humberstone. Warner Bros., 1953.
*Double Edge.* Amos Kollek. Castle Hill Productions, 1992.
*The Dictator.* Larry Charles. Paramount Pictures, 2012.
*Executive Decision.* Stuart Baird Warner Bros., 1996.
*Exodus.* Otto Preminger. United Artists, 1960.
*Eye for an Eye.* John Schlesinger. Paramount Pictures, 1996.
*Fire over Afghanistan.* Terence H. Winkless. Concorde-New Horizons, 2003.
*Gandhi.* David Attenborough. Columbia Pictures, 1982.
*The Garden of Allah.* Richard Boleslawski. United Artists, 1936.
*GI Jane.* Ridley Scott. Buena Vista Pictures, 1997.
*The Godfather.* Francis Ford Coppola. Paramount Pictures, 1972.
*The Godfather Part II.* Francis Ford Coppola. Paramount Pictures, 1974.
*The Gold Bracelet.* Kavi Raz K.R. Films Hollywood, 2006.
*The Golden Blade.* Nathan H. Juran. Universal Pictures, 1955.
*La Grand Illusion.* Jean Renoir. Realisations d'Art Cinematographique (RAC), 1937.
*The Greatest.* Tom Gries. Columbia Pictures, 1977.
**Green Zone. Paul Greengrass. Universal Pictures, 2010.**
*He Got Game.* Spike Lee. Buena Vista Pictures, 1998.
*Heat and Dust.* James Ivory. Universal Classics, 1983.
*Heathers.* Michael Lehmann. New World Pictures, 1989.
*The Hell with Heroes.* Joseph Sargent. Universal Pictures, 1968.
*Hester Street.* Joan Micklin Silver. Midwest Films, 1975.
**Hidalgo. Joe Johnston. Buena Vista Pictures, 2004.**
*His People.* Edward Sloman. Universal Pictures, 1925.
*Homeland.* Showtime Television, 2011.
**House of Sand and Fog. Vadim Perelman. DreamWorks SKG, 2003.**
*House of Strangers.* Joseph L. Mankiewicz. Twentieth Century–Fox Film Corporation, 1949.
**The Human Shield. Ted Post. Cannon Film Distributors, 1991.**

*The Hunting Party*. Richard Shepard. The Weinstein Company, 2007.
**The Hurt Locker. Kathryn Bigelow. Summit Entertainment, 2008.**
*In the Army Now*. Daniel Petrie Jnr. Buena Vista Pictures, 1994.
*The Incredible Hulk*. Columbia Broadcasting System. 1978–1982.
***Invitation to the Dance*. Gene Kelly. Metro-Goldwyn-Mayer, 1956.**
***Iron Man*. Jon Favreau. Paramount Pictures, 2008.**
*Jackass Number Two*. Jeff Tramaine. Paramount Pictures, 2006.
*Jagged Edge*. Richard Marquand. Columbia Pictures, 1985.
*Jerry Maguire*. Cameron Crowe. TriStar Pictures, 1996.
***The Jewel of the Nile*. Lewis Teague. Twentieth Century–Fox Film Corporation, 1985.**
*Johnny Guitar*. Nicholas Ray. Republic Pictures, 1954.
*The Jungle Book*. Zoltan Korda. United Artists, 1942.
*The Karate Kid*. Harald Zwart. Columbia Pictures, 2010.
*The Keeper: The Legend of Omar Khayyam*. Kayvan Mashayekh. Arrival Pictures, 2005.
*The Killer*. John Woo. Golden Princess Film, 1989.
***The Kingdom*. Peter Berg. Universal Pictures, 2007.**
***Kingdom of Heaven*. Ridley Scott. Twentieth Century–Fox Film Corporation, 2005.**
*Kismet*. Vincente Minelli, Metro-Goldwyn-Mayer, 1955.
*Kismet*. William Dieterle. Metro-Goldwyn-Mayer, 1944.
***The Kite Runner*. Marc Forster. Paramount Vantage, 2007.**
*Klute*. Alan J. Pakula. Warner Bros., 1971.
*The Last King of Scotland*. Kevin Macdonald. Fox Searchlight Pictures, 2006.
*Last of the Mohicans*. Michael Mann. Twentieth Century–Fox Film Corporation, 1992.
*Last Tango in Paris*. Bernardo Bertolucci. United Artists, 1972.
***Lawrence of Arabia*. David Lean. Columbia Pictures, 1962.**
*Little Big Man*. Arthur Penn. National General Pictures, 1972.
*Live from Baghdad*. Mick Jackson. HBO, 2002.
*The Long Kiss Goodnight*. Renny Harlin. New Line Cinema, 1996.
*Looking for Comedy in the Muslim World*. Albert Brooks. Warner Independent Pictures (WIP), 2005.
***Malcolm X*. Spike Lee. Warner Bros., 1992.**
*Man on Fire*. Tony Scott. Twentieth Century–Fox Film Corporation, 2004.
***Man Push Cart*. Ramin Bahrani. Koch Lorber Films, 2005.**
*The Manchurian Candidate*. Jonathan Demme. Scott Rudin Productions, 2004.
*Manhattan*. Paul Strand and Charles Sheeler. Kino Video, 1921.
*Mean Streets*. Martin Scorsese. Warner Bros., 1973.
*The Message*. Moustapha Akkad. Filmco International Productions Inc., 1976.
*Mississippi Masala*. Mira Nair. The Samuel Goldwyn Company, 1991.
*The Molly Maguires*. Martin Ritt. Paramount Pictures 1970.
*Mooz-lum*. Qasim Basir. Peace Film, 2010.
*Munich*. Steven Spielberg. Universal Pictures, 2005.
*The Next Man*. Richard C. Sarafian. Allied Artists Pictures, 1976.
*The Night Of*. HBO, 2016.
*Not Without My Daughter*. Brian Gilbert. Metro-Goldwyn-Mayer, 1991.
*Oliver!* Carol Reed. Columbia Pictures, 1968.

*Once Upon a Time in Mexico*. Robert Rodriguez. Columbia Pictures, 2003.
*The Other Son*. Lorraine Levy. Cohen Media Group, 2012.
*Our Gang*. MGM, 1938–1944.
*Out of Reach*. Po Chih Leong. Screen Gems, 2004.
*Paris*. Auguste and Louis Lumiére, 1895.
*A Passage to India*. David Lean. Columbia Pictures, 1984.
*A Perfect Murder*. Andrew Davis. Warner Bros., 1998.
**Pretty Persuasion. Marcos Siega. Samuel Goldwyn Films, 2005.**
*Prince of Persia: The Sands of Time*. Mike Newell. Walt Disney Studios Motion Pictures, 2010.
*Quick Change*. Howard Franklin and Bill Murray. Warner Bros, 1990.
*The Raid*. Gareth Evans. Sony Pictures Classics, 2012.
*Raid on Entebbe*. Irvin Kershner. National Broadcasting Company (NBC), 1977.
*Raiders of the Lost Ark*. Steven Spielberg. Paramount Pictures, 1981.
*Rambo 3*. Peter MacDonald. TriStar Pictures, 1988.
*Redacted*. Brian De Palma. Magnolia Pictures, 2007.
**Rendition. Gavin Hood. New Line Cinema, 2007.**
*Resident Evil*. Paul W.S. Anderson. Sony Pictures Entertainment, 2002.
*Road to Morocco*. David Butler. Paramount Pictures, 1942.
*Rules of Engagement*. William Friedkin. Paramount Pictures, 2000.
**Sahara. Andrew V. McLagren. Cannon Film Distributors, 1983.**
*Salt of this Sea*. Annemarie Jacir. Lorber Films, 2008.
*The Searchers*. John Ford. Warner Bros., 1956.
*Sex and the City*. HBO, 1998–2004.
**Sex and the City 2. Michael Patrick King. New Line Cinema, 2010.**
**The Sheik. George Melford. Paramount Pictures, 1921.**
*The Siege*. Edward Zwick. Twentieth Century–Fox Film Corporation, 1998.
*The Silence of the Lambs*. Jonathan Demme. Orion Pictures, 1991.
*Sinbad the Sailor*. Richard Wallace. RKO Radio Pictures, 1947.
*Sirocco*. Curtis Bernhardt. Columbia Pictures, 1951.
*Six Million Dollar Man*. Universal Television, 1974–1978.
*Skyfall*. Sam Mendes. Sony Pictures Releasing, 2012.
*Slingshot Hip Hop*. Jacqueline Reem Salloum. 48 RecordZ, 2008.
*Slumdog Millionaire*. Danny Boyle. Fox Searchlight Pictures, 2008.
*Solomon and Sheba*. King Vidor. United Artists, 1959.
*The Son of Sinbad*. Ted Tetziaff. RKO Radio Pictures, 1955.
**Sorry, Haters. Jeff Stanzler. IFC Films, 2005.**
*Spy Kids*. Robert Rodriguez. Dimension Films, 2001.
*The Stoning of Soraya M*. Cyrus Nowrasteh. Roadside Attractions, 2008.
*Street Scene*. King Vidor. United Artists, 1931.
*The Sunchaser*. Michael Cimino. Regency Enterprises, 1996.
**Syriana. Stephen Gaghan. Warner Bros., 2005.**
*Taken 2*. Olivier Magaton. Twentieth Century–Fox Film Corporation, 2012.
*Team America: World Police*. Trey Parker, Matt Stone. Paramount Pictures, 2004.
*Tears of the Sun*. Antoine Fuqua. Columbia Pictures, 2003.

*The Ten Commandments*. Cecil B. DeMille. Paramount Pictures, 1956.
*Ten Pickaninnies*. Thomas A. Edison. Edison Manufacturing Company, 1904.
*The Terminal*. Steven Spielberg. DreamWorks Distribution, 2004.
*Terminator 2: Judgment Day*. James Cameron. TriStar Pictures, 1991.
*The Thief of Baghdad*. Raoul Walsh. United Artists, 1924.
*The Thief of Baghdad*. Ludwig Berger, Michael Powell. United Artists, 1940.
*The Thief of Baghdad*. Clive Donner. NBC Television, 1978.
*The 13th Warrior*. John McTiernan. Buena Vista Pictures, 1999.
*Three Kings*. David O. Russell. Warner Bros., 1999.
*Three Veils*. Rolla Selbak. Peccadillo Pictures, 2009.
*The Thousand and One Nights*. Alfred E. Green. Columbia Pictures, 1945.
*Towelhead*. Alan Ball. Warner Independent Pictures, 2007.
*Traitor*. Jeffrey Machmanoff Overture Films, 2008.
*True Lies*. James Cameron. Twentieth Century–Fox Film Corporation, 1994.
*Uncle Tom's Cabin*. Harry A. Pollard. Universal Pictures, 1927.
*United 93*. Paul Greengrass. Universal Pictures, 2007.
*The Visitor*. Tom McCarthy. Overture Films, 2007.
*When We Were Kings*. Leon Gast. Gramercy Pictures, 1996.
*White Savage*. Arthur Lubin. Universal Pictures, 1943.
*Wrong Is Right*. Richard Brooks. Columbia Pictures, 1982.
*You Don't Mess with the Zohan*. Dennis Dugan Columbia Pictures, 2008.
*Zero Dark Thirty*. Kathryn Bigelow. Columbia Pictures, 2012.

# Chapter Notes

## Chapter 1

1. In *Philosophy of Mind*, Hegel (1971, 3) writes: "The knowledge of mind is the highest and hardest, just because it is the most 'concrete' of sciences. The significance of that 'absolute' commandment, 'know thyself'—whether we look at it in itself or under the historical circumstances of its first utterance—is not to promote mere self-knowledge in respect of the particular capacities, character, propensities and foibles of the single self."
2. Slavoj Žižek (1997), for instance, in the paper "The Big Other Doesn't Exist," argues that Lacan's "great Other" is in fact God himself and, similarly to God, it does not exist or, as a counter-claim, exists in everything and everywhere.
3. Referring to Kilpatrick's (1999) work, Mike King (2009, 136), for instance, writes: "It is not until the films of the 1980s and 1990s that Kilpatrick finds a more truly sympathetic portrayal of the Native American, finding for example Cimino's *The Sunchaser* (1996) to be a 'good film' and Jarmusch's *Dead Man* (1996) to be a 'great film.'" Another work that usefully traces this development is that by Michael Hilger (1995, 179), who cites the "kindly eyes" of Old Lodge Skins as an example of the image of the Native American in film that dominates his imagination, though it is still a stereotype.
4. The criticisms of Said's *Orientalism* (2003) made by Bernard Lewis (1993) have been discussed earlier in this chapter. More significant in the present context is the criticism made on the grounds that Orientalism is a polemical discourse that leaves out some significant elements related to the Muslim world. "Black Orientalism," coined and described by Jackson (2005) as a reaction to the newly deployed relationship between Islam, Black Americans and the Muslim world, is one such element. Said's (2003) work does not refer to new developments such as American Exceptionalism (Ceaser 2012) or the New Orientalists (Keshavarz 2007).
5. This concept was first developed by Benedict Anderson (1983) to define nationalism but in time has become widely used to refer to the image manipulation exercised by the media.
6. The full cast and crew is available on the IMDb website: http://www.imdb.com/title/tt0120188/fullcredits?ref_=tt_cl_sm#cast (accessed 26/11/2017). Jack Shaheen's name is under "Other Crew."

## Chapter 2

1. Associating Arabs with camels is equivalent to the Indian's totemic relationship with the horse and buffalo. In the same way that Native Americans are presented in an arid landscape as, at worst, brutal, scalping warriors, sexually violating white women, and at best as unsmiling, untalkative primitives, with tropes of tepees, peace pipes, handmade knives and

feathery headbands, the desert has also been propped with peculiarities consisting of "an oasis, oil wells, palm trees, tents, fantastically ornate palaces, sleek limousines, and of course, camels," as mentioned in Chapter 1 (Shaheen 2003a, 8).

2. One exception is *Adventure in Iraq* (1943), which narrates the story of two Americans and one Englishman kept in captivity by the sheikh of an Iraqi Kurdish tribe. The tribesmen in this case are presented as "devil worshippers" and not as traditional believers in Islam. The film thus presents a strange mixture of Muslim Arabs and Kurdish Yazidis.

3. The narratives are similar, even to the point of having lookalike minor characters—for instance, Ahmed in *The Sheik* (1921) has a French valet, and Jaffar in *Sahara* (1983) has an English valet called Cambridge.

4. Ella Shohat's (2006, 55) interpretation of this ending is based on the female instinct for submission: "At the end the courageous winner of the race decides 'on her own' to return to the noble light-skinned sheik who had rescued her from cruel Arabs at the risk of his own life. The woman, who could have won independence, still 'voluntarily' prefers the ancient ways of gender hierarchies."

5. Samuel Scurry's (2010) selection of films includes *The Thousand and One Nights* (1945), *The Thief of Baghdad* (1940), *Arabian Nights* (1942), *Aladdin* (1992), *Live from Baghdad* (2002) and *Body of Lies* (2008).

6. http://www.nytimes.com/movie/review?res=9F04E4D61E3EE03BBC4C51DFB4678 382659EDE (accessed 12/12/2016).

## Chapter 3

1. An abridged version of this chapter has been published: Kerem Bayraktaroğlu, "The Muslim Male Character Typology in American Cinema Post–9/11," *Digest of Middle East Studies* 23.2 (2014): 345–359.

2. In comparison, the current analysis spreads Muslim representation across a broad spectrum, starting with the "Arab terrorist" and ending with the "respectable Arab," with no harsh divisions between them, and with some typologies overlapping with others in the range.

3. I have purposefully excluded *Mooz-lum* (2010) from the numerous case studies as it was never given a full theatrical release in the United States.

4. Personal conversation with Dr. Jaime Robles, University of Exeter.

5. This information comes from http://www.pewresearch.org/fact-tank/2016/01/06/a-new-estimate-of-the-u-s-muslim-population/ (accessed 24/11/2017).

6. This enemy type has come very much to the forefront with current reports that a sizeable part of the calamity that the world has been experiencing since 2013 under the name of ISIS is made up of nationals from the Western world.

7. Describing how these heads of intelligence work, Ignatius writes: "They're patient and meticulous in preparing operations.... And they are very good at interrogation—not at beating people up ... but at eliciting information through other means" (http://davidignatius.com/body-of-lies/, accessed 26/11/2017).

## Chapter 4

1. One of many examples is President Bush's address to the nation at the start of the second Gulf War: "To all the men and women of the United States armed forces now in the Middle East, the peace of a troubled world and the hopes of an oppressed people now depend on you. That trust is well placed" (https://www.theguardian.com/world/2003/mar/20/iraq.georgebush, accessed 26/11/2017).

2. However, the female characteristics have not been totally overlooked. In both *Aliens* (1986) and *Terminator 2: Judgment Day* (1991), there are female protagonists whose primary

maternal instincts are not relinquished as they protect children from an overwhelming threat and elements outside their control.

3. Based on a 1996 doctrine, a product of the National Defense University in the United States written by Harlan K. Ullman and James P. Wade, "Shock and Awe" (otherwise known as "Rapid Dominance") was frequently used by the media in March 2003 to describe the first Iraqi campaign.

4. It cannot be a coincidence that Bank Street station is made to resemble the location—recognizable by resident New Yorkers—in close proximity to ground zero and the financial district.

5. Retrieved from http://news.bbc.co.uk/1/hi/world/middle_east/4632495.stm (accessed 26/11/2017).

6. Waterboarding has been a particularly common method used against Muslim suspects during the U.S. War on Terror. Further information regarding America's use of waterboarding can be found online: Leonard Doyle, "Waterboarding Is Torture—I Did It Myself, Says U.S. Advisor," *The Independent*, Thursday, 1 November 2007 (http://www.independent.co.uk/news/world/americas/waterboarding-is-torture—i-did-it-myself-says-us-advisor-398490.html, accessed 26/11/2017).

7. "Woman castrator" is a concept originally presented by Freud (1976) and later developed by Barbara Creed (1993) as one of the faces of the "monstrous feminine."

8. In July/August 2007, Barack Obama was reported to have said, "We must bring the war to a responsible end and then renew our leadership—military, diplomatic, moral—to confront new threats and capitalise on new opportunities" (http://users.metu.edu.tr/utuba/Obama.pdf, accessed 1/12/2017).

## Chapter 5

1. In the "It's a Man's (Celluloid) World" survey, Martha M. Lauzen (2014) reports that Muslim women, as film characters, were allocated minimum screen time and speaking parts in the period leading up to 9/11. http://womenintvfilm.sdsu.edu/files/2013_It's_a_Man's_World_Report.pdf (accessed 26/11/2017).

## Chapter 6

1. In 1995, the Library of Congress commissioned the Motion Picture/Broadcasting/Recorded Sound Division to catalogue films by type and thus a report/guide was produced on 12 February 1997. The board of members that helped compile the report consisted of Brian Traves (Chair), Judi Hoffman and Karen Lund. The quotation is taken from https://www.loc.gov/rr/mopic/miggen.html#Youth (accessed 26/11/2017).

2. Retrieved from http://www2.anglistik.uni-freiburg.de/intranet/englishbasics/NarrativeSituation01.htm (accessed 3/3/15).

3. Retrieved from Harriet Beecher Stowe, *Uncle Tom's Cabin; or, Life Among the Lowly*, Volume II (Boston: John P. Jewitt, 1852). https://books.google.si/books?id=TukRAAAAYAAJ&dq=uncle%27s+tom+cabin+volume+2&hl=sl&pg=PR1#v=onepage&q=uncle's%20tom%20cabin%20volume%202&f=false (accessed 26/11/2017).

4. This comment by S. Lichter and D. Amundson (1997) is mentioned in Yurii Horton, Raagen Price and Eric Brown's (1999) online published work with no page number at https://web.stanford.edu/class/e297c/poverty_prejudice/mediarace/portrayal.htm (accessed 26/11/2017).

5. Figueroa (2008) refers to several sources in defining the Spanish stereotypes in American cinema, including Woll (1980), Berumen (1995), and Keller (1994).

6. Some of the films that Sabu appeared in are *Jungle Book* (Korda 1942), *White Savage* (Lubin 1943), and *Cobra Woman* (Siodmak 1944).

7. In fact, it is referred to as "Aladdin, the Animated Racism" (Shaheen, 2003a, 50).

8. Singer (2006) reports that, although the use of young boys as child soldiers and suicide bombers initially started in African countries, they were first used in the Middle East during the Iran-Iraq war.

## Chapter 7

1. Arti (2007) produces a chronology of five historical periods marked by specific events, which have influenced the redesign of the representation of Muslims. He begins with the early 1920s when the Middle East was represented by American filmmakers as a "world of fantasy" (6). Quoting from McAlister (2005, 5), he says this world is bundled with funny caricatures of Arabs. This stage is followed by the period right after World War II, when the State of Israel was founded. During this time, Hollywood produced films with Biblical references such as *The Ten Commandments* (1956), *Exodus* (1960) and *Solomon and Sheba* (1959). The third stage was marked by the 1970 oil embargo, encouraging films in support of Israel and denouncing PLO terrorists. The fourth stage, in the aftermath of the Iranian revolution, gave birth to productions with hijacking and hostage-taking themes. The final stage before 9/11 witnessed the First Gulf War and the end of the Cold War, instigating the characterization of Islamic fundamentalism in films.

2. In a shocked reaction on the day after the incident (12/9/2001), the *New York Times* reported that "for several panic-stricken hours yesterday morning, people in Lower Manhattan witnessed the inexpressible, the incomprehensible, the unthinkable." A language of hysteria is apparent in the whole of this reporting. "Buildings Burn and Fall as Onlookers Search for Elusive Safety," *New York Times*, 12 September 2001. https://global.nytimes.com/2001/09/12/nyregion/12SCEN.html?pagewanted=print&position=top (accessed 20/06/2014).

3. Yenigün (2004, 47) suggests that the source of this division is in fact G.W. Bush who said in one of his speeches, "The enemy of America is not our many Muslim friends; it is not our many Arab friends. Our enemy is a radical network of terrorists, and every government that supports them."

4. Jeffrey L. Thomas (2015, 103) attests that the few and far between images of "good" Muslims in films were deceptive in terms of reflecting the true psyche of the American public. Almost all of the major broadcast and cable networks presented post–9/11 programmes with "Muslim characters that conformed to traditional negative stereotypes."

## Chapter 8

1. Franklin D. Roosevelt.

2. On this subject, in addition to the social and political reasons listed in the previous chapters, one of the conclusive accounts comes from Teo (2011, 138–139):

"The Middle East ceased to be the domain of contemporary Orientalist romantic stories in American films after the Second World War.... The reasons for this were probably ... sheer fatigue with the genre, the growing complexity of political events in the Middle East, a growing fascination with international intrigues and thrillers during the period of the Cold War, and preoccupation with the political and economic effects of the Middle East on American society beginning in the late 1960s. Oil politics became increasingly important for Americans in the post–Second World War period, while successive American governments became entangled in the process of decolonialization in the region during the Cold War."

3. In the Behrani household in *House of Sand and Fog* (2003), for instance, apart from a typically Iranian round brass tray and the cups for Turkish coffee, there is not much to signify the East. The same can be said about Ahmad's New York City room in *Man Push Cart* (2005).

4. This trend continued into 2011 when Season One of the popular TV series *Homeland* (developed by Howard Gordon and Alex Gansa) was premiered, and 2012 when *Zero Dark Thirty* was theatrically released, both being high-profile examples of U.S. audio-visual texts with strong female protagonists.

# Works Cited

Abu-Lughod, Lila (2013). *Do Muslim Women Need Saving?* Cambridge: Harvard University Press.
Adra, N. (2005). "Belly Dance: An Urban Folk Genre," in A. Shay and B. Sellers-Young, eds., *Belly Dance: Orientalism Transnationalism and Harem Fantasy*. Costa Mesa, CA: Mazda, 28–50.
Aguayo, Michelle (2009). "Representations of Muslim Bodies in The Kingdom: Deconstructing Discourses in Hollywood." *Global Media Journal* 2.2: 41–57.
Ahmed, Leila (1992). *Women and Gender in Islam: Historical Roots of a Modern Debate*. New Haven: Yale University Press.
Aitken, Stuart C., and Leo E. Zonn (1994). "Re-Presenting the Place Pastiche" in Stuart C. Aitken and Leo C. Zonn, eds., *Place, Power, Situation and Spectacle: A Geography of Film*. Lanham, MD: Rowman & Littlefield, 3–26.
Alalawi, Noura (2015). "How Do Hollywood Movies Portray Muslims and Arabs After 9/11? Content Analysis of The Kingdom and Rendition Movies." *Cross-Cultural Communication* 11.11: 58–62.
Alford, C. Fred (2016). *Trauma, Culture and PTSD*. New York: Palgrave Macmillan.
Allport, Gordon W. (1954). *The Nature of Prejudice*. Oxford: Addison-Wesley.
Al-Mahadin, S. (2013). "The Social Semiotics of Hijab: Negotiating the Body Politics of Veiled Women." *Journal of Arab and Muslim Media Research* 6.1: 3–18.
Alsultany, Era Evelyn (2013). "Arabs and Muslims in the Media After 9/11: Representational Strategies for a 'Postrace Era.'" *American Quarterly* 65.1: 161–169.
Anderson, Benedict (1983). *Imagined Communities: Reflections on the Origin and Spread of Nationalism*. London: Verso.
Appadurai, Arjun (1996). *Modernity at Large: Cultural Dimensions of Globalization*. Minneapolis: University of Minnesota Press.
Arti, Suleiman (2007). "The Evolution of Hollywood's Representation of Arabs Before 9/11: The Relationship Between Political Events and the Notion of 'Otherness.'" *Networking Knowledge: Journal of the Media, Communication and Cultural Studies Association Postgraduate Network* 1.2: 1–20. http://ojs.meccsa.org.uk/index.php/netknow/article/viewFile/23/23.
Bal, Mieke (1996). "Focalization," in Susana Onega and Jose Angel Garcia Landa, eds., *Narratology: An Introduction* (Longman Critical Readers). New York: Longman, 115–128.
Balázs, Béla (1970). *Theory of the Film: Character and the Growth of a New Art*. New York: Dover.
———. *Early Film Theory* (2010). Ed. Erica Carter. Trans. Rodney Livingstone. Oxford: Berghahn.
Basch, Linda N., Nina Glick Schiller, and Christina Szanton Blanc (1994). *Nations Unbound: Transnational Projects, Postcolonial Predicaments and Deterritorialised Nation-States*. Basel: Gordon and Breach Science.

Bayraktaroğlu, Kerem (2014). "The Muslim Male Character Typology in American Cinema Post-9/11." *Digest of Middle East Studies* 23.2: 345–359.

———. (2015). "The Portrayal of Muslim Children in American Cinema Post 9/11," in S. Mukherjee and S. Zulfiqar, eds., *Islam and the West: A Love Story?* Newcastle-upon-Tyne: Cambridge Scholars, 67–82.

Bazin, André. *What Is Cinema?* Trans. Hugh Gray. Berkley: University of California Press, 1967.

Bernstein, Matthew, and Gaylyn Studlar, eds. (1997). *Visions of the East: Orientalism in Film*. New Brunswick: Rutgers University Press.

Berumen, Frank J.G. (1995) *The Chicano/Hispanic Image in American Film*. New York: Vantage.

Bhabha, Homi K. (1994). *The Location of Culture*. Oxon: Routledge.

———. (1996). "Culture's in Between," in S. Hall and P. Du Gay, eds., *Questions of Cultural Identity*. London: Sage, 53–60.

Bodenhausen, Galen V., and Robert S. Wyer (1985). "Effects of Stereotypes in Decision Making and Information-Processing Strategies." *Journal of Personality and Social Psychology* 48.2: 267–282.

Boozer, Jack (1999/2000). "The Lethal Femme Fatale in the Noir Tradition." *Journal of Film and Video* 51.3/4: 20–35.

———. (2002). *Career Movies: American Business and the Success Mystique*. Austin: University of Texas Press.

Botz-Bornstein, Thorsten (2015). *Veils, Nudity, and Tattoos: The New Feminine Aesthetics*. Lanham, MD: Lexington Books.

Boyd-Barrett, Oliver, David Herrera, and Jim Bauman (2011). *Hollywood and the CIA: Cinema, Defence and Subversion*. London: Routledge.

Bradshaw, Peter (2011). "9/11 films: How Did Hollywood Handle the Tragedy?" *The Guardian Filmblog*, 8 November. Available at http://www.theguardian.com/film/filmblog/2011/sep/08/9-11-films-hollywood-handle (accessed 26/11/2017).

Braidotti, Rosi (1994). *Nomadic Subjects. Embodiment and Sexual Difference in Contemporary Feminist Theory*. New York: Columbia University Press.

Baudry, Jean-Louis (1986). "Ideological Effects of the Basic Cinematographic Apparatus," in Philip Rosen, ed., *Narrative, Apparatus, Ideology. A Film Theory Reader*. New York: Columbia University Press.

Bronfen, Elisabeth (2004). "Femme Fatale—Negotiations of Tragic Desire." *New Literary History* 35.1: 103–116.

Brudholm, Thomas (2010). *Resentment's Virtue: Jean Amery and the Refusal to Forgive*. Philadelphia: Temple University Press.

Brunsdon, Charlotte, ed. (1987). *Films for Women*. London: BFI.

Bullock, Katherine (2002). *Rethinking Muslim Women and the Veil: Challenging Historical & Modern Stereotypes*. London: The International Institute of Islamic Thought.

Bulman, Robert C. (2005). *Hollywood Goes to High School: Cinema, Schools, and American Culture*. New York: Worth.

Butler, Judith (1999). *Gender Trouble: Feminism and the Subversion of Identity*. New York: Routledge.

———. (2004). *Precarious Life: The Powers of Mourning and Violence*. London: Verso.

Cainkar, Louise (2002). "No Longer Invisible: Arab and Muslim Exclusion After September 11th." *Middle East Report* 224 (Autumn): 22–29.

Carr, Steven Alan (2007). "Wretched Refuse: Watching New York Ethnic Slum Films in the Aftermath of 9/11," in Murray Pomerance, ed., *City That Never Sleeps: New York and the Filmic Imagination*. New Brunswick: Rutgers University Press.

Cavell, Stanley (1976). "The Avoidance of Love: A Reading of King Lear," in Stanley Cavell, ed., *Must We Mean What Say?* Cambridge: Cambridge University Press, 267–356.

Ceaser, James W. (2012). "The Origins and Character of American Exceptionalism." *American Political Thought* 1.1: 3–28. Available http://www.jstor.org/stable/10.1086/664595 (accessed 25/11/2017).

Cettl, Robert (2009). *Terrorism in American Cinema: An Analytical Filmography, 1960–2008.* Jefferson, NC: McFarland.
Chaliand, G., ed. (1989). *Minority Peoples in the Age of Nation-States.* Trans. T. Berrett. London: Pluto Press.
Clark, C.C. (1969). "Television and Social Control: Some Observations on the Portrayals of Ethnic Minorities." *Television Quarterly* 8: 18–22.
Clifford, James (1997). *Routes: Travel and Translation in the Late Twentieth Century.* Cambridge: Harvard University Press.
Cones, John W. (2012). *Patterns of Bias in Hollywood Movies.* New York: Algora.
Considine, David M. (1985). *The Cinema of Adolescence.* Jefferson, NC: McFarland.
Creed, Barbara. (1993). *The Monstrous Feminine: Film, Feminism, Psychoanalysis.* London: Routledge.
_____. (1995). "Lesbian Bodies: Tribades, Tomboys and Tarts," in Elizabeth Grosz and Elspeth Probyn, eds., *Sexy Bodies: the Strange Carnalities of Feminisim.* London: Routledge, 86–103.
Crenshaw, Kimberle (1991). "Mapping the Margins: Intersectionality, Identity Politics, and Violence Against Women of Color." *Stanford Law Review* 43.6: 1241–1299.
Crone, Patricia (1980). *Slaves on Horses: The Evolution of the Islamic Polity.* Cambridge: Cambridge University Press.
Dannin, Robert (2000). "Understanding the Multi-Ethnic Dilemma of African-American Muslims," in Yvonne Yazbeck Haddad and John L. Esposito, eds., *Muslims on the American Path?* New York: Oxford University Press, 263–284.
Deleuze, Gilles (1986). *Cinema 1: The Movement Image.* Trans. Hugh Tomlinson and Barbara Habberjam. Minneapolis: University of Minnesota Press.
Deleuze, Gilles, and Felix Guattari (1987). *A Thousand Plateaus: Capitalism and Schizophrenia.* Trans. Brian Massumi. Minneapolis: University of Minnesota Press.
Devine, Patricia (1989). "Stereotypes and Prejudice: Their Automatic and Controlled Components." *Journal of Personality and Social Psychology* 56.1: 5–18.
Dong, Lan (2013). "Childhood in War and Violence: Turtles Can Fly and The Kite Runner," in Debbie Olson and Vibiana Bowman Cvetkovic, eds., *Portrayals of Children in Popular Culture: Fleeting Images.* Lanham, MD: Lexington Books, 195–206.
Dunphy, Graeme (2001). "Migrant, Emigrant, Immigrant: Recent Developments in Turkish-Dutch Literature." *Neophilologus* 85.1: 1–23.
Durovicová, Nataša, and Kathleen Newman, eds. (2009). *World Cinemas, Transnational Perspectives.* Abingdon: Routledge.
Dyer, Richard (2005). "Don't Look Up Now: The Instabilities of the Male Pin-Up," in Richard Dyer, *Only Entertainment.* Abingdon: Routledge, 131–147.
Edelman, Dennis (2013). "The 'War on Terror' in Contemporary Hollywood Cinema: Ridley Scott's Body of Lies and Jeffrey Nachmanoff's Traitor," in Frauke Reitemeier, ed., *"Deepe Things out of Darknesse": English and American Representations of Conflicts.* Universitätsverlag Göttingen, 93–130.
Ekman, P., and Wallace V. Friesen (1969). "The Repertoire of Nonverbal Behavior: Categories, Origins, Usage and Coding." *Semiotica* 1.1: 49–98. Available at http://homes.di.unimi.it/~boccignone/GiuseppeBoccignone_webpage/CompAff2011_files/EkmanFriesenSemiotica.pdf (accessed 04/02/2015).
el-Aswad, el-Sayed (2013). "Images of Muslims in Western Scholarship and Media After 9/11." *Digest of Middle Eastern Studies* 22.1: 39–56.
Elouardaoui, Ouidyane (2011). "Arabs in Post 9/11 Hollywood Films: A Move Towards a More Realistic Depiction?" Available at http://docs.lib.purdue.edu/cgi/viewcontent.cgi?article=1056&context=revisioning (accessed 17/11/2017).
Fan, Yi-Tu (2011). *Space and Place. The Perspective of Experience.* Minneapolis: University of Minnesota Press.
Fanon, F. (1965). *Algeria Unveiled. A Dying Colonialism.* Trans. A.H. Chevalier. Chicago: University of Chicago Press.

Farrell, Amy, and Patrice McDermott (2005). "Claiming Afghan Women: The Challenge of Human Rights Discourse for Transnational Feminism," in Wendy S. Hesford and Wendy Kozol, eds., *Just Advocacy: Women's Human Rights, Transnational Feminisms, and the Politics of Representation*. New Brunswick: Rutgers University Press, 33–55.

Featherstone, Joseph (1974). "Children and Youth in America." *Harvard Educational Review* 9: 357.

Fernandez, Sonya (2009). "The Crusade Over the Bodies of Women." *Patterns of Prejudice* 43.3: 269–286.

Figueroa, Ramon. G. (2009). "Spy Kids: A New Breed of Latinos in American Cinema." *McNair Scholars Journal* 10: 61–79.

Fitzgerald, Michael Ray (2010). "Evolutionary Stages of Minorities in the Mass Media: An Application of Clark's Model to American-Indian Television Representations." Available at https://www.academia.edu/459949/_Evolutionary_Stages_of_Minorities_in_the_Mass_Media_An_Application_of_Clarks_Model_to_American-Indian_Television_Representations (accessed 19/11/2017).

Foster, Gwendolyn Audrey (1999). *Captive Bodies. Postcolonial Subjectivity in Cinema*. Albany: State University of New York Press.

Foucault, Michel (1977). *Discipline and Punish: The Birth of the Prison*. Trans. Alan Sheridan. London: Penguin.

Francaviglia, Richard V. (2007) "Crusaders and Sarajens: The Persistence of Orientalism in Historically Themed Motion Pictures about the Middle East," in Richard Francaviglia and Jerry Rodnitzky, eds., *Lights, Camera, History: Portraying the Past in Film*. Arlington: University of Texas, 53–90.

Freeburg, Victor Oscar (1918). *The Art of Photoplay Making*. New York: Macmillan.

Freud, Sigmund (1976). "The Dissolution of the Oedipus Complex," in S. Freud, *On Sexuality. Vol. 7, Penguin Freud Library*. Ed. Angela Richards. Trans. James Strachey. Harmondsworth: Penguin, 313–322.

Friedman, Lester D. (1982). *Hollywood's Image of the Jew*. New York: Frederick Ungar.

———. (1991). "Celluloid Palimpsests: An Overview of Ethnicity and the American Film," in Lester D. Friedman, ed., *Unspeakable Images: Ethnicity and the American Cinema*. Urbana: University of Illinois Press, 1–35.

———. (2012). "A Forgotten Masterpiece: Edward Sloman's His People," in Murray Pomerance and Hava Tirosh-Samuelson, eds., *Hollywood's Chosen People: The Jewish Experience in American Cinema*. Detroit: Wayne State University Press, 19–34.

Galbraith, J. K. (1984). *The Anatomy of Power*. London: Hamish Hamilton.

Gazimihal, M.R. (1991). *Turk Halk Oyunlari Katalogu Cilt: 1 (A Catalogue of Turkish Folk Dances Volume: 1)*. Ankara: Kultur Bakanligi Yayinlari.

Gerhard, Jane (2005). "Sex and the City." *Feminist Media Studies* 5.1: 37–49.

Gordon, Milton (1964). *Assimilation in American Life: The Role of Race, Religion, and National Origins*. New York: Oxford University Press.

Graham, Helen (2007). "Post-Pleasure." *Feminist Media Studies* 7.1: 1–15.

Grossberg, Lawrence (1997). *Dancing in Spite of Myself*. Durham: Duke University Press.

Haake, M., and A. Gulz (2008). "Visual Stereotypes and Virtual Pedagogical Agents." *Educational Technology & Society* 11.4: 1–15. Available at http://www.ifets.info/journals/11_4/1.pdf (accessed 18/11/2017).

Hall, Stuart (1997a). "The Spectacle of the Other," in Stuart Hall, ed., *Representation: Cultural Representations and Signifying Practices*. London: Sage in association with the Open University, 223–290.

———. (1997b). "The Work of Representation," in Stuart Hall, ed., *Representation: Cultural Representations and Signifying Practices*. London: Sage in assoc with Open University, 13–74.

Harp, Dustin, and Sara Struckman (2010). "The Articulation of Lynndie England to Abu Ghraib: Gender Ideologies, War, and the Construction of Reality." *Journal of Magazine & New Media Research* 11.2. Available at http://aejmcmagazine.arizona.edu/Journal/Spring2010/HarpStruckman.pdf (accessed 22/11/2017).

Hegel, G.W.F. (1971). *Philosophy of Mind*. Trans. W. Wallace. Oxford: Clarendon Press.
Heidegger, M. (2008). *Being and Time*. Trans. John Macquarrie and Martin Edward Robinson. New York: Harper Perennial.
Helff, Sissy (2016). "Transcultural Affect: Human-Horse Relations in Joe Johnston's *Hidalgo*, Steven Spielberg's *War Horse*, and Belá Tarr's *The Turin Horse*," in Jopi Nayman and Nora Shuurman, eds., *Affect, Space and Animals*. Abingdon: Routledge, 95–106.
Hettich, Katja (2013). "Reorienting Romantic Comedy: Genre Negotiations in Richard Linklater's Before Sunrise," in Julia Eckel et al., eds., *(Dis)orienting Media and Narrative Mazes*. Wetzlar: Majuskel Medienproduktion, 145–164.
Hilger, Michael (1995). *From Savage to Nobleman: Images of Native Americans in Film*. Lanham, MD: Scarecrow Press.
Hills, Elizabeth (1999). "From Figurative Males to Action Heroines." *Screen* 40.1: 38–50.
Holbrook, Morris B., and Elizabeth C. Hirschman (1982). "The Experiential Aspects of Consumption: Consumer Fantasies, feelings, and Fun." *The Journal of Consumer Research* 9.2: 132–140.
Holsinger, Jennifer Leila (2009). *Residential Patterns of Arab Americans: Race, Ethnicity and Spatial Assimilation*. El Paso: LFB Scholarly.
Horton, Yurii, Raagen Price. and Eric Brown (1999). "Portrayal of Minorities in the Film, Media and Entertainment Industries." *Poverty and Prejudice: Media and Race*. Available at https://web.stanford.edu/class/e297c/poverty_prejudice/mediarace/portrayal.htm (accessed 25/11/2017).
Hutchinson, Stuart (1994). *Mark Twain Humour on the Run*. Amsterdam: Rodopi.
Ingram, David (2004). *Green Screen Environmentalism and Hollywood Cinema*. Exeter: University of Exeter Press.
Jackson, Kathy Merlock (1986). *Images of Children in American Film: A Sociocultural Analysis*. Metuchen, NJ: Scarecrow Press.
Jackson, Liz (2014). *Muslims and Islam in U.S. Education: Reconsidering Multiculturalism*. London: Routledge.
Jackson, Sherman A. (2005). *Islam and the Blackamerican: Looking Toward the Third Resurrection*. Oxford and New York: Oxford University Press.
Jawad, Haifa, and Tansin Benn (2003). *Muslim Women in the United Kingdom and Beyond: Experiences and Images*. Leiden: Brill.
Jennings, Ros (1995). "Desire and Design—Ripley Undressed," in Tamsin Wilton, ed., *Immortal/Invisible Lesbians and the Moving Image*. London: Routledge.
Jones, Owain (2008). "True Geography [ ] Quickly Forgotten, Giving Away to an Adult-Imagined Universe. Approaching the Otherness of Childhood." *Children's Geographies* 6.2: 195–212.
Kääpä, Pietari, and Silja Laine, eds. (2013). *World Film Locations: Helsinki*. Bristol: Intellect.
Kamen, Paula (2000). *Her Way: Young Women Remake the Sexual Revolution*. New York: New York University Press.
Kannan, Sweta Madhuri (2011). "Representation of Female Terrorists in the Western Media and Academia." *E-International Relations Students*, 31 August. Available at www.e-ir.info/2011/08/31/representation-of-female-terrorists-in-the-western-media-and-academia/ (accessed 24/11/17).
Kaplan, Ann E. (1997). *Looking for the Other: Feminism, Film and the Imperial Gaze*. New York: Routledge.
Kapur, Ratna (2002). "The Tragedy of Victimisation Rhetoric: Resurrecting the 'Native' Subject in International/Post-Colonial Feminist Legal Politics." *Harvard Human Rights Journal* 15.1: 1–38.
Karim, Karim H. (2000). *Islamic Peril: Media and Global Violence*. Montreal: Black Rose Books.
Keller, Gary D. (1994). *Hispanics and United States Film: An Overview and Handbook*. Tempe: Bilingual Press/Editorial Bilingue,.
Kellner, Douglas (2010). *Cinema Wars: Hollywood Film and Politics in the Bush-Cheney Era*. Oxford: Wiley Blackwell. Available at https://books.google.co.uk/books?id=GrQnyVqW

BzYC&pg=RA2-PA1980&dq=Fatima+in+Rendition&hl=en&sa=X&redir_esc=y#v=onepage&q=Fatima%20in%20Rendition&f=false (accessed 25/11/2017).
Keniston, Kenneth (1965). *The Uncommitted: Alienated Youth in American Society*. New York: Harcourt, Brace & World.
Kennedy, Christina B. (1994). "The Myth of Heroism: Man and Desert in *Lawrence of Arabia*," in Stuart C. Aitken and Leo E. Zonn, eds., *Place, Power, Situation and Spectacle: A Geography of Film*. Lanham, MD: Rowman & Littlefield, 161–179.
Keshavarz, Fatemah (2007). *Jasmine and Stars: Reading More Than Lolita in Tehran*. Chapel Hill: University of North Carolina Press.
Khatib, Lina (2006). *Filming the Modern Middle East: Politics in the Cinemas of Hollywood and the Arab World*. London: I.B. Tauris.
Kilpatrick, Jacquelyn (1999). *Celluloid Indians: Native Americans and Film*. Lincoln: University of Nebraska Press.
King, Geoff (2005). *American Independent Cinema*. London: I.B. Tauris.
King, Mike (2009). *The American Cinema of Excess: Extremes of the National Mind on Film*. Jefferson, NC: McFarland.
Kollin, Susan (2015). *Captivating Westerns: The Middle East in the American West*. Lincoln: University of Nebraska Press.
Kracauer, Siegfried (1959). "National Types as Hollywood Presents Them," in Bernard Rosenberg and David Manning White, eds., *Mass Culture: The Popular Arts in America*. Glencoe, IL: The Free Press.
Kunz, William M. (2007) *Culture Conglomerates: Consolidation in the Motion Picture and Television Industries*. Lanham, MD: Rowman & Littlefield.
Lacan, Jacques (1977). *Écrits. A Selection*. Trans. A. Sheridan. New York: W.W. Norton.
Laderman, David (2002). *Driving Visions: Exploring the Road Movie*. Austin: University of Texas Press.
Lauzen, M.M. (2014). "It's a Man's (Celluloid) World: On-Screen Representations of Female Characters in the Top 100 Films of 2013." Research report, San Diego State University. Available at http://womenintvfilm.sdsu.edu/files/2013_It's_a_Man's_World_Report.pdf (accessed 26/11/2017).
Ledesma, Eduardo (2012). "Through 'Their' Eyes: Internal and External Focalizing Agents in the Representation of Children and Violence in Iberian and Latin American Film," in Carolina Rocha and Georgia Seminet, eds., *Representing History, Class, and Gender in Spain and Latin America: Children and Adolescents in Film*. New York: Palgrave Macmillan, 151–169.
Lee, Martha F. (2011). "The Nation of Islam and Violence," in James Lewis, ed., *Violence and New Religious Movements*. Oxford: Oxford University Press, 295–306.
Lee, Robert G. (1999). *Orientals: Asian Americans in Popular Culture*. Philadelphia: Temple University Press.
Lefebvre, Henri (1991). *The Production of Space*. Trans. Donald Nicholson-Smith. Oxford: Blackwell.
Lefebvre, Martin (2006). "Between Setting and Landscape in the Cinema," in Martin Lefebvre, ed., *Landscape and Film*. New York: Routledge, 19–59.
Lewis, Bernard (1993). *Islam and the West*. New York: Oxford University Press.
Lichter, Robert S., and Daniel R. Amundson (1997). "Distorted Reality: Hispanic Characters in TV Entertainment," *Latin Looks: Images of Latinas and Latinos in the U.S. Media*: 57–79.
Light, Andrew (1999). "Boyz in the Woods: Urban Wilderness in American Cinema," in Michael Bennett and David W. Teague, eds., *The Nature of Cities: Ecocriticism and Urban Environments*. Tucson: University of Arizona Press, 137–156.
Lindner, Christoph (2015). *Imagining New York City: Literature, Urbanism, and the Visual Arts 1890–1940*. New York: Oxford University Press.
Lippmann, W. (1967). *Public Opinion*. 1922. New York: Free Press Paperbacks.
Lisiak, Agata Anna (2010). *Urban Cultures in (Post)colonial Central Europe* (Comparative Cultural Studies Series). West Lafayette: Purdue University Press.

Lury, Karen (2010). *The Child in Film: Tears, Fears and Fairy Tales*. London: I.B. Tauris.
MacDonald, Megan (2014). "Surveil: The Veil as Blank(et) Sgnifier," in Lisa K. Taylor and Jamin Zine, eds., *Muslim Women, Transnational Feminism and the Ethics of Pedagogy*. Abingdon: Routledge, 25–58.
Macey, Marie (1999). "Religion, Male Violence and the Control of Women: Pakistani Muslim Men in Bradford." *Gender and Development* 7.1: 48–55.
Marks, Laura U. (2006). "Asphalt Nomadism: The New Desert in Arab Independent Cinema," in Martin Lefebvre, ed., *Landscape and Film*. New York: Routledge, 125–148.
Mastro, Dana E., and Bradley S. Greenberg (2000). "The Portrayal of Racial Minorities on Prime Time Television." *Journal of Broadcasting and Electronic Media* 44.4: 690–703.
McAlister, M. (2005). *Epic Encounters: Culture, Media, & U.S Interests in the Middle East Since 1945*. Berkeley: University of California Press.
McArthur, Colin (1997). "Chinese Boxes and Russian Doll," in David Clarke, ed., *The Cinematic City*. London: Routledge, 19–45.
McCarthy, Todd (2010). "Review: Green Zone." *Variety*, 4 March. Available at http://variety.com/2010/film/markets-festivals/green-zone-1117942351/ (accessed 19/11/2017).
McCloud, Aminah B. (1994). "Racism in the Ummah," in Mohammad A. Siddiqui, ed., *Islam: A Contemporary Perspective*. Chicago: NAAMPS, 73–80.
McCloud, Beverly Thomas (1991). "African-American Muslim Women," in Yvonne Yazbeck Haddad, ed., *The Muslims of America*. New York: Oxford University Press, 177–187.
McKee, A. (2003). *Textual Analysis: A Beginner's Guide*. London: Sage.
McLean, A.L. (1997). "The Thousand Ways There Are to Move: Camp and Oriental Dance in the Hollywood Musicals of Jack Cole," in M. Bernstein and S. Gaylyn, eds., *Visions of the East: Orientalism in Film*. New Brunswick: Rutgers University Press, 130–157.
Meiloud, Ahmed O. (2007). "The Image of Arabs in Hollywood Films." Master's thesis, Graduate School of the University of Wyoming. https://books.google.co.uk/books?id=nIsSb8IKBl4C&pg=PP2&lpg=PP2&dq=Meiloud,+Ahmed+O.+%E2%80%9CThe+image+of+Arabs+in+Hollywood+films%E2%80%9D.&source=bl&ots=BouZ3mSbCt&sig=dE82rRL5E2HRnJkXDZX_LLxRuaw&hl=en&sa=X&ved=0ahUKEwjyn_b-1ezMAhWC6xoKHRN3D0YQ6AEIHDAA (accessed 22/05/2016).
Melbye, David (2006). *The Contemplative Landscape: Allegories of Space in Cinema*. Ann Arbor: ProQuest Information and Learning.
Metcalf, Barbara D. (1996). "Introduction," in Barbara D. Metcalf, ed., *Making Muslim Space in North America and Europe*. Berkeley: University of California Press, 1–30.
Metz, Christian (1982). *Imaginary Signifier: Psychoanalysis and the Cinema*. Bloomington: Indiana University Press.
Michalak, Laurence (2010). "Improvements in the images of Arabs and Muslims." *Annual Meeting of the Middle East Studies Association*. San Diego, 18–21 November.
Mingant, Nolwenn (2014). "Beyond Muezzins and Mujahideen: Middle-Eastern Voices in Post-9/11 Hollywood Movies," in Iraj Omidvar and Anne R. Richards, eds., *Muslims and American Popular Culture, Volume One: Entertainment and Dijital Culture*. Santa Barbara: Praeger, 167–194.
Mohanty, Chandra T. (2003). "Under Western Eyes: Feminist Scholarship and Colonial Discourses," in Chandra T. Mohanty, ed., *Feminism Without Borders: Decolonizing Theory, Practicing Solidarity*. Durham: Duke University Press.
Mokdad, Linda Y. (2013). "Imaginary Geography: Mapping the History of the Middle East in Post-9/11 American Cinema," PhD thesis, University of Iowa. Available at http://ir.uiowa.edu/cgi/viewcontent.cgi?article=5754&context=etd (accessed 25/11/2017).
Morey, Peter (2010). "Terrorvision: Race, Nation and Muslimness in Fox's 24." *Interventions* 12.2: 251–264. Available at http://www.tandfonline.com/doi/abs/10.1080/1369801X.2010.489699 (accessed 17/11/2017).
Morey, Peter, and Amina Yaqin (2011). *Framing Muslims: Stereotyping and Representation After 9/11*. Cambridge: Harvard University Press.

Moxley Rouse, Carolyn (2004). *Engaged Surrender. African American Women and Islam.* Berkeley: University of California Press.

Mulvey, Laura (1975). "Visual Pleasure and Narrative Cinema." *Screen* 16.3: 6–18.

———. (1996) *Fetishism and Curiosity: Cinema and the Mind's Eye.* London: Palgrave MacMillan.

Muscati, Sina A. (2002). "Arab/Muslim 'Otherness': The Role of Racial Constructions in the Gulf War and the Continuing Crisis in Iraq." *Journal of Muslim Minority Affairs*: 1–18.

Naber, Nadine (2000). "Ambiguous Insiders: An Investigation of Arab American Invisibility." *Ethnic and Racial Studies* 23.1: 37–61.

Natali, Maurizia (2006). "The Course of the Empire: Sublime Landscapes in the American Cinema," in Martin Lefebvre, ed., *Landscape and Film.* New York: Routledge, 125–148.

Nittle, Nadra Kareem (2014). "Five Common Asian-American Stereotypes in TV and Film." www.about.com. Available at http://racerelations.about.com/od/hollywood/a/Five-Common-Asian-american-Stereotypes-In-Tv-And-Film.htm (accessed 17/11/2017).

Nuruddin, Yusuf (2000). "African-American Muslims and the Question of Identity Between Traditional Islam, African Heritage, and the American Way," in Yvonne Yazbeck Haddad and John L. Esposito, eds., *Muslims on the Americanization Path?* New York: Oxford University Press, 267–330.

Omanson, Lisa G. (2013). "African-American and Arab American Muslim Communities in the Detroit *Ummah*." Master's thesis, University of Iowa. Available at http://ir.uiowa.edu/cgi/viewcontent.cgi?article=4726&context=etd (accessed 21/11/2017).

Pickering, Michael (2001). *Stereotyping: The Politics of Representation.* Basingstoke: Palgrave.

Pink, Sarah (2008). "Analysing Visual Experience," in Michael Pickering, ed., *Research Methods for Cultural Studies.* Edinburgh: Edinburgh University Press, 125–149.

Place, Janey (1998). "Women in Film Noir," in E. Ann Kaplan, ed., *Women in Film Noir.* London: BFI, 35–68.

Pratt, Mary Louise (1992). *Imperial Eyes: Travel Writing and Trans-Culturation.* London: Routledge.

Quindlen, Anna (1994). "Public & Private; and Now, Babe Feminism," *New York Times*, 19 January. Available at http://www.nytimes.com/1994/01/19/opinion/public-private-and-now-babe-feminism.html (accessed 22/11/2017).

Qutub, Afnan (2013). "Harem Girls and Terrorist Men: Media Misrepresentations of Middle Eastern Cultures." *Colloquy* 9: 139–155. Available at http://www.calstatela.edu/sites/default/files/users/u2276/qutub_essay8.pdf (accessed 23/11/2017).

Ramirez-Berg, Charles (2002). *Latino Images in Film: Stereotypes, Subversion, Resistance.* Austin: University of Texas Press.

Ramji, Rubina (2016). "Examining the Critical Role American Popular Film Continues to Play in Maintaining the Muslim Terrorist Image, Post 9/11." *Journal of Religion and Film* 20.1: 1–19.

Rhines, Jesse Algeron (1996). *Black Film/White Money.* New Brunswick: Rutgers University Press.

Richards, Jeffrey (2015). "Sabu, the Elephant Boy," in Noel Brown and Bruce Babbington, eds., *Family Films in Global Cinema: The World Beyond Disney.* London: I.B. Tauris,. 87–102.

Rimmon-Kenan, Shlomith (1983). *Narrative Fiction: Contemporary Poetics.* London: Methuen.

Rinne, Craig (2001). "White Romance and American Indian Action in Hollywood's The Last of The Mohicans." *Studies in American Indian Literatures Series* 2. 13.1: 3–22.

Robe, Chris (2010). *Left of Hollywood: Cinema, Modernism and the Emergence of U.S. Radical Film Culture.* Austin: University of Texas Press.

Rogin, Michael (1992). "Blackface, White Noise: The Jewish Jazz Singer Finds His Voice." *Critical Inquiry* 18.3: 417–444.

Rusbult, C.E., and P.A.M. Van Lange (2008). "Why We Need Interdependence Theory." *Social and Personality Psychology Compass* 2: 2049–2070.

Said, Edward W. (1997). *Covering Islam: How the Media and the Experts Determine How We See the Rest of the World.* London: Vintage.

———. (2003). *Orientalism.* 1978. London: Penguin Classics.

Salazer, A. (2004). "Arabs in Hollywood: US Films' Cultivation of Viewers—Perceptions and Attitudes Toward Arabs." Master's Thesis, University of Texas, El Paso.

Schwarzer, Mitchell (2000). "The Consuming Landscape: Architecture in the Films of Michelangelo Antonioni," in Mark Lamster, ed., *Architecture and Film*. New York: Princeton Architectural Press, 197–215.

Scott, A.O. (2009). "Neo Neo-Realism." *New York Times Magazine*, 17 March. Available at http://www.nytimes.com/2009/03/22/magazine/22neorealism-t.html?_r=1 (accessed 19/11/2019).

Scurry, Samuel (2010). "Orientalism in American Cinema: Providing an Historical and Geographical Context for Postcolonial Theory." Thesis, Clemson University. Available at http://tigerprints.clemson.edu/cgi/viewcontent.cgi?article=1789&context=all_theses (accessed 19/11/2017).

Semmerling, Tim Jon (2006). *"Evil" Arabs in American Popular Film: Orientalist Fear*. Austin: University of Texas Press.

Shaheen, Jack G. (1993). "The Arab World as Place," in Paul Loukides, ed., *Beyond the Stars: The American Material World in American Popular Film*. Bowling Green: Bowling Green State University Press, 80–85.

_____. (2000). "Hollywood's Muslim Arabs." *The Muslim World* 90, 22–42.

_____. (2003a). *Reel Bad Arabs: How Hollywood Vilifies a People*. Gloucestershire: Arris Books.

_____. (2003b). "Arab Americans," in Peter C. Rollins, ed., *The Columbia Companion to American History on Film: How the Movies Have Portrayed the American Past*. New York: Colombia University Press, 218–224.

_____. (2008a). *Guilty: Hollywood's Verdict on Arabs After 9/11*. Northampton: Olive Branch Press.

_____. (2008b). *Reel Bad Arabs: How Hollywood Vilifies a People* (updated version). New York: Olive Branch Press.

Shanahan, James, and Michael Morgan (1999). *Television and Its Viewers: Cultivation Theory and Research*. Cambridge: Cambridge University Press.

Shaw, Deborah (2013). "Deconstructing and Reconstructing 'Transnational Cinema,'" in Stephanie Dennison, ed., *Contemporary Hispanic Cinema: Interrogating Transnationalism in Spanish and Latin American Film*. Woodbridge: Tamesis Books, 47–66.

Sherif, M. (1966). *Group Conflict and Co-Operation: Their Social Psychology*. London: Routledge & Kegan Paul.

Shiel, Mark (2001). "Cinema and the City in History and Theory," in Mark Shiel and Tony Fitzmaurice, eds., *Cinema and the City: Film and Urban Societies in a Global Context*. Oxford: Blackwell, 1–18.

Shohat, Ella (1997). "Gender and Culture of Empire: Towards a Feminist Ethnography of Cinema," in Matthew Berstein and Gaylyn Studlar, eds., *Visions of the East: Orientalism in Film*. New Brunswick: Rutgers University Press, 19–66.

_____. (2006). *Taboo Memories, Diasporic Voices*. Durham: Duke University Press.

Shohat, Ella, and Robert Stam (2014). *Unthinking Eurocentrism: Multiculturalism and the Media*. London: Routledge.

Singer, P.W. (2006). *Children at War*. Berkeley: University of California Press.

Sinyard, Neil (1992). *Children in the Movies*. New York: St. Martin's Press.

Sjoberg, L. (2007). "Agency, Militarized Femininity and Enemy Others: Observations from the War in Iraq." *International Feminist Journal of Politics* 9.1: 82–101.

Smith, Sharon (1972). "The Image of Women in Film: Some Suggestions for Future Research." *Women and Film* 1: 13–21.

Sokoloff, Naomi B. (1986). "Interpretation: Cynthia Ozick's Cannibal Galaxy." *Prooftexts* 6.3: 239–257.

Spivak, G. Chakravorty (1985). "The Rani of Sirmur: An Essay in Reading the Archives." *History and Theory* 24.3: 247–272.

Stacey, Jackie (1993). "Textual Obsessions: Methodology, History and Researching Female Spectatorship." *Screen, Reports and Debates* 34.3: 260–274.

_____. (2002). "Hollywood Cinema: The Great Escape," in J. Stacey, ed., *Star Gazing: Hollywood Cinema and Female Spectatorship*. Abingdon: Routledge, 80–125.

Stewen, Christian (2012). "Childhood, Ghost Images, and the Heterotopian Spaces of Cinema: The Child Medium," in Debbie Olson and Andrew Scahill, eds., *The Others Lost and Othered Children in Contemporary Cinema*. Lanham, MD: Lexington Books, 265–286.

Sultana, Parvin (2013). "Essentialising the Other—Representing Muslims in Media Post 9/11." *The Indian Journal of Media Studies* 7.1–2: 63–71.

Tajfel, Henri (1981a). "Social Stereotypes and Social Groups," in John C. Turner and Howard Giles, eds., *Intergroup Behaviour*. Oxford: Blackwell, 144–167.

_____. (1981b). *Human Groups and Social Categories*. Cambridge: Cambridge University Press.

Tasker, Yvonne (1993). *Spectacular Bodies: Gender, Genre and the Action Cinema*. London: Routledge.

_____. (1998). *Working Girls: Gender and Sexuality in Popular Cinema*. London: Routledge.

Tayyara, Abed el-Rahman (2014). "The Representations of Arab-Muslims Through the Language Lens." *Cultural Encounters, Conflicts and Resolutions* 1.2: Article 7. Available at http://engagedscholarship.csuohio.edu/cgi/viewcontent.cgi?article=1024&context=cecr (acc 19/11/2017).

Tehranian, M. (2000). "Islam and the West: Hostage to History?" in Kai Hafez, ed., *Islam and the West in Mass Media*. Creskill: Hampton Press, 201–18.

Teo, Hsu-Ming (2012). *Desert Passions: Orientalism and Romance Novels*. Austin: University of Texas Press.

Thomas, Jeffrey L. (2015). *Scapegoating Islam: Intolerance, Security, and the American Muslim*. Santa Barbara: Praeger.

Thompson, Lisa B. (2009). *Beyond the Black Lady: Sexuality and the New African American Middle Class*. Urbana: University of Illinois Press.

Tischler, Barbara L. (2016). *Muhammad Ali: A Man of Many Voices*. New York: Routledge.

Tocqueville, Alexis de (1836). *Democracy in America*. New York: George Dearborn.

Toles-Patkin, T. (2004). "Explosive Baggage: Female Palestinian Suicide Bombers and the Rhetoric of Emotion." *Women and Language* 27.2: 79–89.

Turner, Richard Brent (2003). *Islam in the African-American Experience* (2nd Edition). Bloomington: Indiana University Press.

Ullman, Harlan K., and James P. Wade (2003). *Shock and Awe: Achieving Rapid Dominance*. N. Charleston, SC: CreateSpace.

Wilkins, Karin Gwinn (2009). *Home/Land/Security: What We Learn about Arab Communities from Action-Adventure Films*. Lanham, MD: Lexington Books.

Wilkins, Karin, and John Downing (2002). "Mediated Terrorism: Text and Protest in the Interpretation of The Siege." *Critical Studies in Media Communication* 19.4: 419–37.

Wolf, Naomi (1991). *The Beauty Myth: How Images of Beauty Are Used Against Women*. New York: William Morrow.

_____. (1993). *Fire with Fire: The New Female Power and How It Will Change the 21st Century*. New York: Random House.

Wolfenstein, Martha, and Nathan Leites (1950). *Movies: A Psychological Study*. Glencoe, IL: The Free Press.

Woll, Allen L. (1980). *The Latin Image in American Films*. Los Angeles: UCLA Latin American Center Publications,

Yenigün, Halil İbrahim (2004). "Muslims and the Media After 9/11: A Muslim Discourse in the American Media?" *The American Journal of Islamic Social Sciences* 21.3: 39–69.

Zaccak, Hady (2003). "Les Arabes dans 'le western.'" *Regards* 5: 53–58.

Zeiger, Dinah (2008). "That (Afghan) Girl! Ideology Unveiled in *National Geographic*," in Jennifer Heath, ed., *The Veil: Women Writers on its History, Lore, and Politics*. Berkeley: University of California Press, 266–281.

Zine, Jasmin (2002). "Muslim Women and the Politics of Representation." *American Journal of Islamic Social Sciences* 19.4: 1–22.

Žižek, Slavoj (1997). "The Big Other Doesn't Exist." *Journal of European Psychoanalysis* (Spring–Fall). Available at http://www.lacan.com/zizekother.htm (accessed 27/11/2017).

_____. (2002). *Welcome to the Desert of the Real! Five Essays on September 11 and Related Dates*. London: Verso.

# Index

action woman  101, 104, 105–106, 116–119, 120
Ali Baba kit  24
American cinema  102, 103, 106, 127, 147, 150, 152, 156, 159, 178, 179, 188, 189, 190, 196, 197, 206, 207, 210, 211, 212, 214, 215–217
American female character  4, 98, 113, 107, 121, 129, 135
antagonist (antagonistic)  21, 52, 58, 62, 63, 80, 81, 82, 85, 97, 103, 110, 112, 115, 117, 191
Arab-land  24, 25
Asian stereotypes  22
attributes (character)  12, 17, 38, 65, 67, 115, 124, 125, 135, 132, 133, 135, 137, 144, 145, 165, 180, 192, 194
attribution (theory of)  134, 135, 193

Baghdad  4, 27, 28, 46–59, 63, 128, 182, 190, 191, 201, 203, 206
belly dancer  126–129, 138, 140
Black African American Muslims  72, 73, 135, 144, 158, 161, 193
Blaxploitation  20
*burka*  49, 54, 56, 89, 122, 125–127, 132, 138, 147, 193
Bush administration  44, 95, 107, 113, 183
butch *femme*  116

changeability  7, 13, 14, 34, 117, 197
childlike (childish)  22, 93, 146, 153, 155, 157, 161, 165, 170, 177
Civil Rights Movement  25, 71, 74, 75
colonial rescue fantasy  45, 82, 94
colonizing practice  153
comedy  36, 60, 66, 69, 92–94, 95, 96, 128, 201, 213
commercial cinema  9

control (actor, interdependence, partner, joint)  135, 136, 148, 193
cultural diversity  19, 39, 60
*cura*  129, 130, 141, 142, 139, 143, 146

deconstruction (of the Muslim image)  66, 94, 95
desert  14, 19, 24, 27, 28, 29, 32–46, 48, 49, 52, 58, 62, 63, 82, 90, 91, 121, 126, 161, 164, 189, 190, 200, 206, 214, 215, 218
desolate/abjection (space)  62, 173
discourse  8, 15, 21, 34, 68, 70, 74, 81, 82, 89, 90, 94, 129, 134, 135, 163, 171, 184, 205, 209, 212, 215, 218

emancipation  136, 143, 193
emigrant  163, 169, 211
ethnonormativity (ethnonormative)  9, 83
ethnoscape  19

fanaticism (Islamic, Muslim, religious)  5, 25, 65, 68, 128, 188
femininity  17, 36, 114, 116, 117, 131, 217
feminism (first wave, second wave, third wave, fourth wave)  3, 4, 12, 14, 16–18, 44, 96, 97, 98, 101, 106, 119, 120, 123–125, 141, 143, 145, 181,188, 189, 192, 196, 197, 210–213, 215, 216
*femme fatale*  101, 104–105, 107–112, 114, 117, 120, 210
fetishism  104, 105, 118, 216
*film noir*  31, 104, 115, 216
focalization (internal, external)  5, 155–157, 166, 168, 170, 171, 174, 176–178, 209

gaze (male, colonial, imperial)  13, 33, 61, 62, 66, 67, 81, 84, 93, 102–104, 106, 107, 109, 112, 116, 120, 121, 129–132, 136, 139, 140, 143, 147, 153, 193, 213 globalization 4, 12, 14, 18–19, 94, 209

*hijab* 25, 126, 140, 142, 147, 193, 209
Hispanic 157–159, 178, 194, 210, 213, 214, 217
Homeland Security 5, 87, 88, 157, 165, 195
hybrid "Otherness" 5, 154, 163, 166, 170, 178
hybridity 76, 154, 178, 195
image formation 7, 12, 74, 96, 180
immigrant (American) Muslims 18, 19, 21, 22–24, 27, 41, 59–62, 63, 66, 71–79, 80, 93–95, 107–110, 112, 134, 135, 139, 140, 148, 150, 152, 154, 157, 159, 163, 166, 169, 172, 182, 190, 192, 195, 211
imperialism 15, 18, 83, 109
in-group 20, 23, 179
independent cinema 8, 185, 214, 215
informative setting 31, 39
interpretative approach 7
Islamic rage boy 65, 83, 86, 94, 132

Jessica Lynch 99, 100, 119, 192
Jews (Jewish) 20, 23–25, 59, 78, 93, 94, 184, 212, 216

*keffiyah* 83, 109

landscape 4, 19, 22, 28–46, 53, 54, 57, 61, 63, 74, 86, 90, 145, 173, 174, 177, 190, 196, 205, 214–217
Lynndie England 99, 100, 107, 115, 119, 192, 212

masculinity 17, 37, 88, 101, 117, 118, 192
methodology 6, 217
Michalak, L. 70, 81, 96, 180, 182, 215
misrepresentation 14, 23, 33, 82, 93, 127, 216
monolithic (image, representation) 5, 23, 66, 74, 91, 95, 140, 147, 162, 181, 182, 186, 189, 191, 192
Morey, P. 9, 65, 68, 80, 83, 85, 179, 182, 191, 215
Muslim children 5, 56, 150–178, 194–196, 210
Muslim female character(s)/Muslim women 5, 17–19, 118, 124–149, 192 Muslim male character(s)/Muslim men 4, 5, 17, 18, 62, 65–96, 97–123, 124, 125, 127, 128, 162, 184, 192, 206, 210, 215
Muslim world 3, 4, 6, 9, 11–14, 16, 18, 24, 26, 27, 58, 65, 66, 69, 92, 96, 98, 179, 181–184, 186–189, 196, 197, 201, 205, 217

Nation of Islam 72, 73, 75, 76, 144–146, 214
national security 58, 113, 115, 116, 123, 190
Native American 20, 21, 23, 24, 33, 38–40, 43, 44, 101, 205, 213, 214
natural (space, wilderness) 28, 31, 32, 39, 43, 47
neutral setting 31

objective reality 11, 12, 19
occident 5, 62, 186
Orient (Oriental) 4, 5, 11, 15, 16, 22, 24, 27, 30, 33, 34, 46, 49, 58, 62, 68, 85, 89, 93, 94, 109, 121, 122, 125, 127, 128, 160, 179, 188, 192
Orientalism (Orientalist) 1, 4, 12, 14–16, 19, 24, 26, 28, 33, 40, 41, 46, 56, 62, 64, 72, 74, 80, 90, 95, 96, 109, 117, 121, 123, 124, 128, 131, 136, 143, 148, 149, 151, 159, 164, 167, 177, 181, 184, 186, 188–190, 194, 196, 197, 205, 208–210, 212, 215–218
"Other" ("Othering," "Other-ness") 4–6, 13, 16, 19, 20, 24, 29, 30, 45, 48, 64–68, 75, 78, 79, 81, 85, 88, 89, 92–94, 100–104, 107, 108, 110, 143, 148, 154, 155, 163, 164, 166, 170, 171, 178, 180, 186, 189, 191, 195, 197, 205, 209, 212, 213, 216–218
Ottoman empire 16, 127
out-group 4, 23, 67
overseas Muslim 5, 70, 72, 94, 134, 135, 143, 164

patriarchy (patriarchal) 17, 18, 38, 106, 107, 109, 113, 117, 135, 136, 148
(post) colonialism 3, 15, 33, 40, 125, 180, 211
power 13–15, 29, 41, 98, 101, 103, 106, 108, 112–115, 118, 134, 190, 209, 212, 214, 218

qualitative approach 6
quantitative approach 6

reconstruction (of the Muslim image) 95, 107, 117, 130, 192
rescue agent 150, 160, 161, 162
rescue fantasy 45, 82, 94
romance films 35

Said, E.W. 9, 12, 13, 15–16, 24, 26, 33, 72, 85, 96, 103, 126, 151, 173, 180, 205, 216
savage (savagery) 7, 20, 21, 28, 31, 34, 37, 38, 47–49, 59, 62, 65, 70, 74, 82, 171, 174, 203, 207, 213
self (as opposed to "Other") 13, 67, 75, 89, 92–94, 107

Semmerling, T.J. 7, 9, 29, 36, 37, 65, 85, 113, 127, 132, 180, 217
Shaheen, J. 4, 9, 16, 24–26, 29, 30, 47, 59, 60, 66, 67, 69, 71, 81, 82, 85, 126, 128, 151, 161, 180, 186, 205–207, 217
Shohat, E. 12, 19, 33, 34, 45, 67, 89, 206, 217
space (Muslim) 3, 4, 6, 12, 26, 27–64, 145, 169, 191, 182, 188, 189, 190, 215
stereotypes (ethnic, cultural) 4, 19–24, 26, 135
superrat 101, 104, 106–107, 120–122

taqiyah 109, 110
terrorism (terrorist) 45, 46, 60, 62, 65, 68, 70, 81–83, 86, 87, 92, 93, 95, 98, 101, 104, 113, 114, 116, 118, 119, 131–134, 141, 162, 170, 171, 180–184, 186, 189, 190, 192, 193, 196, 206, 208, 211, 213, 216, 218
third space (of enunciation) 15, 154
transnational cinema (transnationalism) 3, 4, 18–19, 27, 40, 44, 45, 59, 63, 94, 109, 154, 163, 177, 181, 188, 189, 195–197, 209, 217

trauma (traumatic) 1, 64, 82, 98, 107, 112, 120, 126, 132, 133, 134, 137, 181, 209
*Trümmerfilm* 61, 172, 173

urban (space) 28, 29–31, 47, 56, 59, 61, 209, 214, 217
use value Muslim 65, 85–87, 89, 95, 182

veil (unveil) 19, 25, 42, 87, 88, 119, 122, 125–127, 129, 140, 142, 143, 147, 186, 192, 203, 209–211, 215, 218
vilification (vilified) 4, 16, 25, 70, 90, 93, 162, 180, 185, 188, 194, 196
visual media 14, 184

War on Terror 88, 95, 107, 163, 183, 189, 207, 211
wilderness (urban, natural) 12, 28, 29, 31–34, 37, 39, 41, 43, 47, 56, 59, 62, 63, 171, 174, 189, 190, 214
world politics 3, 148

Yaqin, A. 9, 65, 68, 80, 83, 85, 179, 182, 191, 215

www.ingramcontent.com/pod-product-compliance
Lightning Source LLC
Chambersburg PA
CBHW032053300426
44116CB00007B/717